Jazz Cultures

DAVID AKE

Jazz Cultures

UNIVERSITY OF CALIFORNIA PRESS

BERKELEY LOS ANGELES LONDON

The following chapters have appeared previously in somewhat different form: Chapter 1 appeared as "Blue Horizon: Creole Culture and Early New Orleans Jazz," in *Echo: A Music-Centered Journal* 1:1 (Fall 1999); chapter 3 appeared as "Re-Masculating Jazz: Ornette Coleman, 'Lonely Woman,' and the New York Jazz Scene in the Late 1950s," in *American Music* 16:1 (1998), 25–44; and chapter 5 appeared as a chapter of *The Cambridge Companion to Jazz* (Cambridge: Cambridge University Press, 2001).

University of California Press
Berkeley and Los Angeles, California

University of California Press, Ltd.
London, England

Library of Congress Cataloging-in-Publication Data

Ake, David Andrew.
  Jazz cultures / David Ake.
     p.   cm.
  Includes index.
   ISBN 0-520-22887-1 (alk. paper)—ISBN 0-520-22889-8 (pbk. : alk. paper)
    1. Jazz—History and criticism.   2. Jazz musicians—United States.   I. Title.

ML3507 .A44   2002
781.65—dc21   2001027443

Manufactured in the United States of America

11 10 09 08 07 06 05 04 03 02
10 9 8 7 6 5 4 3 2 1

CONTENTS

ILLUSTRATIONS

WHEN I ENTERED GRADUATE school at UCLA, in 1994, it was with hopes of answering a question that had dogged me in one way or another since I had relocated to New York in early 1990. Before that move and its resulting quandary, I had enjoyed a certain amount of professional success as a jazz pianist in Los Angeles and Munich. But somehow the notion that "real jazz" resided only in New York grabbed hold of me, and I set forth for "The City" with my friend, the outstanding saxophonist and composer John Schroeder.

Like so many jazz pilgrims before me, I experienced New York as a daily roller coaster of glorious little victories and discouraging little defeats. Supremely inspiring rehearsals, gigs, and recording sessions with like-minded players (they deserve mention: Ralph Alessi, Ben Allison, Jeff Ballard, Chuck Braman, Scott Colley, Ravi Coltrane, Mark Feldman, Gerry Gibbs, Philip Harper, Mike Karn, Kiyoshi Kitagawa, Jeff Lederer, Ben Monder, Scott Neumann, John Schroeder) redeemed the tedious day-to-dayness of subsistence living. During that New York period—I don't know when, exactly—this question presented itself to me: How did I get here?

Now, this wasn't posed in the metaphysical sense of "where does life come from?" but in the very literal sense of "how did a white, beer-drinking Cubs fan from Chicago's Northwest suburbs, who grew up with the music of Elton John, Rod Stewart, Joe Walsh, Yes, Jimi Hendrix, Lynyrd Skynyrd, Charlie Daniels, Muddy Waters, the Kinks, the Who, Little Feat, and Led Zeppelin, wind up sleeping on a pull-out bed in the converted front room of an apartment on Bergen Street in Brooklyn, writing and playing music that sounds something like a cross between Ornette Coleman, Thelonious Monk, Keith Jarrett, Bill Frisell, Hampton Hawes, Paul Bley, John Coltrane, Charlie Haden, Johnny Hodges, Kenny Wheeler, Wynton Kelly, Dewey Redman, Dave Holland, and, alas, Led Zeppelin?" It would take another book to recount all the steps that took me from those best and worst of times in New York to UCLA's Department of Musicology (by way of its Ethnomusicology Department), driven by that question. But I will say one thing: I still don't know the answer.

And this isn't so bad. True, all the time I spent reading, listening, writing, teaching, and (even and still) performing during my four-plus years of study didn't seem to bring me any closer to resolving my existential dilemma. Yet somehow the need to explain it all doesn't force itself as urgently on me as it once did. In its place have come dozens of different questions, and the book that follows represents my effort to address some of these newer problems. That is not to say that the issues I outline here are unimportant to me, or even that they bear no relation to the first question, only that they remain a little less personal. Ultimately, I hope that anyone interested in jazz as both a musical practice and as a site where individuals and cultures construct, display, and challenge their identities can find in these pages, if not their own answers, at least some new questions.

ACKNOWLEDGMENTS

THIS BOOK IS A REVISION and expansion of my Ph.D. dissertation in musicology at UCLA, and, not surprisingly, much of it was shaped and inspired by my interactions at that school. Seminars under the direction of Robert Walser, Susan McClary, and Roger Savage opened vast territories of music and thought. Post-seminar pizza-and-beer "debriefings" in Westwood Village with fellow grad students Steve Baur, David Borgo, Durrell Bowman, Francesca Draughon, Daniel Goldmark, Mai Kawabata, Glenn Pillsbury, Jacqueline Warwick, and Nadya Zimmerman nurtured fruitful debate (while supplying a big dose of fun). Many of those same students also participated in Susan McClary's weekly dissertation group, which provided an incredibly helpful forum to test new ideas and an invaluable means of staying committed to the task at hand (I would strongly recommend such a study group for any Ph.D.-granting program). My dissertation committee—Raymond Knapp, Christopher Waterman, Susan McClary, and chair Rob Walser—always offered timely, insightful, and practical suggestions on how to focus and strengthen my theses. Mitchell Morris brought his wit and seemingly limitless store of knowledge to the department just in time to help me with some finishing touches.

I'm grateful to David Borgo, Dale Chapman, Larry Engstrom, Robert Fink, Chuck Garrett, Mark Gridley, Roger Kendall, Richard Leppert, Ralph Locke, Roger Savage, Jacqueline Warwick, James Westby, and Nadya Zimmerman for providing helpful comments on specific written or lecture versions of these chapters. Chapter 1 originally appeared in *Echo* (on-line); chapter 3 appeared in *American Music;* chapter 5 comes from an essay written for *The Cambridge Companion to Jazz.* Thanks to the editors of those publications for their sound advice and for allowing me to revise and reprint my earlier publications. Todd Sickafoose deserves credit for converting my very sloppy musical notation into neat digital manuscript (sadly, his fine work cannot appear in this book), as do Durrell Bowman and John Schroeder for supplying computer assistance when all technological hell seemed to be breaking loose around me. A very special thanks to Lynne Withey at the University of California Press for taking on this project in the first place, and to Mary Francis, Laura Harger, David Severtson, and the Press's readers for guiding me toward producing the best book possible.

I wish to thank the following people for contributing valuable information and/or resources: Ralph Alessi, Paul Astin, David Borgo, Lisa Bourne, Jennifer Cady, Ravi Coltrane, Gail Crum of the Music Educators National Conference, Francesca Draughon, Larry Engstrom, Daniel Goldmark, Billy Higgins, Ray Knapp, Susan McClary, Dan Morgenstern and the staff at the Institute for Jazz Studies at Rutgers University in Newark, Bruce Rayburn and the staff at the William Ransom Hogan archive at Tulane University, the UCLA Department of Musicology, the UCLA Division of Graduate Studies, Robert Walser, and Andrew White.

Friends Heidi Bayer, James Carney, Alan Ferber, Mark Ferber, Marc Free, Pete and Pam Hanasz, Bob Oesterreich, John Schroeder, Todd Sickafoose, and David Wittman brought music, moral support, and meals when I seemed to need them the most. Former roommates Leslie Jon Martinez, Frank Duggan, and Rebecca Scanlan deserve medals for putting up with my very difficult habits during the dissertation years in L.A. Thanks to the people at the Urth Caffé on Melrose Avenue for supplying the best green tea in the world and a perfect place to read, think, and revise.

Since moving to the University of Nevada, Reno, I've been fortunate to work alongside a remarkable group of colleagues and musicians. In particular, Catherine Parsons Smith and department chair Michael Cleveland have enthusiastically supported my research since day one here, while Francis Vanek, Hans Halt, Gerry Genuario, and Andrew Heglund have reminded me how important it is to play on a regular basis with outstanding musicians. I'd especially like to acknowledge Larry Engstrom, who, as a great trumpeter, family man, friend, colleague, teacher, and baseball fan, acts as a role model to us all.

This book would not be what it is if not for the inspiration and guidance provided by my former piano and composition teachers. I'm particularly grateful to Roger Goodman, Reed Arvin, David Roitstein, Vince Maggio, Ron Miller, Charlie Haden, James Newton, and the late Robert Gersch. Unfortunately, I can't pay my individual respects to all the great musicians I've worked with and learned from over the years, but they've given me many of my life's most memorable experiences and I can't thank them enough.

I feel very lucky indeed to have been raised within an extraordinary family. To sister Dea, brother Ted, brother Stu, their respective spouses and children, and, above all, to Beatrice and Theodore Ake (my mom and dad): thank you so much for all the love and support you've provided and continue to provide. By the time this book goes to press I'll have married into another wonderful household. My gratitude to Marie, Clint, and Annette Case and Anita Abraham for welcoming me so warmly into the fold. To Hillary Louise Case, my best friend and confidante: *je t'aime.*

Finally, I want to single out Robert Walser. Many of you already appreciate Rob's eminent work as a scholar and journal editor. You should also know that he's an outstanding lecturer, a devoted committee chair, a strong musician on many instruments (but only an average pool player), and the best mentor one could ever hope for. Rob, this book's for you.

INTRODUCTION

UNLIKE PSYCHOLOGY OR American literature (or the music of Milton Babbitt, for that matter), jazz scholarship has yet to find a comfortable home in the academy. Though seemingly an obvious fit for music departments, no one appears sure which area of music research should claim jazz as its own. As my friend David Borgo, the outstanding saxophonist and ethnomusicologist, likes to say, "Jazz is too 'Other' for musicology and not 'Other' enough for ethnomusicology." Consequently, while some excellent work on jazz has emerged from those two disciplines, a significant percentage of the serious research on the subject has originated outside of music departments, produced by individual scholars working in English, film, American, and African-American studies.

To be sure, the seeming fragmentation of jazz research to date has created a rather untidy body of work. But multidisciplinary does not necessarily mean antidisciplinary: scholars reveal their fields' traditional interests and methodological emphases through the works they produce. That is to say, ethnomusicologists have tended toward ethnographies of jazz communities; musicologists have leaned toward producing historical studies and editions of early composers; and humanities scholars have broached subjects ranging from constructions of subjectivity and racial identity to the impact of commodification on understandings of jazz.

Given the complex history of cross-cultural interaction in this country, it seems almost inevitable that jazz—perhaps the most culturally promiscuous music of the twentieth century—would provide the focal point for so many different claims and interpretations from the academy. From its beginnings, jazz has presented a somewhat contradictory social world: Jazz musicians have worked diligently to tear down old boundaries, but they have just as resolutely constructed new ones; jazz provided one of the first locations of successful interracial cooperation in America, yet it has also served to perpetuate negative stereotypes and to incite racial unrest.[1]

So it should come as no surprise that, much like the conflicts that have arisen among jazz communities over the way the music should sound or who should serve as its rightful figureheads, the research from today's multicultural academies often presents conflicting findings and narratives. What is surprising (and pleasantly so) is the many ways in which these seemingly disparate studies can serve to illuminate one another, displaying a multifaceted picture of jazz almost as rich as the music itself. Of course, I hope that my work will contribute to the ongoing, if somewhat messy, debate characterizing contemporary jazz scholarship.

To this end, *Jazz Cultures* explores some of the diverse musics and related identities that jazz communities have configured over the past century, covering a wide range of issues. Jazz always encompasses an array of practices. And I follow a number of recent scholars in suggesting that we can study it most productively by looking at the evolving meanings, values, and ideals—as well as the sounds—that musicians, audiences, and critics have carried to and from the various activities they have called jazz. Such a view necessarily results in a historical narrative marked by contestation, contradiction, and plurality. All eras of the music are considered here in an effort to illuminate the ever-changing nature of jazz. But rather than a broad-based survey of stylistic innovation, each of the book's chapters concentrates on a specific moment or institution, focusing on the historical, cultural, technological, and musical phenomena that gave rise to different ways of playing and understanding jazz.

I use the term "identity" frequently throughout the book. That term refers to the ways in which jazz musicians and audiences experience and understand themselves, their music, their communities, and the world at large. Although Paul Gilroy's work concerns African-diasporic cultures in particular, it provides a useful description of identity in general:

> Identity is not simply a social and political category to be used or abandoned according to the extent to which the rhetoric that supports and legitimizes it is persuasive or institutionally powerful. . . . It is lived as a coherent (if not always stable) experiential sense of self. Though it is often felt to be natural and spontaneous, it remains the outcome of practical activity: language, gesture, bodily significations, desires.[2]

Gilroy's description of an "experiential sense of self" neatly illustrates the fact that identity always goes beyond conscious personal choice. Rather, it both reflects and shapes all understandings of one's self and one's relationships to the world. This book, then, explores those "practical activities" that work to differentiate one jazz identity or jazz culture from another and, more broadly, jazz cultures from nonjazz cultures.

The word "images" also appears throughout and refers to the many public representations and projections of jazz: photographs, feature films, advertisements, and published stories, both journalistic and fictional. Issues of meaning always extend beyond the borders of "the music itself," and the nonsonic aspects of jazz have played a vital role in influencing perceptions. For example, the various recorded media in jazz (LPs, CDs, prerecorded cassettes, videos) serve as more than just documents of musical performances. The pictures and liner notes that adorn each disc's or tape's protective sleeve also shape impressions of the genre, and I look to these as one kind of jazz imagery.

Still, the sounds preserved on recordings remain central to all understandings of this genre, and these form the foundation for many of the discussions here. The ephemerality of a performance-based music such as jazz distinguishes recordings—with their repeatability, replicability, and portability—as one of the few grounds for shared listening experiences, and so they constitute a fitting basis for exploration. Evan Eisenberg has gone so far as to suggest that "records not only disseminated jazz, but inseminated it—that in some ways they created what we call jazz."[3] Eisenberg demonstrates that jazz performances, the technology to preserve and reproduce them, the market forces involved in distributing them, and the understandings effected by listening to them remain so inextricably interrelated that the category "jazz" simply would not exist as it does today were it not for recordings. However, recognizing the fact that records may outlive the time and place of their origin (we can still listen to John Coltrane's *Live at Birdland* album, though neither Coltrane nor the original Birdland nightclub survive) does not necessarily presuppose that their meanings remain stable. One of the tasks of this book is to reveal the tangled web of understandings surrounding the various performances discussed here, to try to reclaim meanings as they may have existed at the time of their release, as well as to discuss later interpretations.

Indeed, the idea that musical and cultural values and practices continually evolve guides this work and explains its very broad scope. Framing these chapter subjects expansively allows us to view each topic in detail but also serves to illuminate certain themes that a more specialized study may overlook. For instance, the chapter on New Orleans Creole musicians at the turn of the twentieth century and the chapter on John Coltrane's reputation within jazz education programs since the 1970s offer insight into two very different (and largely overlooked) jazz cultures. But juxtaposing these chapters offers a perspective on more general issues as well, such as the gradual elevation of the genre's prestige or the continued rise of the "great soloist" as the music's institutionalized ideal. Such a broad field of inquiry almost inevitably calls for a broad critical approach, and no single methodology dominates this book. Instead, my goal is to shape the analytical tools to the subject at hand. And while this results in not-so-subtle shifts from chapter to chapter, I am confident that the reader will not suffer too much methodological "whiplash."

Throughout this project, I hope to elucidate notions of jazz as a type of narrative involving the question of "who." Not only is this meant in the sense that some historians would have us understand it—as a listing of exemplary performers in the music—but it also involves the broader issues of who participates, who belongs. History isn't collected; it's told. Each jazz musician, critic, and listener tells a slightly different story of the music's past and present, emphasizing this participant, ignoring another. In this way, we should see that jazz does not simply entail a smoothly evolving series of musical styles but rather an array of individuals and communities engaging with diverse, oftentimes conflicting, actions, ideals, and attitudes.

I've based much of this study on my continued participation as professional pianist and composer in the jazz communities of Los Angeles, New York, and elsewhere. Although performing ability is not essential to critical writing on music and its relationships to the broader social and cultural spheres, a scholar possessing practical knowledge of the field will certainly bring a different outlook on musical practices than will a nonmusician. This combined perspective of scholarship and performance (still fairly rare in jazz studies) creates new possibilities, ideally joining the invaluable insights of a player writing about his experiences in music with those opened by working through a variety of academic discourses.

By the same token, while my musical background enables many of these discussions—allowing me to discern the musical details that lead to the formation of differing jazz identities—I have tried to ensure that it does not dominate them. I've purposely avoided using musical notation or jargon unless I felt it was absolutely necessary to illustrate my point. In this way I hope that readers from a wide range of backgrounds, with or without musical training, can follow the arguments I've drawn here. For *Jazz Cultures* broaches issues that stretch well beyond the everyday concerns of musicians on the bandstand. And just as the members of a good jazz group participate in a kind of nonstop musical conversation among themselves and with their audience, this study represents my ongoing interaction with scholars in a number of fields. Many of the same concerns I raise here (racial identity and difference, gender construction, cultural hierarchy) have been raised elsewhere, sometimes in very different contexts, and I invoke these broader academic debates and concerns throughout this study along with my continued focus on jazz performance, criticism, and scholarship.

It should be clear to the reader by now that by pursuing this project I am pursuing a cultural critique as well as a musical one. And, as Joseph Kerman has observed, "The way we think about music—as professionals or as amateurs; as critics, historians, theorists, whatever—is important at least partly because of the way it impinges on music that is composed, performed, and listened to. Ideas can influence music: though it is just as glaringly obvious that the flow also runs the other direction."[4] For this reason, I find it important to acknowledge that my own ideas, bounded by my own finite horizon of experiences, will guide my interpretation of the albums and other media presented in this project. But the recognition that no individual possesses "the Truth" does not reduce musicological discourse to a simple collection of subjective opinions. While none of us share identical histories—each having grown up within a unique network of economic, geographical, educational, and physical factors—we have encountered many of the same cultural works, we do live in a common era, and, more important, we must continue to live in that era. How we mediate our differences will depend to a large extent on how we understand these shared experiences. *Jazz Cultures* involves interplay among many voices—past and present—contributing contrasting interpretations of its topics. I hope it serves to inspire still more ideas and viewpoints regarding this music's ongoing relationships to historical events, social forces, and cultural practices.

The chapters that make up this study could not possibly represent an exhaustive survey of jazz identities and cultures. Instead, I intend to present an overview of some of the most consequential of these as shaped and exemplified by some of the most influential musicians and institutions. Jazz scholar John P. Murphy, challenging and modifying

Harold Bloom's celebrated 1973 study of poetry, *The Anxiety of Influence,* has shown that every jazz musician holds a greater or lesser degree of sway over his or her peers. For example, to many saxophonists—and not only saxophonists of the 1940s and 1950s—Charlie Parker carried a high degree of "gravity": His behavior and attitudes, as well as his ways of playing, served as powerful models for countless performers. With the 1959 arrival of Ornette Coleman's group in New York, however, a startlingly different manner of jazz presentation opened the possibility (and threat) of new understandings.[5] These sorts of compelling and competing identities form the basis of this project.

I've presented the chapters in a loosely chronological fashion—beginning with early-twentieth-century New Orleans and ending in the 1990s—an arrangement that in many ways reflects only the general order in which selected performances were recorded (as well as my own historical location as author). Rather than re-creating a jazz timeline, the chapter topics are meant to raise issues that remain relevant to our own era. For in many ways, jazz finds itself in the midst of a general identity crisis. Contemporary players, listeners, critics—even record companies and radio stations—often seem uneasy about the immense profusion and diffusion of jazz styles, attitudes, performance venues, and institutions. But what I hope to demonstrate is that the questions now confronting today's various jazz communities echo many of the same conflicts and tensions experienced throughout the music's history. Despite the arguments implicit in most textbooks and history classes, jazz identities do not simply emerge, prosper, and disappear in an orderly fashion. True, players did and do act in response to their predecessors, but many generations of musicians co-exist in close proximity to one another, listen to one another, and respond in a variety of ways. Identities overlap, recede, blend, resurface.

Chapter 1 explores the complex relationship during the first decades of this century between the Uptown, English-speaking African Americans of New Orleans and their neighbors, the Downtown, Francophone "Creoles of color." The attitudes and interactions of these two groups problematize our prevalent and naturalized notions of a black/

white racial binary. The chapter also raises issues of "folk music," lineage, and tradition in jazz, issues to which I return in various ways throughout this book.

Chapter 2 studies the ideals and assumptions of jazz promoted by many recent historiographers by looking to a figure who rarely shows up in their works: saxophonist/singer Louis Jordan. It shows that although Jordan's music readily featured the swing feel, improvisation, and other "purely musical" aspects of formalist definitions of jazz, Jordan's historical location and stage demeanor necessarily preclude him from discourses that promote jazz as high art.

Chapter 3 looks to the controversy surrounding Ornette Coleman's appearances in New York in the late 1950s, arguing that musical differences alone cannot explain the furor that surrounded Coleman and his group at that time. The chapter investigates a "regendering" of established jazz identities opened by Coleman's music and presentation that may help to account for some of the extreme reactions, pro and con, by musicians, critics, and audiences.

Chapter 4 builds on Robert Walser's article on "Deep Jazz" criticism, as well as on studies by Richard Leppert, Susan McClary, and others regarding the "visuality" of music, to illustrate the relationship between performance demeanor and musical meaning in jazz. Focusing on pianists Bill Evans and Keith Jarrett, the essay investigates the ways in which jazz musicians' postures and attitudes while playing may shape understandings of them as profound and serious artists.

Chapter 5 uses the example of saxophonist John Coltrane to examine the musical values and ideals promulgated by college jazz-education programs. The chapter shows that though improvisation teachers and manuals acclaim Coltrane, they expound only a selected segment of that musician's creative output, ignoring other important aspects of his work and life. In particular, the essay contrasts jazz pedagogy's emphasis on Coltrane's "Giant Steps" and "Impressions" and its relative dismissal of the saxophonist's later styles and compositions.

Chapter 6 investigates the concept of the jazz "standard" in the 1990s, as well as the differing senses of "tradition" implied in some recent standards-oriented recordings by Wynton Marsalis and Bill Frisell. Though both of these musicians draw their repertoire from established American composers, they use their chosen works in very different ways and to very different musical and cultural ends. In addition, this chapter offers some concluding remarks on the project as a whole.

The reader may notice that I've devoted no section exclusively to bebop culture. This is not to suggest that bop styles and attitudes are unimportant. Quite the opposite, for as Scott DeVeaux notes, "to understand jazz, one must understand bebop,"[6] and the ideals and images associated with that style play a crucial role in each of these chapters as the current standard against which contesting identities rub. Similarly, figures such as Louis Armstrong, Duke Ellington, Charlie Parker, and Miles Davis—certainly some of the most recognizable names in the music—are not to be found in the chapter headings. As with the discussions of bebop, however, these and other canonical musicians appear throughout the book.

Jazz Cultures isn't meant to "define" the various topics it raises. These issues remain much too complex to nail down definitively, and anyway, meanings, identities, and understandings evolve constantly. Instead, I hope that the reader comes away from this book with new ways of hearing and seeing jazz and perhaps a renewed respect for the richness of these musics and the men and women who play them.[7] For the world of jazz remains as culturally fascinating and musically beautiful as any that we have enjoyed over the past century.

One

"BLUE HORIZON"

Creole Culture and Early New Orleans Jazz

But that's what the music is . . . a lost thing finding itself.
It's like a man with no place of his own. He wanders the world
and he's a stranger wherever he is; he's a stranger right in the place
where he was born. But then something happens to him and he finds
a place, his *place. He stands in front of it and he crosses the door,*
going inside. That's where the music was that day—it was taking
him through the door; he was coming home.

SIDNEY BECHET,
Treat It Gentle

As HISTORIAN GWENDOLYN Midlo Hall has noted, "New Orleans remains, in spirit, the most African city in the United States."[1] At the same time, however, cultural identity among peoples of African extraction in that city has remained anything but uniform. In fact, two distinct African-diasporic communities—the Francocentric *gens du couleur,* or "Creoles of color," and the English-speaking slaves and their descendants—have coexisted in the Crescent City for centuries, each group embodying very different norms and ideals.[2]

Although the subject of racial/cultural identity in jazz has been conceived largely in terms of a black and white binary, this chapter looks to the New Orleans Creole community's participation in and attitudes toward early jazz as a moment when alternative understandings were in play. Not that racial politics weren't a part of that environment, or even that the situation was always less malevolent than in other settings—bassist Pops Foster ruefully recalled the hierarchy of colors when he remarked, "The worst Jim Crow around New Orleans was what the colored did to themselves."[3] But recognizing that jazz musicians and audiences have configured identities outside of our all-too-sedimented understandings of race should make us reconsider our past (musical and social) as well as alternative, hopefully more equitable and constructive, possibilities for the future.

As I've suggested, this is hardly the first study to explore racial issues in jazz. Indeed, the vast majority of critical discourse placing the music in broader cultural and social contexts has emphasized matters of race, and, given the complex and contentious history of racial interaction in this country, this emphasis is neither surprising nor misplaced. Yet critics dealing with these issues generally characterize jazz in terms of two mutating but self-contained worlds: black and white. On the one hand, black jazz is most typically seen as an expression of a unified community ("the people"). On the other, white jazz is often understood as the creation of a rag-tag group of outsiders, misfit individuals forced together by and alienated from an equally unified but incurably unhip metaculture (Bix Beiderbecke, that "tragic" early cornetist from Davenport, Iowa, appears as the quintessential example here). The two jazz communities may listen to each other, even influence each other, and slowly evolve as historical events dictate; but the sphere encompassing each community and separating the two remains somehow homogeneous in these accounts.

For many, jazz has played an especially strong role in representing "blackness" in America, and musicians such as Louis Armstrong, Duke Ellington, Charlie Parker, Nat "King" Cole, Miles Davis, Archie Shepp, and Wynton Marsalis have long exemplified the evolving hopes, fears, dangers, joys, and frustrations of living as African Americans. At the same time, writers have wrestled in various ways with the problem of "whiteness" in jazz, that is, the participation, appreciation, appropriation, and innovation by non-African Americans within what is often understood as a purely "black music."[4]

For instance, in his preeminent survey of American musics, *Music in the New World,* Charles Hamm lists as founding fathers of jazz such New Orleans natives as Buddy Bolden, King Oliver, Freddie Keppard, Sidney Bechet, Johnny Dodds, Kid Ory, and Louis Armstrong.

After describing some early recordings, Hamm writes, "All performers discussed to this point were black, and many histories of jazz have assumed the attitude most pointedly expressed in the opening statement of a book by André Hodier: 'Jazz is the Negro's art and almost all the great jazz musicians are Negroes.'"[5] Hamm then notes that the first jazz recordings were made by (the non-black) Original Dixieland Jazz Band and concludes that "the New Orleans jazz style of the 1910s and '20s encompassed both black and white performers, then. If there is a difference in the playing of the two races, it must be sought at a level other than general style."[6] Meanwhile, in *The Music of Black Americans,* historian Eileen Southern lists Jelly Roll Morton and his sidemen, Omer Simeon and Barney Bigard, as well as Armstrong and Oliver, as important New Orleans innovators. The title and scope of Southern's study leave no question that all of the musicians cited are to be understood as black.[7]

No doubt, all of the men listed by Southern and Hamm were outstanding musicians, largely responsible for taking jazz from New Orleans and disseminating it in a very brief time throughout the United States and, only slightly later, to Europe as well. However, to characterize all of these individuals as black (excepting the O.D.J.B.), as these and many other writers have, disregards the importance of Creole culture in New Orleans history. For there were not two racial categories in that city but at least three, and of the musicians of color listed above, a number of them—including seminal figures Bechet, Morton, and Keppard—did not consider themselves to be black at all but Creole.

This widely overlooked circumstance raises some consequential questions for jazz historiography. First, should scholars relate their takes on history through the lens of present conditions, or should they attempt, instead, to recount the past by bringing forward the terms and identities through which those individuals and communities in question understood themselves to be living? Second, and more pointed, if the overwhelming majority of people outside New Orleans have ignored the cultural differences between African-diasporic cultures in that city, should historians also downplay those cultural differences (as Hamm and Southern seem to have done), using those mischaracterizations as tools to refigure unequal power relations?

Certainly, any historical narrative that emphasizes the immense contributions to jazz by individuals of color is understandable and well founded—it remains irrefutable that the vast majority of the genre's most influential players have originated from African-diasporic communities. This Afrocentric historiographical stance appears especially warranted in light of the deplorable "white washing" of the music's history that has surfaced on occasion (e.g., Paul Whiteman as the "King of Jazz"?). However, such narratives tend to ignore the fact that racial identity among jazz musicians and their attendant audiences within the various camps of this supposed black/white dichotomy has been marked by contradiction and antagonism as well as by cultural pride and unity. And what I hope to demonstrate in this chapter is that lived realities in the jazz world—as in the broader American social and cultural world—are more complex than our simple biracial categories would lead us to believe. Moreover, given the present tendencies to anoint jazz as "America's classical music" and its practitioners as "treasured artists," it might be useful to recall that these lofty understandings developed only recently (and not just in the mainstream white community). As we'll see, the prestige granted early jazz musicians in their own day was significantly less than the "cultural heroes" moniker now bestowed upon them.[8]

James Lincoln Collier has been one of the few jazz scholars to address at length the knotty topic of Creole identity and jazz history. His discussion of the rural roots of many Creole musicians serves as an especially welcome addition to the growing literature on early jazz.[9] Yet while I follow many of Collier's historical observations on this subject, we differ on some fundamental conclusions. Most significant, unlike Collier, I do not argue that calling jazz a "black music" mischaracterizes the genre. True, Europeans, European Americans, Latin Americans, Asian Americans, Asians, and Australians have contributed significantly to all aspects of the music, increasingly so over the past four decades. But so many of the significant figures and practices in jazz derive from African and African-diasporic communities that to ignore these roots signals at the very least a gross injustice to historical accuracy. Unfortunately, as Ingrid Monson has rightly pointed out, some efforts on the part of white writers and musicians to "universalize" jazz—highlighting the fact that the music is performed and enjoyed all over the world by a wide diversity of peoples—"can be perceived as power plays rather than expressions of universal brotherhood."[10]

Non-African-diasporic participants need not feel threatened by the "black music" designation. This is much the same type of historical situation that allows us to speak of, say, a "European classical tradition" even if the music is performed in Chicago, composed by Heitor Villa-Lobos, conducted by Seiji Ozawa, and played by Yehudi Menuhin (or, in the case of his celebrated renditions of the art-music repertoire, even by Wynton Marsalis). "Blackness," then, should be taken as a cultural category rather than a genetic one. And if we understand jazz this way, the labels "black music" or "African-American music" are not biologically exclusionary but simply readily discernible historical realities.

My goal in this chapter is not to retell the "origins" of jazz in New Orleans per se; scholars have produced studies of varying degrees of detail that attempt to uncover the complex events and interactions that gave rise to jazz as a distinct genre in that place.[11] Also largely absent from this discussion is the role played by "white" musicians in New Orleans, though it is clear that we need to reconsider our conception of that aspect of race as well. In fact, many of those players whom we now consider rather routinely as white identified themselves more often in different terms, stemming from a diversity of ethnic backgrounds including Italian, Irish, Hungarian, Canary Island, Mexican, Filipino, and European-Jewish.[12]

Instead, by focusing on Creole musicians active during the time that jazz became recognized as such, I hope to present a richer, more multifarious narrative of the fascinating era and place when and where jazz emerged most forcefully. Showing the cultural transgressions, tensions, and contradictions—as well as new senses of kinship—experienced by Creole jazz players should cause us to rethink some deeply ingrained perceptions of the music. Resuscitating Creole identity will help to challenge today's too neatly circumscribed racial categories.

And, just as important, it upsets many prevalent notions of New Orleans jazz—and, by extension, *all* jazz—as "folk music" and its participants as "natural," if somewhat backward, folk heroes, notions that persist in many ways to this day, though mostly in subtle and unacknowledged guises. To begin, it helps to recount briefly the musical and cultural environment in which Creole musicians developed their craft.

TWO "BLACK" CULTURES IN NEW ORLEANS

I contend that Creoles are a unique race of people . . . [with]
specific traits and traditions that have been transmitted
from generation to generation by Creole speaking
people, a unique nation of mixed bloods.

CREOLE NATIONALIST GILBERT MARTIN,
in Mary Gehman, *The Free People of Color of New Orleans*

The emergence of a distinct Creole community in New Orleans stems from the issue of the first *Code Noir,* or Black Code, by the French monarchy in the seventeenth century. This series of edicts—first signed into French law in 1685 and adopted in modified form in Louisiana in 1724—spelled out the rights, responsibilities, and rules of conduct regarding the interactions of free persons and slaves in France's New World colonies. As Joseph Roach's work on the subject has shown, rather than banning racial interaction, the code's original framers sought to promote a unified French "body politic" with "One Blood." Indeed, Roach argues that "miscegenation was . . . a geopolitical strategy of Louis XIV's France." [13] More than a document of law, the code activated a Franco-acculturation of African-diasporic peoples, permeating all areas of public and private life. For example, the code stipulated that masters baptize their slaves in and teach them the ways of the Catholic church; this conversion would later serve as one of the ways that New Orleans Creoles differentiated themselves from their black Protestant neighbors.

While the Louisiana version of the *Code Noir* omitted certain articles of the original proclamation providing for the manumission of slaves and racial intermarriage, it did leave open the possibility of the emergence of a group of freed peoples of color in that region. Legally, for instance, children born to free women and slave men were deemed free. On a more practical level, the ever-increasing mixed-race population tolerated by the relatively liberal policies of both the French and Spanish colonial governments nurtured an environment in which skin tone did not necessarily determine social status. Meanwhile, the turn of the nineteenth century brought a dramatic influx from St. Domingue of free, French-speaking Creoles into New Orleans.[14] The arrival of these Creoles—many of whom, significantly, had fought unsuccessfully on the side of the white French colonists against the slaves in the uprising of 1791—further ensured a certain amount of socioeconomic mobility for individuals of color. The fact that Creole ownership of slaves was not uncommon by the late eighteenth century illustrates quite clearly the emergence of a separate and increasingly prosperous African-diasporic cultural community in the region. This phenomenon marks a profound difference between the French-dominated territories and the British-ruled North American colonies and states such as Virginia and the Carolinas where being "colored" remained virtually synonymous with being a slave.

The political power and social prestige held by the Louisiana Creole community fluctuated with the changing local governments but generally fell somewhere between the various European-American ethnicities on the one extreme and the English-speaking, African-American population on the other. Even as their economic status began to wane in the nineteenth century, however, Creole society strove to maintain staunchly middle-class values, priding itself on appearing well mannered and well educated (in the European sense) and living within an overall Francocentrism. As LeRoi Jones (now Amiri Baraka) notes: "The Creoles, in much the same manner as the house Negroes on plantations in other areas, adopted as much of the French culture as they could and turned their backs on the "darker" culture of their half-brothers. It is safe to assume, for instance, that there were no black Creoles dancing in Congo Square."[15]

We should read Jones's use of the term "darker" somewhat metaphorically here. For the conflicts that arose between these two communities in New Orleans stemmed as much from differences in language and religious and even culinary customs—that is to say, cultural customs—as well as urban geography (the two groups remained largely segregated for some time) as from skin tone.[16] If, however, we should understand these conflicts as "Francophone versus Anglophone" rather than "brown versus black," the fact remains that the rift between the two populations was a very real one and different individuals negotiated it in different ways.

With the influx of Anglo-Americans after the Louisiana Purchase of 1803, city officials increasingly amended and began stringently enforcing the code's articles. By the last decade of the nineteenth century, anyone possessing any degree of African blood heritage was deemed legally "Negro," ignoring the reality that the vast majority of Creoles considered themselves to be more French than anything else. Subsequent to these pronouncements, Creoles found themselves without the relative legal privilege and elevated social standing they had enjoyed among the Euro-American populations in the city and were often forced into unfamiliar arenas of social interaction among their cross-town antagonists.

Regardless of—or, more accurately, because of—their new "official" standing, many Creoles chose to close ranks, emphasizing and valorizing the differences between the two groups in order to strengthen their own sense of cultural identity and supposed superiority. This attitude existed to the extent that Creole banjo and guitar player Johnny St. Cyr could remark in 1938 that "the mulattoes [Creoles of color] were actually more prejudiced than the white people at that time."[17] Creole historian Arthé Agnes Anthony clarifies this situation, writing that

> the [Creole] community . . . refused to be classified with the publicly maligned freedmen and their descendants. Underlying this perception—a view that was carried over into the twentieth century—was a refusal to submit to the dichotomy explicit in segregation: that all Caucasians were superior and all negroes were inferior.

Rather than accept this view Creoles created a middle ground for themselves; even though they were not legally granted the rights afforded whites by no means would they tolerate categorization with blacks. . . . Creoles sought—and to a certain extent found—if not protection at least comfort in their own world because they were able to exercise a degree of control over it. By avoiding extensive contact with Afro-Americans they were able to separate themselves—at least psychologically—from other blacks, thereby reaffirming in their own minds that they were different from them.[18]

Anthony's work reveals the serious differences separating the two predominant African-diasporic communities in New Orleans and, as we will see, challenges notions of jazz as the product of a unified, Southern black "folk" culture.

TWO "BLACK" MUSICS IN NEW ORLEANS

See, us Downtown people . . . we didn't think so much of this Uptown jazz until we couldn't make a living otherwise.

PAUL DOMINGUEZ,
in Alan Lomax, *Mister Jelly Roll*

By the turn of the twentieth century, New Orleans' Canal Street had come to symbolize the division between the two groups: blacks lived on one side of Canal, or "Uptown"; the Creoles occupied the other, or "Downtown," side.[19] Given the Eurocentrism of most Downtown families, it seems inevitable that European, particularly French, instrumental music and opera would serve as that community's common musical fare.[20] And it follows that, having been raised on the aesthetics attached to the European art-music tradition, most Creoles ridiculed the Uptown musicians as "unschooled." Uptown players were usually less adept at sight reading musical notation than their neighbors, and they incorporated a number of instrumental effects (blues-inflected slurs, "growls," etc.) that conservatory-trained Downtown musicians of the time found to be primitive, distasteful, or otherwise inferior.

The condescending attitude toward blacks fostered by some Creole musicians carried well into the twentieth century, regardless of the legal edict uniting the two groups. Alan Lomax's interview with early-twentieth-century violinist Paul Dominguez reveals the prevailing Creole attitude toward their forced interaction with the Uptown music community:

> You know what happen to us musicians—I mean us real musicians from the Seventh Ward where we were all educated in music and *knew* our instruments—when we came in here, we had to change.[21] Why, my daddy, he was recognized king bass player in this town, but he wouldn't play *ratty*. He wouldn't play unless you put his part in front of him, and then he could make a monkey out of the average player of today. Well, he couldn't make it here in the District. He couldn't make a *living!* . . . [Uptown cornetist Buddy] Bolden cause all that [to change]. . . . He cause these younger Creoles, men like [Sidney] Bechet and [Freddie] Keppard, to have different style altogether from the old heads like [Lorenzo] Tio and [Emanuel] Perez. I don't know how [the improvisers] do it. . . . But goddam, they do it. [They] can't tell you what's there on the paper, but just play the hell out of it.[22]

While Creoles grudgingly acknowledged the superiority of the Uptown musicians' improvisational ability and expressive "fire," in all other respects they scorned, or at least viewed with suspicion, their crosstown rivals. This derision only intensified as Creoles saw the demand for their more polite brand of musicking shrink in favor of "hotter," "dirtier" styles. Their forced musical interaction must have struck many Downtown players as particularly galling because most of them did not even consider Uptown players to be "musicians" at all. "Real musicians" (as Dominguez called his colleagues) could read notation, knew the "classics," and sought a "refined" tone, none of which applied to typical black American players of the time.

Legendary Creole jazzman Jelly Roll Morton—one of those musicians cited by both Hamm and Southern as "black"—was notorious for his anti-Uptown invectives. Morton's chronicler, Alan Lomax, defends the pianist/composer's position, arguing that "Jelly Roll's race prejudice was not . . . a singular defect, but a commonly accepted Creole attitude, considered normal by Creoles and non-Creoles alike." [23] Contradictory as it may seem, Morton and his bands borrowed a number of devices from Uptown styles (he was, for instance, a very fine blues player and singer). [24] Still, he invariably chose to emphasize in his interviews the European side (that is, as he saw it, the "classy" side) of his music, as in the following passage:

> There is nothing finer than jazz music because it comes from everything of the finest-class music. Take the *Sextet* from *Lucia* and *Miserere* from *Il Trovatore,* that they used to play in the French Opera House, tunes that have always lived in my mind as the great favorites of the opera singers; I transformed a lot of those numbers into jazz time, using different little variations and ideas to masquerade the tunes. [25]

JAZZ AS A PROFESSION

Of course, my folks never had the idea they wanted a musician in the family. They always had it in their minds that a musician was a tramp, trying to duck work, with the exception of the French Opera House players which they patronized.

JELLY ROLL MORTON,
in Lomax, *Mister Jelly Roll*

Musicking in turn-of-the-century New Orleans entailed virtually citywide participation. And while the extraordinary vibrancy of musical life in that town was most conspicuously and most famously demonstrated by the frequent parades that wound through the streets, these events constituted only one realm in which musicians developed and displayed their craft. For apart from the parades and the more prestigious concert-hall genres, instrumentalists (male instrumentalists, at least) played whenever and wherever community events called for their services: on riverboats, at birthday parties, picnics, social clubs, weddings, funerals, in brothels, nightclubs, and stage shows.[26] Repertoire ranged from rags and popular songs to marches, spirituals, and classical fare. And if their music wasn't exactly jazz, one branch of the early jazz musicians' immediate forebears frequently utilized a "ragged" performance style that present-day listeners, musicians, and scholars would consider to be, at the very least, jazzlike. These players relied heavily on "growls," scoops, and other effects derived from blues-style vocalizations while incorporating varying degrees of rhythmic swing and greater or lesser amounts of improvisation.

As I've noted, music played a central role in New Orleans life, and Creole society was no exception. Yet while many Creoles enlivened social events and earned extra money by performing, their community generally frowned upon jazz musicking as a career choice. Indeed, despite all of the music, jazz historian Burton Peretti has suggested that there was an overall paucity of *professional* musicians in New Orleans during the early jazz years. He cites figures showing that "in 1870, among the city's 40,000 blacks, only 7 listed their major occupation as musician in the census survey. This compared to 177 black policemen, 397 cigarmakers, and 249 shoemakers. Ten years later the number of black musicians rose to only 53."[27]

Peretti's comments raise a number of points. First, given that cigarmaking and shoemaking are Creole traditions, it is likely that that community figured more prominently in the census readings than the Uptown population. Second, while fifty-three musicians in 1880 may not sound like a significant figure, it *is* almost eight times the number of the previous decade. Consequently, it seems plausible that, during the height of jazz activity in New Orleans in the two decades after the turn of the century, a reasonably large contingent worked in the city as professionals.

But even if we follow Peretti in his numerical assessments, his conclusions—that economics dictated such low numbers of professional musicians, and that envy from the city's poor and condescension from its wealthy accounted for the lowly social status those musicians suffered—bear reconsideration. To be sure, it was difficult to make a living as a player (it still is). But evidence suggests that, as with most middle-class white families in the America of the time, it was the "unsavory" individuals with whom one might mingle during the late-night gigs, rather than the financial unpredictability of the full-time musician's life, that marked music as a less-than-honorable profession among New Orleans Creoles.

For one, John Chilton has shown that by the age of thirteen, Creole reedman Sidney Bechet was earning around $15 per week—"a little more than the average wage for a working adult"—and contributing some of that income to his mother and father.[28] Similarly, Johnny St. Cyr recalled that while most players did hold other jobs,

> a musician was paid $1.00 for riding on a truck and playing for five hours, $2.50 if he played a ball, from 8 P.M. until 4 A.M., with one hour intermission. House parties paid $1.50 to $2.00 and you played about five hours—8 P.M. to 1 A.M., or 9 P.M. to 2 A.M. This does not sound like much money today, but it was good money in those days. A popular musician in those days would make a good living.[29]

At the same time, Arthé Anthony has pointed out the degree to which the elitist stance characterizing the Downtown population extended to their views on employment:

> The Creole community was cognizant of the relationship between race and occupational opportunity. Their attitudes toward jobs—those that were respected and those that were not—were influenced by the city's racially determined occupational patterns. Aware of the limited range of job opportunities, Creoles tended to value those jobs that appeared to set them apart from the larger black community.[30]

In line with this thinking, Chilton, Sidney Bechet's biographer, writes of the disposition of Bechet's parents toward their son's chosen—and at that time only—source of income: "no amount of money compensated the family for the fact that Sidney was working regularly in 'the District': such employment was thought of by them as a stigma."[31] Jelly Roll Morton also encountered antagonism from his family when they learned of his activities (not all of which were strictly musical):

> In those days everybody was playing what they call ragtime, and I wanted to play too. But my daddy caught me trying one day and took off his belt and tanned me good and proper. He said: "Son, if you ever play that dirty stuff again I'll throw you out of here on your ear!" But man, I couldn't no more stop playing it than I could stop eating. So I used to go to the cabaret called "The Frenchman" and boy—I used to really beat it out.[32]

Of course, Morton continued his pursuits, and his grandmother eventually refused to put up with the resulting social humiliation. She rebuked him, "A musician is nothing but a bum and a scalawag. I don't want you round your sister," and Morton was forced to move out of the family home.[33]

These and many similar reminiscences reveal that identity, not economics, was the primary factor in discouraging certain types of musical participation. In this way, Peretti's citing of an unnamed source regarding the highly regarded Creole clarinetist Alphonse Picou—"'He never considered himself a musician as such until he was asked to join the Bloom Symphony,' a Creole classical group,"[34]—tells us more about the favorable attitudes held by Creoles toward European musics (and the concomitant distaste for jazzlike musics) than about the fiscal hardships of that time and place.

By contrast, Uptown families did not seem to view the choice to pursue music as a profession as an unforgivable transgression against the community. As those occupying the lowest rung on the socioeconomic ladder, these performers simply had less (or nothing) to lose by overstepping the social norms observed by their Downtown neighbors. Indeed, Scott DeVeaux has shown that "by the beginning of the twentieth century, the profession of musician was taking its place alongside barber, caterer, and Pullman porter as one of a handful of occupations outside unskilled manual labor open to blacks."[35] But a Creole considering music as a lifestyle faced a much greater likelihood of provoking familial discord, even in those instances, like Bechet's, in which a musician could support himself or herself comfortably through playing.[36]

SIDNEY BECHET

I have touched already upon the famous Creole reedman Sidney Bechet (1897–1959), but his situation is worth exploring more closely, for Bechet's music and writing intimate some of the earliest interactions among jazz cultures. Though Bechet's status in recent jazz history texts does not equal that granted to Uptown trumpeter Louis Armstrong, Bechet's own contemporaries regarded him as a player of startling brilliance. Bechet was also one of the first jazz musicians to spend extensive time in Europe, ultimately achieving the status of a cultural hero in France. In doing so, he served as one of the primary role models for succeeding generations of European jazz musicians at the same time that he nurtured an environment that would become amicable to the many expatriate American players who made Europe, particularly Paris, their home from the 1920s onward.[37]

Through his autobiography, *Treat It Gentle* (published posthumously in 1960), Bechet left behind a wonderfully rich firsthand account of musical and cultural life in turn-of-the-century New Orleans. *Treat It Gentle* stands as one of the true gems of autobiography—jazz or otherwise—it is a beautiful story, beautifully told. If, as John Chilton has pointed out, Bechet's tale does not always correlate with what we might regard as historical fact, the work does tell us what Bechet would have us believe to be true, and so serves as an invaluable account of his ideals and aspirations.[38] It helps, too, that Bechet played on numerous recordings over many decades, a circumstance that allows for critical discussions of his music making. In this way, he differs from many of his New Orleans–raised colleagues and predecessors; the now-mythical Buddy Bolden stands as only the most notable of the lamentably unrecorded or underrecorded innovators of the early jazz era.

Despite his Creole background, Bechet always remained an "ear" player, staunchly refusing to learn musical notation, an aspect of his musicianship roundly criticized by many of his fellow Downtown players, with their pride in European-style "professionalism." Jazz historians Lewis Porter and Michael Ullman understood Bechet's inability to read music as a "failing" about which he was "sensitive." But far from being defensive about this issue, Bechet makes it plain in his autobiography that his decision not to read was a conscious one. Such a stance can be seen as evidence of his desire to be linked with what he must have regarded as the more "pure" Uptown style of musical expression.[39] He was not alone in his mistrust of reading. Nat Hentoff and Nat Shapiro quote Jack Weber as saying of early New Orleans clarinetists that "some of them thought that if they learned how to read, it would ruin their ability to improvise."[40] One explanation for this stance may be that the Uptown players, those most inclined to rely solely on their "ears," were by necessity the strongest improvisers, and improvisational ability remained one of the traits that Bechet and like-minded players esteemed most highly in a musician.[41]

Bechet's case frequently reveals such culturally transgressive allegiances, as he maintained a decidedly more Uptown, even Afrocentric, position than the one taken by most Creoles of his day. And this stance extended beyond music; for example, Bechet went so far as to assert, "my grandfather, he was Africa,"[42] and to claim that one of the reasons behind his relocation to France in the early 1950s was the proximity of that country to the African continent.[43]

However, Bechet's position on his racial heritage was neither unremittingly Afrocentric nor uncomplicated. In spite of his apparent Uptown ties, he never disavowed his Creole-French roots, as can be seen in his assertion about the confluence that created jazz: "The rhythm came from Africa, but the music, the foundation, came from right here in France."[44] Indeed, even with someone who often patterned himself after Uptown ways, Bechet could occasionally revert to the virulent racism that characterized Downtown attitudes. Saxophonist Bob Wilber, a longtime friend and student of Bechet's, discussed his teacher's complex, often contradictory, stance toward his own cultural heritage. Bechet, he wrote,

> never thought of himself as a black man. . . . Creoles like Bechet and Jelly Roll [Morton] did not see themselves as black, yet they

were not accepted as white men. This sometimes resulted in strange statements from Sidney, like, "Them Goddam niggers, doin' this and doin' that, and givin' us all a bad name." We once sat down in front of the tape recorder while he expounded on the subject, extolling the virtues of the infamous southern racist senator, the notorious Senator Bilbo, who had connections with the Ku Klux Klan and all the worst aspects of that business. Sidney said, "Bilbo's doin' a good job. He's for law and order. He keepin' all them people in their places."[45]

These outbursts notwithstanding, Bechet's stance on his lineage differed greatly from that of his fellow Creole, Jelly Roll Morton. In the Library of Congress–sponsored interviews with Alan Lomax, Morton explicitly emphasized the European side of his ancestry. He noted, "As I can understand, my folks were in the city of New Orleans long before the Louisiana Purchase, and all my folks came directly from the shores of France, that is across the world in the other world, and they landed in the New World years ago."[46] Similarly, a note from Richard B. Allen, former curator of the William Ransom Hogan Jazz Archive at Tulane University in New Orleans, states that Morton often insisted to singer Lizzie Miles that he was white. Allen adds: "She [Miles] had good reason to believe otherwise, having grown up in the same neighborhood [as Morton]."[47]

The differing attitudes of Bechet and Morton toward both jazz and even their own respective Creole ancestries are reflected to a large degree in the music each emphasized. Morton played piano, an instrument closely associated with the European classical tradition, considered himself a "composer," and openly ridiculed musicians who couldn't read notation (though his own skill as a reader has been questioned). Conversely, Bechet, while a composer in his own right (presumably he would play or sing his tunes to someone able to transcribe his melodies into notation), made his mark primarily as an outstanding improvising reed player. And though the clarinet and saxophone originated in Europe, both may more readily approximate the slurs and bends of African-derived blues vocalizations than the piano, with its keyboard organized in fixed, discrete pitches. In fact, Bechet's attitude toward musicking directly opposed European ideals. His playing leaned heavily toward the Uptown, that is to say "unschooled," "low-down," or "blacker" styles, and it is precisely these "rough" techniques that Bechet saw as essential to jazz.

For instance, of his first clarinet teacher, Creole George Baquet, Bechet remarked,

> Baquet was a hell of a fine musicianer; he played awful fine. But he wasn't exactly a real ragtime player. What he played, it wasn't really jazz . . . he stuck real close to the line in a way. He played things more classic-like, straight out how it was written. And he played it very serious. . . . When Baquet played it, there wasn't none of those growls and buzzes which is a part of ragtime music, which is a way the musicianer has of replacing different feelings he finds inside the music and inside himself . . . all those interpreting moans and groans and happy sounds. There wasn't none of that in the way he played. I don't know if it was that Baquet *couldn't* do it, all I know is he *didn't* do it.[48]

Bechet respected Baquet's smooth and "straight" Downtown-style playing but felt that it lacked the "interpreting sounds" preferred by Uptown stylists. Similarly, Richard Hadlock's descriptions of his lessons under Bechet suggest that his teacher believed that a jazz musician finds his or her "voice" by learning to manipulate pitch and timbre:

> "I'm going to give you one note to play today," he once told me. "See how many ways you can play that note—growl it, smear it, flat it, sharp it, do anything you want to it. That's how you express your feelings in this music. It's like talking."[49]

BECHET AND THE BLUES

The most notable means Bechet found to express his sense of identity musically was, significantly, through that very un-European musical form: the blues. The blues have been described as "revenge," a response to the incessant trials and tribulations of a group living under relentless racism.[50] To be sure, there is a sense of revenge about the blues. The music and lyrics can function as an act of defiance toward the dominant values, laws, and rules that would keep a people exploited. And, by creating their own aesthetic precepts, many New Orleans musicians did, consciously or unconsciously, turn their backs on those practices that both white and Creole society deemed "cultured," demonstrating as they did this that those in power are not necessarily the wisest, most creative, or most imaginative.

But the term "revenge" does not adequately describe the full range of the blues, for revenge remains, by definition, only a re-action. Participation among the blues-based, Uptown-style musicians, listeners, and dancers attracted peoples of disparate cultural lineages and opened the possibility for new senses of community. Their musicking constituted, therefore, a generative action in its own right. Through the blues, like-minded musicians from both Uptown and Downtown could imagine, and even configure, a world comprising different (and not merely inverted) relationships among cultures. This phenomenon helps to explain why jazz practices became ever more closely monitored by the white arbiters of taste as the music attracted increasing numbers of white participants. Any alternative to the prescribed notions of identity (and, therefore, possible action in the world) would be seen as threatening to those whose interests it serves to maintain the status quo. It shows, too, why the blues were, and remain, a powerful draw for groups of people exploited or otherwise disenfranchised, regardless of racial heritage.[51]

Dwight Andrews has suggested that "the blues form evolved unfettered by any aesthetic obligations outside of the African-American traditions and the community it was destined to serve."[52] But while the musical and cultural gap separating blues from European models remains wide, no African-diasporic communities have ever existed in total isolation. The blues, after all, went unheard in Africa until it reached there via recordings, and blues legend Howlin' Wolf even cited white "hillbilly" star Jimmie Rodgers as a formative influence.[53] Even the predominantly white-owned record companies played a role. They decided what material would and would not be recorded and released by such seemingly "pure" blues artists as Robert Johnson and

Bessie Smith, both of whom knew and performed the full range of popular musics of the day. These points aside, Andrews is right to celebrate the sense of self-empowerment that accompanies blues making and the possibilities that that sense opens.

Recordings abound of Bechet playing the blues, almost all of which achieve a degree of that very elusive quality called "soul" attained by few others. He belongs to a group of "jazz" and "blues" players—oftentimes the boundary where one genre ends and the other begins is blurred or erased altogether—whose playing speaks of joy as well as, indeed, in spite of, pain.[54] Musicians as seemingly disparate as Bechet, Mississippi John Hurt, Louis Armstrong, Charlie Parker, Hampton Hawes, Big Joe Turner, Johnny Hodges, Louis Jordan, Ray Charles, Taj Mahal (Henry Saint Claire Fredericks), Wynton Kelly, Lester Bowie, Ornette Coleman, and, for that matter, Jaco Pastorious and Dr. John (Mac Rebennack), gain not only a certain amount of "revenge" but also, more important, a sense of dignity, affirmation, and, ultimately, identity that flies in the face of those who would insist on a perpetually "downtrodden" people.

These are not "angry" or even consistently "sad" blues; rather they represent, in Bechet's own words, "what you'd send to your son in trouble if he was on earth and you was in Heaven."[55] Bechet's approach to the blues parallels his theory of effective autobiographical narration, wherein the good stories need to be told "the long way."[56] His celebrated 1944 recording of "Blue Horizon" demonstrates this philosophy put to practice.

"BLUE HORIZON"

Bechet most often relied on his loud and brash soprano saxophone sound in performance, but he used "Blue Horizon" to feature his warm, woody clarinet playing.[57] Accompanying him here are Sidney DeParis on trumpet, Uptown–New Orleans bassist Pops Foster, pianist Art Hodes, drummer Manzie Johnson, and trombonist Vic Dickenson. Although Bechet receives credit as the composer of "Blue Horizon," that recording exemplifies less a composed blues song—with melodic "heads" serving as bookends for a string of solo statements—

than it does a complete blues performance, a distinction that I will clarify below.

Bechet begins in the lower, chalumeau register of the clarinet and slowly unfolds his statement over six choruses. The manner in which he shapes each successive twelve-bar harmonic cycle—gradually manipulating dynamics and range, pushing toward the last chorus for his loudest playing and most sustained upper register work—typifies his "story-teller" approach.

In particular, Bechet's work here displays an extraordinary use of musical "space," emphasizing sustained notes and extended silences to add dramatic weight to his phrases. Recollections of his former students confirm that he focused on this aspect of playing. Richard Hadlock, who studied under Bechet, recalled that his teacher would admonish him: "Always try to complete your phrases and ideas. There are lots of otherwise good musicians who sound terrible because they start a new idea without finishing the last one." [58] Bechet's suggestions reveal one of the ways in which he formed his highly rhetorical style; recall his advice to Bob Wilber: "It's like talking." He relies less on long strings of eighth-note lines, such as one would find in Swing and bop styles, than on the exploration, even delectation, of sound in itself.

We've seen that an essential trait distinguishing a jazz musician from a typical Downtown musician of the time is the incorporation of what Bechet described as the "interpreting moans and groans and happy sounds." "Blue Horizon" overflows with such sonorities, as Bechet colors and shapes each phrase—indeed, virtually every tone— with a long, slow, rising glissando, a gentle "scoop" from below, a "fall" from above, or a throaty growl. Of course, it is just these devices, the slurs, rips, and buzzes, that bear some of the most African-related traits of early jazz. [59] Bechet's famous wide and rapid vibrato further accentuates the flexibility of pitch and dramatic flair characterizing his playing, a technique he applies liberally throughout all his performances and one that would have put off most of his more traditional Creole colleagues.

These Uptown-derived "scoops" and exaggerated vibrato would become Bechet's trademarks and exert a tremendous influence on other players, particularly on alto saxophonist Johnny Hodges. [60] Significantly, those musical gestures fell out of favor during the rise of bebop in the 1940s as musicians began to favor "thinner" vibratos (or none whatsoever) and more "centered" pitch articulation. This shift was a response in part to the bop era's emphasis on faster tempos and greater use of "extensions" (ninths, flatted fifths, thirteenths) but also to a desire to sound less "melodramatic." Scott DeVeaux has pointed out the ambivalence of bop-era players to such blues stylings, noting that "as brash New Yorkers with an attitude, they were keenly aware that the blues embodied a certain social inertia, a rural passivity, that they were determined to overcome." [61]

The boppers' take on blues-oriented players may have been somewhat misplaced, for Bechet was no "hick." He experienced and enjoyed at close hand cosmopolitan French life, with its abundance of fine wines, rich foods, and available women, far more frequently than most of the bop hipsters ever came close to doing. Nor was he a reactionary, never denying the necessity of stylistic changes in jazz, always believing in the need for each generation to tell its own stories.

> You know, there's this mood about the music, a kind of need to be moving. You just can't set it down and hold it. Those Dixieland musicianers, they tried to do that; they tried to write the music down and kind of freeze it. Even when they didn't arrange it to death, they didn't have any place to send it; that's why they lost it. You just can't keep the music unless you move with it. [62]

Bechet suggests here that to ensure the survival of a viable—which is to say expressive, relevant, and entertaining—musical style, players must not only draw upon the past but also give sound to the present while moving toward an imagined future. Not until the emergence of Charles Mingus and Ornette Coleman as band leaders in the late 1950s and early 1960s did jazz styles shift again to reincorporate the overtly expressive slurs, glisses, and scoops that were common in earlier jazz eras. [63]

"Blue Horizon," like most of Bechet's recordings, clearly illustrates the "problem of transcription" pointed out in recent scholarship dealing with non-European musics. The excruciatingly slow glissandi and other gestures so crucial to this style simply resist reduction to notes on a page. The fact that Bechet himself never relied on notation may contribute here. Rather than seeing discrete notes, Bechet necessarily approached playing more broadly in terms of sonorities, and these did not necessarily—in fact rarely—fit into centered, stable pitches. Similarly, his rhythmic conception in this performance seems less bound by equal subdivisions. To be sure, all musicians stretch or contract note values to some degree, but Bechet's gestural blues playing lends his phrasing a freer quality than one would hear from a more "linear" jazz player, Clifford Brown, say, or the early John Coltrane.[64]

In fact, this loose aural/oral sense seems to inform the piece as a whole. As I've remarked, "Blue Horizon" lacks the sort of clearly stated head-solo-head arrangement that frames most jazz. The only hint that Bechet may have had an actual "tune" in mind comes in his return to a brief melodic fragment in bars nine and ten (the V chord and IV chord respectively) of each chorus, though he never plays these fragments the same way twice. And while the contour of his phrases and gestures follows the cycling of the blues form, a larger musical narrative guides his work, as his playing pushes toward a multichorus resolution rather than through a succession of self-contained twelve-bar cycles. That is why I've suggested that we consider "Blue Horizon" a performance rather than a song whose melody can be fixed onto a lead sheet and played one way this time and differently the next. The entirety of Bechet's long-term blues trajectory looks toward, well, the "horizon," and, in many ways, is the piece.

Crucial to the effectiveness of this approach is the subtle accompaniment provided by his colleagues, who act as a sort of congregation/ choir to Bechet's "preacher." Beginning in the third chorus, each rhythm-section player, in turn or in tandem, supports the clarinetist's blues rhetoric with some sort of pedal point (right-hand tremolos in the piano, steady roots bowed on the bass, subtle snare drum rolls). Their contributions serve to generate a remarkably relaxed intensity, enabling the soloist to take his "story" to the next dramatic level. Manzie Johnson's understated drumming lends particularly subtle and effective support. By 1944, when this track was recorded, contemporary drumming styles had turned busier, most noticeably through left-hand snare-drum interjections and "bombs" dropped by the right-foot/bass drum. By contrast, Johnson seems content to provide a firm but unobtrusive pulse throughout.

The horn players too, though remaining in the background, provide crucial backing to the soloist, following his narrative thread. Trombonist Vic Dickenson enters in the second chorus with a simple background two-bar riff figure. Trumpeter Sidney DeParis enters in the following chorus, harmonizing with Dickenson for twelve bars before improvising a light counterpoint to Bechet. Both horn players lay out for the fifth chorus. But as Bechet's solo peaks in both register and dynamics in the final twelve bars, the horn players reenter with their most animated counterpoint, underlining the climax of the clarinetist's performance. Bechet clearly stands as the focus of this recording, but the work of the others enables him to make the most of his prodigious skills. Though not virtuosic in the "showy" sense, "Blue Horizon" represents a masterful performance, demonstrating a deep understanding of blues rhetoric, an ease of expression, and a cooperative spirit from all of the players.

"WAITING TO UNDERSTAND WHAT THE OTHER MAN IS DOING"

Bechet made it clear that his joy and creativity were piqued when playing among musicians like those mentioned above who were his peers in improvisational-interplay abilities. And it was the continual challenge of creating sounds that complemented and inspired bandmates that he found to be most satisfying.

> That's the thing about ragtime. . . . It ain't a writing down where you just play what it says on the paper in front of you, and so long as you do that the arranger, he's taken care of everything else. When you're really playing ragtime, you're feeling it out, you're playing to the other parts, you're waiting to understand what the other man's doing, and then you're going with his feeling, adding what you have of your feeling.[65]

In this regard, Lewis Porter and Michael Ullman rightly suggest that "one of the great tensions in [Bechet's] life was between his natural competitiveness and his lifelong desire to assemble a collectively swinging, New Orleans band. He never quite succeeded. . . . But he never gave up!"[66]

Examples of Bechet working within a more classically New Orleans polyphonic approach run throughout his work, from his 1924 recording of "Texas Moaner Blues" with Louis Armstrong and trombonist Charlie Irvis, to his outstanding Blue Note sessions from two decades later such as "Old Stack O'Lee Blues" in which he interweaves lines with fellow clarinetist Albert "Nick" Nicholas.[67] We can even hear Bechet's love of interplay on his 1941 self-accompanied multitracked performances (the first of their kind) of "Blues of Bechet" and "The Sheik of Araby."[68] These recordings display a complex moment in Bechet's jazz ideals: while proud of his acclaim as the first to explore the most recent recording technologies, Bechet's comments on these sessions make it clear that the spirit of jazz exploration was somehow lost in the overdubbing process. For he esteemed not only the musical texture of counterpoint but also the engagement with like-minded—yet not "identical"—musicians in order to mutually challenge, inspire, and surprise. As Bechet remarked in the 1950s, "In the old days there wasn't no one so anxious to take someone else's run. We were working together. Each person, he was the other person's music: you could feel that really running through the band, making itself up and coming out so new and strong. We played as a group then."[69]

The degree to which jazz behavior gradually drifted away from this New Orleans musical-social ideal can be seen in this passage from Ralph Ellison's 1958 paean to the late nascent-bop-era guitarist Charlie Christian:

> There is . . . a cruel contradiction implicit in the art form itself. For true jazz is an art of individual assertion within and against the group. Each true jazz moment (as distinct from uninspired commercial performance) springs from the contest in which each artist challenges all the rest; each solo flight, or improvisation, rep-

resents (like the successive canvases of a painter) a definition of his identity: as individual, as member of the collectivity and as a link in an endless chain of tradition.[70]

Bechet would not have seen group play as a "cruel contradiction" but rather as an arena of mutually satisfying cooperation and the very foundation for his love of playing music. To be sure, musicians did push each other; rivalries (some not so friendly) did spring up. But Ellison's essay illustrates a profound shift in jazz aesthetics in the rise of the soloist and, specifically, the public "cutting contest" in the period just before and through the bop era, a type of battle very different from the sort of mutual challenging for which Bechet strove.[71] Ironically, this shift in emphasis was facilitated, though almost certainly unwittingly, by the tremendous strength and beauty of Bechet's (and, obviously, of Armstrong's) playing. Of course, as Ingrid Monson has noted, even in bop and post-bop styles, interaction and cooperation remain crucial to effective and satisfying musical experiences for musicians as well as their audiences.[72] Monson's work serves as a much-needed reminder that jazz is, at its best, an arena in which very close musical and personal relationships are formed and tested. Still, there can be little question that the "cutting" mentality played an integral role in "separating the men from the boys" in bebop's formative years, and that mentality did and does survive.[73]

One could argue that the stance taken by Bechet and other Creole musicians who modeled themselves on Uptown styles did resonate in one important sense with that taken by most early bop-oriented musicians in the 1940s. For both sought to create an alternative to a mainstream, dominant (white Protestant and/or Francocentric Creole) society of the time, challenging those African-diasporic communities that saw integration and assimilation of European and Euro-American ideals as the most fruitful means to redress power imbalances.

But bebop and Bechet differ in their ideals in many other significant ways, most noticeably so in the attitude taken by each toward their respective audiences. Unlike bop performers who expressed their unity by withdrawing into a hermetic subculture marked by exclusivity on many levels, Bechet and his cohorts sought to openly proclaim and celebrate their sense of comfort and community to all those who would hear.[74] Bechet's circle looked upon a large, diverse, and joyful audience as a musical and professional achievement, a marked contrast from bop ideals wherein widespread popularity could be (and still is to a degree) perceived as "selling out," even by those who pushed to have their music recorded and sold. For Bechet, playing the blues was not merely the individual musician's expression of an "inner self" but a simultaneous exploration, revelation, and narration of a community looking for, and becoming, itself. Coming from a relatively "foreign" Creole background, such musicking is not simply a playing about a people but a way of playing a new jazz/cultural identity into being.

This idea of allowing the music, the musicians, and the audience to "find each other"—in a sense, to define a socially shared moment—should not be understood as an endless jazz "orgasm," or "enormous present," as Norman Mailer describes it in his account of the post–World War II "white Negro" hipster world.[75] Mailer saw late bop-era jazz musicians—black and white—and their listeners as engaging in a nihilistic rejection of bourgeois ideals, forsaking the middle-class world for a string of never-ending "kicks." Disregarding for now the question of whether the musicians and audiences ever really did "drop out" as fully as Mailer proposes, this view misses two points crucial to an understanding of jazz as it was conceived by Bechet and his circle, if not by jazz communities in general. First, if Mailer's essay is useful in depicting some of the listeners and hangers-on of the post–World War II jazz scene, we should remember that the performers themselves—that is, the individuals around whom this purported hip scene revolved—worked diligently to acquire the skills on their instruments necessary to project the apparent "disengaged" affect. One does not simply pick up a horn and play from one's beat/hip soul—at least not if one wants to hold an audience for any length of time (though this may be a difference between Bechet's conception of jazz freedom and that of some of the less "entertainment"-minded practitioners of the 1960s avant garde). Second, and more important, though Bechet does look outside of his "birth" culture (i.e., Creole) to

Uptown, more African-rooted ways of musicking and acting, he is claiming, even refiguring, a strong sense of lineage and tradition, a concept very different from Mailer's depiction of jazz life as a seemingly rootless existence. Bechet's assertion, "My story goes a long way back. It goes further back than I had anything to do with. My music is like that," illustrates only one such manifestation of his position.[76]

NEW ORLEANS JAZZ AS "FOLK MUSIC"

Duke Ellington once wrote of early jazz:

> *Call* was very important in that kind of music. Today, the music has grown up and become quite scholastic, but this was *au naturel,* close to the primitive, where people send messages in what they play, calling somebody, or making facts and emotions known. Painting a picture, or having a story to go with what you were going to play, was of vital importance in those days.[77]

Ellington's depiction of early players, though perceptive in its recognition of the rhetorical richness of their style, seems to cast the New Orleans musician as a type of "savage" straight from the backwater "jungles" of the South. His comments reveal just how deeply the identities of even the earliest Swing-era musicians differed from their predecessors (even Ellington, with whom Bechet played and for whom the reed player had great admiration!).

Jazz scholar Bernard Gendron has recently located a similar perception toward New Orleans players in a branch of 1940s jazz criticism that painted early jazz as a "folk music," or at least one possessed of a folklike authenticity. For these writers, as Gendron notes, "the transition from New Orleans jazz to swing represented the disintegration of an authentic folk culture" into a watered-down commercialized bastardized version of the "real thing."[78] Yet as "natural" as the early players sounded to Ellington (a middle-class, African-American pianist/composer from Washington, D.C.) and the white critics of the 1940s, or, indeed, as natural as they sound to us now, these musicians had to learn to sound that way.

Sidney Bechet, for instance, was clearly talented (he was overheard playing at the age of six by a number of Creole players who were astonished at his prowess even then). But music—much less blues stylings—did not just flow from him. Bechet's own words of advice to Richard Hadlock on approaches to practicing his instrument (cited above) demonstrate that the reed player had given a great deal of thought to the ways in which musicians achieve a style that sounds both expressive and natural. In other words, Bechet and others like him (Morton, Keppard, Ory, Bigard, Wellman Braud) were not just "emoting" through their instruments; each had to experiment in order to develop the technique, time feel, and devices that would be heard as emotional by their various audiences.

Their example illustrates the fundamental lesson to be learned from Albert Murray's outstanding *Stomping the Blues.* Murray suggests that blues/jazz playing on a level such as these players achieved is far from a natural "folkiness." Rather, their playing is "precisely an artful contrivance, designed for entertainment and aesthetic gratification; and its effectiveness depends on the mastery by one means or another of the fundamentals of the craft of music in general and a special sensitivity to the nuances of the idiom in particular."[79]

Moreover, the blues—the form and aesthetic with which Bechet is most associated and in which he developed many of his most profound recordings—represented a relatively "foreign" form in his Creole neighborhood. Bechet had to seek out and learn the blues idiom from his cultural "rivals" or, at the very least, from Creole musicians who were themselves rebelling against their cultural norms. And though Bechet played "for the people," even he writes, "I can remember back in New Orleans when people who first heard our music just didn't know what to think. They'd never heard anything like it in their lives; they didn't even know how to dance to it. . . . But they learned the music, it made itself important to them; it made them want to learn."[80] Clearly, this desire to learn the music was as true for Bechet himself as it was for his audiences.[81]

All of these circumstances problematize LeRoi Jones's (Amiri Baraka's) famous hypothesis that early "Negro" jazz musicians simply mirrored and expressed their own cultural ideals while early white jazz musicians rebelled against theirs.[82] Jones/Baraka and like-minded critics overlook those important early New Orleans Creole players who rebelled, though in different ways and to differing degrees, against their culture just as they claim Bix Beiderbecke and his Northern white crowd had rebelled against theirs. Although one may argue that early jazz drew some white participants because of its taboo coding of "otherness/blackness," we have seen that contentions suggesting that this allure separates a clear-cut "white jazz" from an equally unambiguous black counterpart does not hold true. For one must consider the very complex perceptions of identity as experienced by Uptown and Downtown cultures in New Orleans. Indeed, the very concept of "blackness" was contested and redefined at this time, not only by legal decree but by and among musicians and their audiences as well.

It appears ironic, too, given certain "folk" arguments surrounding early jazz, that many of these players were, at heart, quite "progressive." Bechet, for instance, claimed repeatedly that jazz should change as musicians respond to a changing world, and he practiced his preaching by at least exploring (if not enjoying) technological advances in mass mediation: not only recording but multitracking!

Contrary, then, to popular accounts, early jazz players were not simply "folk musicians" unconsciously expressing the realities of "black life in the South." These individuals were not merely playing the music of "their people," because in flux at this time was the very notion of who exactly was one's "people," an evolution accelerated by the oftentimes painful confluence of differing attitudes and ideals regarding racial and musical identity. In this light, we need to reconsider any historical narrative that identifies jazz as a wholly natural, serendipitous, and joyous intersection of schooled, literate Downtown Creole musicians with the unschooled but fiery Uptown Black improvisers, creating a unified African-American musical form. While such theories are not altogether false, they brush aside the crucial reality that individuals from these two very different communities often had to endure difficult moments in which musicians and their audiences found themselves engaging with ideals and musical aesthetics that were at odds with their "birth" cultures. The two groups did eventually move closer together, especially after the massive migration to urban areas in the North in the 1920s when professional and practical circumstances necessitated they do so. However, this coming together was often a contentious one and, ironically, was facilitated by Northern whites who would recognize no cultural distinctions and who simply labeled all of these individuals as "black."

Finally, we should note that this complex racial circumstance has not completely disappeared to this day. Mary Gehman's work on the subject demonstrates the ongoing cultural ambiguity facing individuals and communities in New Orleans. Her thoughts on media representation (or nonrepresentation) of this phenomenon mirror similar trends in jazz historiography and are worth quoting at length.

> Today [1994] in New Orleans the press and other media use the terms "black" or "African-American" to refer to anyone of African descent. Technically then, there is no more distinction between Creole and American blacks. . . . But to anyone who observes New Orleans social, political and racial patterns, it is very clear that "Creole" is a term used frequently by blacks among themselves for those who carry on the names, traditions, family businesses and social positions of the free people of color, and as such that they continue to face some of the same issues at the end of the twentieth century that their ancestors did two hundred years ago. Light skin, European features, long straight hair or wavy black hair and a French surname earn some blacks privilege and status above others among whites, yet they also evoke disgust and anger among darker skinned blacks with English surnames who feel discriminated against by such favored members of their own race. Though rarely discussed in the media or other open forums, this intra-racial situation affects the politics, social order, jobs and businesses of the city in many ways.[83]

The binary racial opposition of black and white is not a "natural" one; it is socially and culturally constructed. The many jazz histories, however well meaning, that depict the genre wholly in terms of these categories necessarily overlook this unique and important cultural moment in New Orleans. In doing so, they miss one of the primary responsibilities and most productive possibilities of historical writing: to help us to understand how things got the way they are by imaginatively but carefully exploring the ways things once were and opening new possibilities to the ways things might yet be. The alternative only reduces individuals and historical communities to impermeable if internally mutating constructs and hampers opportunities for increased understanding across, and even within, cultural boundaries.

I raise these points not to erase differences among peoples (that would simply create yet another "universalist" jazz narrative) but rather to show the multiplicity, interaction, interdependence, and fluidity—and not mere biology—of cultural and musical identity. Like the assessments by American-studies scholar Sieglinde Lemke of the influence of African art and artifact on modernist painters, jazz, as we know it, "could never have been conceived but for an act of cultural transgression."[84] To present early jazz musicians in any other way not only distorts the realities of turn-of-the-century New Orleans but demeans the efforts of those individuals whom we now laud rather automatically as "early greats." For the example of Creole musicians reminds us that, far from a quaint Southern folk tradition, jazz cultures, even in the genre's formative years in New Orleans, entailed an oftentimes conflicted interaction that ultimately helped to shape and express new senses of personal and communal identity in and beyond jazz.

Two

JAZZ HISTORIOGRAPHY AND
THE PROBLEM OF LOUIS JORDAN

> *To judge from textbooks aimed at the college market, something like an*
> *official history of jazz has taken hold in recent years. On these pages,*
> *for all its chaotic diversity of style and expression and for all the com-*
> *plexity of its social origins, jazz is presented as a coherent whole, and*
> *its history as a skillfully contrived and easily comprehensible narrative.*
>
> SCOTT DEVEAUX,
> *"Constructing the Jazz Tradition"*

SAXOPHONIST AND SINGER Louis Jordan emerged as one of the most
influential and commercially successful bandleaders of the 1940s. His
buoyant music and affable stage presence garnered him a large and diverse following in an America still characterized by stark social and
cultural divisions. The "problem" suggested in this chapter's title refers to the fact that although Jordan's hugely popular bands featured a
hard-swinging rhythmic drive and outstanding improvised solos—
two cornerstones of formalist definitions of jazz—he remains largely
ignored in jazz history books, recording anthologies, and video docu-
mentaries. My goal here is not merely to argue that Louis Jordan was
a musical giant deserving of expansive coverage in jazz texts (though I
suggest that he certainly warrants some mention) but rather to discern
the implications of his general absence in these works. That is, what
current assumptions, ideals, and aesthetics of jazz would Jordan's presence threaten or undermine?

It would be unfair to suggest that music scholars as a whole have
overlooked Louis Jordan's contributions. George Lipsitz, Reebee Garo-

falo, Nelson George, Arnold Shaw, and others have cited Jordan as a founding father of both rhythm and blues and rock and roll.[1] But those scholars' works neither explain nor excuse Jordan's absence from jazz-oriented studies, unless we concede that jazz writing by definition omits those musicians deemed as indispensable to other genres. Clearly this is not the case, for if jazz historians faithfully followed such an exclusionary approach, they would be forced to pass over such rhythm and blues progenitors as Lionel Hampton, Fats Waller, and even Count Basie, all of whom appear frequently and justifiably throughout the jazz literature.

Still, Louis Jordan's name barely rates mention as a jazz player at all. The history texts by Frank Tirro, Mark Gridley, and Lewis Porter and Michael Ullman all cite Jordan's name, but only in passing and only in blues or rhythm and blues contexts. Ted Gioia ignores Jordan altogether, as did the late Martin Williams, editor of the widely used *Smithsonian Collection of Classic Jazz* recording anthology.[2] If others who have been credited as r&b forefathers merit attention by jazz historians, and if, as I show below, Louis Jordan's influential bands attracted extraordinarily large audiences, swung furiously, and featured fine soloists, how can we explain historians' reticence to also grant Jordan credit as a significant *jazz* musician?

I suggest that this phenomenon involves a number of factors—both "musical" and "extramusical" (to the extent that one can make such distinctions)—but that it hinges predominantly on Jordan's historical location. That is to say, while r&b precursors Hampton and Basie continued to perform through the rise of the bebop style in the 1940s and for many years thereafter, they had already established themselves as significant contributors. Louis Jordan's fame, however, coincided almost perfectly with the emergence of bop, and I argue that the seeming lightheartedness of Jordan's music flags him as a problematic figure for critics attempting to paint jazz since the 1940s as a serious art form.

One may be tempted to question at this point what difference it makes whether Louis Jordan garners acclaim as a "jazz" musician or as a "rhythm and blues" musician, so long as his accomplishments receive credit in some manner. But again, my interests here lie less in correcting what I perceive to be merely some sort of historiographical

oversight than in exploring the assumptions and positions that under-
lie certain historiographical decisions. Music-genre designations function as more than convenient partitions in record stores: more important, they help to construct individual and cultural identity. In many
ways, musicians, listeners, scholars, and institutions define and orient
themselves in terms of who counts and who does not count within
a certain category. So before turning to the specific causes underlying jazz historians' ambivalence regarding Louis Jordan, let us explore
briefly the question of genre and the interests at stake in constructing
and guarding these categories.

PATROLLING THE BORDERS

No inherent qualities separate one musical category from another.
Genres are historical and cultural constructs, and evolving ones at
that. For this reason, genre labels always refer to a great deal more than
simply a musical style, as a variety of meanings and associations coa-
lesce around and even help to form each category. For instance, there
can be little doubt that an aura of prestige hangs over the designation
"classical music." The "classical" category still represents in many circles a unified, smoothly evolving tradition reflecting musical sophistication and cultural refinement, despite the almost bewildering array
of composers, historical periods, geographical regions, musical languages, and performance situations that come under its umbrella.
Separate listening areas in record stores, government and corporate
sponsorship of symphony orchestras, and the use of European musics
in all manner of "high-end" advertising illustrate the lofty reputation
that that genre carries in public discourse.

To be sure, the construction and elevation of the classical category
has involved a broad range of individuals and institutions, but historians have clearly played a significant role in this process, most notably
through their emphasis on "serious music." For example, the extensive space granted to German symphonies in so many music-history
texts and buying guides paints a brooding and profound picture of
European music making during the nineteenth century. By contrast,
Sir Arthur Sullivan and Johann Strauss Jr., composers of some of the

most popular works of that century, receive little or no attention in those same music texts, as their works have been deemed mere "entertainment." Indeed, one writer recently lamented of Sir Arthur, "A jaunty Symphony in E hints at what he might have achieved, had Gilbert never turned up."[3] If historians and critics are to present a unified, austere, and complex European art-music tradition, "lighter" fare such as that composed by Sullivan, Strauss, and, in our own time, John Williams, must be brushed aside regardless of that music's significance to its audiences.[4]

While classical music still stands well in front of other genres in terms of worldwide esteem (if not in record sales), jazz has narrowed the gap in recent years and currently enjoys the highest prestige of its existence.[5] The 1987 Congressional Act declaring jazz "a rare and valuable national American treasure," along with the fact that jazz performers increasingly share performance spaces and grant dollars with their more established classical colleagues, both symbolizes and solidifies jazz's prominence in and beyond this country.[6] And while this newfound respect has allowed increasing numbers of jazz musicians to command substantial concert fees, the status shift affects more than just the music's performers. For those writing on jazz, just as for those playing it, an elevation in the genre has enhanced professional reputations, job security, and financial resources (witness the many jazz books currently published by prestigious university presses, of which, of course, this book is one example). Consequently, some writers apparently feel it is their duty to ensure that jazz retain this privileged position, for they seemingly remain on constant vigil so that "America's classical music"—as jazz is so often called today—appears as "cultured" as its European cousin.

"Is Jazz Popular Music?"—an essay written by jazz historian Mark Gridley and directed to college-level music educators—reveals some of the stakes involved in such categorization and hierarchy:

> The moral of the story is, don't assume that anyone understands
> the differences between jazz and pop. If you run into resistance establishing a jazz curriculum or in trying to obtain funding for a jazz
> concert series, remember those who hold the purse strings might be

withholding the money only because they are confused about what jazz is and because they see the music as so commercially successful and plentiful that it does not need their patronage. *They may also see it as not warranting study because pop music by definition is not serious.*[7]

The passage above should make it clear that Gridley proudly answers his own question "Is jazz popular music?" in the negative. And with his stance in mind, we can return to the specific problem of Louis Jordan.

"WHO'S THE TALK OF RHYTHM TOWN?"

While jazz historians may ignore Louis Jordan's accomplishment, by all other accounts his efforts proved enormously successful and influential. Born in Brinkley, Arkansas, in 1908, Jordan traveled as a singer, woodwind player, and comedian with various bands and minstrel shows before joining Chick Webb and His Orchestra in 1936. During his two-year stay with Webb, Jordan polished his vocal skills and developed into a highly accomplished alto saxophonist in the mold of Benny Carter. Jordan's musical talents and amiable stage persona drew ever-increasing public recognition, resulting in growing friction with his apparently jealous bandleader. Jordan left Webb in 1938 to form his own unit.

Within a decade, Louis Jordan and his Tympany Five, as the group came to be called, had risen to become one of the most popular recording acts in the country, and one of the very few African-American bands of the time to "cross over" to white audiences. Between 1944 and 1949 Jordan's recordings reached the broader pop charts nineteen times, with both "G.I. Jive" and its flip side, "Is You Is or Is You Ain't (Ma' Baby)" reaching number 1. His million sellers also included "Caldonia," "Choo Choo Ch'Boogie," and "Saturday Night Fish Fry."[8] During this extraordinary period, Jordan appeared in a handful of black-oriented feature films, starred in numerous short-subject "soundies" (precursors to modern-day music videos), and received equal billing on recorded collaborations with the music world's biggest stars, including Louis Armstrong, Ella Fitzgerald, and Bing Crosby.

Even given this widespread popularity—and in contrast to other crossover artists such as the Mills Brothers or the later Nat Cole—Jordan's sound and subject matter remained deeply rooted in African-American forms and styles. Like the music of so many groups out of the South and the Midwest, Jordan's music of this period relied heavily on short riff figures, often involving a call and response between the horn players or between the horns and the rhythm section.[9] And, like those same Midwest "territory bands," Jordan's group maintained a strong connection to the blues and an insistent, eminently danceable beat, two crucial points to which I'll return. While Jordan retained these musical features of the territory bands, in one important way his units stood as an exception, for the Tympany Five generally featured only two or three horns. Like the bop configurations that would emerge around the same time, his small ensemble offered a lighter and more flexible texture than the prevalent big bands, emphasizing a hard-swinging rhythm section over dense, multihorn arrangements.

Neither surprisingly nor insignificantly, Jordan's small-group setting also proved more economically viable than big bands. The Tympany Five (so named even when the group stretched to six or seven members) could perform in any size room, while all financial burdens—band uniforms, arrangement copying, travel expenses—remained minimal. As one might expect, given their almost immediate commercial success, this pared-down orchestration proved highly influential. Recounting tough times in the mid-1940s, former bandleader Dud Bascomb remarked, "Things began to get rough for big bands and we weren't doing too well. Louis Jordan had come out with a small band, and everybody began to talk about small bands in different [booking-agency] offices and say they couldn't do anything with the big bands."[10]

Other oral histories substantiate Jordan's prominence at the time. Trumpeter Benny Bailey, when asked about his musical experiences in the middle 1940s, recalled, "Oh, yeah, we had a group, and we were trying to play like Louis Jordan—because it was very simple. We had a sort of quintet, and we would copy the arrangements and copy the solos, exactly. It was a lot of fun."[11] When Bailey characterizes the music as "simple" and "fun" he offers some of the first clues to Jordan's tenuous position among jazz historians, for as we've seen with European musics, issues of seriousness and complexity can play important roles for writers wishing to elevate a genre's prestige.

JAZZ AND THE AESTHETICS OF COMPLEXITY

In *Jazz Styles,* the biggest-selling textbook on the music (now in its seventh edition), author Mark Gridley expands on the theme of his article cited above, tracing explicit boundaries separating jazz from popular music. Among other points, he writes that jazz musicians are not of the "common people" (in contrast, he suggests, to folk and blues musicians) but represent a "highly versatile and specially trained elite whose level of sophistication is not common to the population at large." Gridley argues, too, that jazz is not primarily "utilitarian in nature" (by which he means it is not dance music, film music, or party music). "Instead, it is appreciated for its esthetic and intellectual rewards, and it is approached with some effort." [12]

As Lawrence Levine's insightful work on cultural hierarchy has shown, use of the term "popular" has not meant only that a work or genre has been widely accepted and enjoyed. Critics have also employed that term pejoratively to cover that which was not deemed sufficiently "highbrow." Clearly, Gridley invokes this somewhat patronizing notion of the popular when he compares pop music to what he sees as the extraordinary sophistication of jazz. Ironically, Gridley's policy for why jazz should not be considered popular—that it is complex and appreciated only through difficult study—echoes the identical sentiments voiced by European-oriented music critics in the early decades of the twentieth century as a way of relegating jazz to the ash heap of lowbrow culture. [13]

I should note that jazz writers are not the only ones who have promulgated this strict jazz/popular dichotomy; some rock critics have adopted a similar stance. For example, Nick Tosches of the *Village Voice* wrote in 1992 that Louis Jordan dealt a "resounding smack to the face of all self-serious art and a smack as well on the ass of that newborn baby, conceived in rhythm and baptized in wine, called rock and roll. It was a sundering smack, leaving the paradigm of hep forever cleft in twain."[14]

Tosches differs from many jazz historians in that his divisions run less along hierarchical lines than along parallel degrees of "self-consciousness." But his position still maintains a clear and seemingly irreconcilable split in African-American musicking. In this view, jazz must, by necessity, be that music enjoyed by only a few navel-gazing, soul-tortured hipsters. Any music that did not exert these angst-ridden qualities, that inspired audiences to dance or romance or laugh, could be called race music, r&b, rock 'n' roll, soul, pop, in fact almost anything but jazz. How did a tradition that produced—even since World War II—such tremendously entertaining and frequently hilarious figures as Sonny Rollins, Thelonious Monk, Sun Ra, Roland Kirk, Don Cherry, Lester Bowie, and Henry Threadgill acquire such a stuffy reputation?

BLUES IN THE BOP NIGHT

Writing in 1956, French authors Hughes Panassie and Madeline Gautier stood as some of the first—and, indeed, only—jazz historians to recognize Jordan's accomplishments. They observed that "since 1937 the success of two groups specializing in blues, those of Count Basie and Louis Jordan, brought forth fresh respect for this form of music which for some years before had been somewhat in eclipse."[15] These comments, written only a year after the death of bop innovator Charlie Parker, highlight the first specifically musical problem involving contemporary jazz historiography and Louis Jordan, that is, Jordan's penchant for heavily blues-inflected material and styles. I noted in the previous chapter that most New York-based bebop musicians consciously avoided traditional blues chord changes and stylistic devices. With the notable exception of Charlie Parker (a Kansas City native), early bop players largely sought to distinguish themselves from the perceived backwardness of their Southern relatives, displaying a new sense of independence and worldliness.[16]

But even in pre-bop styles, few musicians from the Northeast earned reputations as outstanding blues players.[17] In the 1920s and 1930s, the Harlem-based community of stride-piano players tended to favor transformed ragtime pieces and Tin Pan Alley songs and largely dismissed blues and boogie-woogie pianists, most of whom hailed from the South and Midwest, as "hicks." Never mind that those pianists from Chicago, St. Louis, New Orleans, and Memphis could drive an entire room full of people to dance, New York players prized harmonic invention and a more fluid pulse over what they heard as crass and obvious "pounding." Even that eventual blues proponent par excellence Count Basie—a native of New Jersey—came to the blues later in life. He recalled of the late 1920s that, "I had heard the blues Bessie, Mamie, and Trixie Smith, Viola McCoy, Victoria Spivey, and Ida Cox, and singers like that were putting out on records back in those days, but I hadn't ever really paid any attention to them, and I hadn't ever played the blues. I hadn't got my first real taste of the blues until the burlesque show I first left New York with played Kansas City." [18]

Jazz historiography has tended to reinforce these prevailing East Coast attitudes toward the blues-rich traditions of other regions. Most notably, historians have largely left the borderline between "blues" and "jazz" less distinct with regard to the earliest recordings (those made by New Orleans-, Chicago-, or Kansas City–based musicians). However, their genre demarcations become increasingly clearer with representations of music since the 1940s, that is, since the time when New York took over as the unquestionable center of jazz in the United States. For example, Martin Williams included in his *Smithsonian* anthology two tracks from Bessie Smith, that Tennessee-born "Empress of the Blues." Similarly, the CD accompanying Frank Tirro's book opens with a cut from Mississippi Delta blues legend Robert Johnson. Yet neither Williams nor Tirro programmed performances from more recent musicians generally affiliated with the blues.

Why would these editors include Smith's 1920s recordings or Johnson's raw Delta sound but not Louis Jordan's (or, for that matter, Ray Charles's or T-Bone Walker's or "Cleanhead" Vinson's) swinging work from the 1940s or 1950s? The most plausible explanation is that these historians adhere to a type of musical evolutionary theory, suggesting that jazz emerged from a black-and-bluesy primordial soup, gradually developing into an increasingly complex and sophisticated "art music." Williams's *Smithsonian Collection* neatly traces such a line. He promotes bebop in the 1940s, followed by Miles Davis's orchestrated collaborations with Gil Evans, Lennie Tristano's astringent counterpoint, Cecil Taylor's explorations, and so forth, all the while ignoring the more accessible and commercially successful stylings of Stan Getz, Dave Brubeck, and Les McCann.

Frank Tirro's editorial decisions reflect a similar historical teleology. As shown in table 1, he arranges all but one of the cuts—the opening Robert Johnson selection—in chronological order. Like Williams, Tirro seems to treat the Delta blues as a sort of primitive ancestor to jazz. For if he had held to a strict chronology, Johnson's "Dust My Broom," recorded in 1936, would be placed not first, but at least fourth. Both Ellington's "Clarinet Lament" and Basie's "Tickle-Toe" originated at the same moment as Johnson's work, a full ten years after Armstrong's "Cornet Chop Suey," and three years after Art Tatum's virtuosic "Tiger Rag"!

It's worth noting that, in contrast to these jazz narratives, blues historians have tended to guard their genre borders somewhat less strictly. The blues has never attained the level of prestige enjoyed by jazz, and writers haven't seemed overly concerned with elevating or protecting its image. For instance, in his *The History of the Blues,* Francis Davis grants suitably ample space to canonic blues legends Charley Patton, Muddy Waters, and Ma Rainey, but he also pays tribute to figures less directly associated with the genre, including Ornette Coleman, Chuck Berry, and Elvis Presley. Similarly, the chapter entitled "The Musicians" in Johnny Otis's chronicle of the rhythm and blues scene on Los Angeles' Central Avenue focuses on Lester Young and Count Basie, as well as on T-Bone Walker, Wynonie Harris, and Little Esther Phillips.[19]

As virtually every jazz musician plays the twelve-bar blues form at one time or another, a clear jazz/blues division can prove difficult for historians to justify. To counteract ambiguities, some jazz scholars have sought to explicitly outline the difference between the blues genre and blues forms incorporated by jazz players. Grover Sales, author of

Track Number	Artist	Song	Recording Year
1	Robert Johnson	"I Believe I'll Dust My Broom"	1936
2	Louis Armstrong	"Cornet Chop Suey"	1926
3	Frankie Trumbauer	"Ostrich Walk"	1927
4	Art Tatum	"Tiger Rag"	1933
5	Duke Ellington	"Clarinet Lament (Barney's Concerto)"	1936
6	Count Basie	"Tickle-Toe"	1936
7	Benny Goodman	"Mission to Moscow"	1942
8	Dizzy Gillespie	"Groovin' High"	1945
9	Lee Konitz	"Marshmallow"	1949
10	Charlie Parker	"Confirmation"	1953
11	Gerry Mulligan	"I Can't Believe That You're in Love with Me"	1953
12	Jazz Messengers [should be listed as the Horace Silver Quintet]	"The Preacher"	1955
13	George Russell	"All about Rosie"	1957
14	Miles Davis	"Dr. Jekyll"	1958
15	John Coltrane	"Giant Steps"	1959
16	Ornette Coleman	"Change of the Century"	1959
17	Thelonious Monk	"Bemsha Swing"	1964
18	Miles Davis	"Circle"	1966
19	Weather Report	"Tears"	1971
20	Wynton Marsalis	"Delfeayo's Dilemma"	1986

SOURCE: Frank Tirro, *Jazz: A History*, back cover.

Jazz: America's Classical Music, adopts such an approach when he compares Charlie Parker's "Now's the Time" with Louis Jordan's "Buzz Me Blues." Both are medium tempo, twelve-bar blues forms recorded in 1945; but Sales writes:

> "Buzz Me" is a straight-ahead jump blues and vocal, tailor made to get the dancers up and moving—and to top record sales charts. "Now's the Time" shows how Parker enriched the blues with a new and complex harmonic-rhythmic language that made intellectual demands on its listener. Like "Buzz Me," "Now's the Time" is body-based . . . but its main appeal is not to the feet but to the head and heart.[20]

True enough, Charlie Parker's approach to the saxophone differs significantly from Louis Jordan's. Parker's lines evince a wider variety of intervals, incorporating chromatic passages and the suggestion of alternative chord progressions, as well as blues licks. Moreover, he offsets his phrases from typical starting and ending points, resulting in a rhythmic feel that seems to float over the beat rather than outlining it distinctly. But Jordan's cut also remains firmly grounded in a traditional jazz dialect. His deep scoops and wide vibrato borrow liberally from Johnny Hodges's renowned alto sound. And the performance in general retains all of the features of the Swing-era "head arrangement" style, built around a steady rhythmic flow and simple background riffs. Such an approach to jazz performance and composition clearly suggests a scaled-down version of the "classic" Count Basie ensembles of the 1930s that Sales had praised earlier in his book.[21]

Sales's somewhat dismissive reference to the danceability of Jordan's style points to a related historiographical issue: that "real jazz" and "dance music" somehow remain mutually exclusive, a stance echoing one of Mark Gridley's aforementioned assertions regarding the supposed nonfunctionality of authentic jazz. Yet while historians rightly cite the big bands of Basie, Duke Ellington, Billy Eckstein, and Dizzy Gillespie as among the most creative of the 1930s and 1940s, they tend to overlook the fact that those same ensembles were also, sometimes primarily, outstanding dance bands.

New rhythmic conceptions certainly had begun to emerge by the middle 1940s. New York–based drummers such as Kenny Clarke and Max Roach moved away from their traditional role as strict time-keepers. They developed a more dialogic manner of accompaniment, breaking up the flow of the beat through unusually placed accents on the snare and bass drums, all of which made dancing to this music a somewhat precarious endeavor. But again, jazz historians have turned these East Coast musical practices into genre-wide aesthetic ideals. For even while most jazz fans of the time still identified with a smooth, danceable swing beat, bop-oriented writers viewed the new rhythmic techniques as qualitative evolutions, dismissing as unhip, or unjazzy, a steady bounce such as Jordan's band featured. Lost, too, in such narratives is the fact that not all jazz musicians celebrated the change in audience roles from dancers to listeners that bop practices precipitated. Indeed, though Count Basie's later experience fronting the house band for Alan Freed's Rock 'n' Roll Dance Party radio show proved short-lived, he relished the role, remarking that, "Rock 'n' Roll started the kids dancing again—that's certainly a blessing for us."[22]

Grover Sales also reveals his tendency toward a type of jazz-as-autonomous-art historiography when he refers to commercial aspirations only with regard to Louis Jordan's recording, implying that Charlie Parker's "complex" and "intellectual" style stood above such tainted concerns. Yet while Sales's narrative does serve to highlight the tremendous technical skills achieved by Parker and other bop players, it overlooks the reality that bebop musicians remained professional musicians. That is, each player's economic survival necessitated accepting and negotiating most of the same institutions and circumstances as his or her forebears. To be sure, by configuring a more complex melodic and harmonic vocabulary and a less jovial stage manner than Swing stylists, bop musicians of the 1940s did help to shape notions of the jazz "artist"—that genius of spontaneous musical creation. But we should bear in mind that this stance was always played out, and even helped to enhance professional prospects, within a commercial marketplace. For no matter what the musical language or attitude, the situation remained that jazz musicians needed to work. Sales's "bop for art's sake" position is further problematized by the fact that bop founders Charlie Parker and Dizzy Gillespie reached number 22 on the pop music charts with Gillespie's "Salt Peanuts" in that same year of 1945.

SINGERS AND "REAL" MUSICIANS

The final factor I discuss here concerns the disparity between public perceptions of jazz singers on the one hand and jazz historians' attitudes toward those same singers on the other. Vocalists have always ranked among the most popular artists in jazz. Billie Holiday, Ella Fitzgerald, Louis Armstrong, Frank Sinatra, and Joe Williams stand as some of the most recognizable names, faces, and sounds in the music, even decades after their passing. To many listeners, these musicians embody jazz, while figures such as Coleman Hawkins, Clifford Brown, and Bud Powell remain virtually unknown to the general public. Yet the fact that the audience attention lavished on singers far exceeds that bestowed on their instrumentalist colleagues has not altered the equally inescapable fact that vocalists go largely overlooked in jazz history texts. With the exception of Armstrong, Holiday, and to a lesser extent Sarah Vaughan, singers are viewed with suspicion by jazz writers: Singers aren't "real musicians," they're "entertainers."

Louis Jordan's role as a singer, and a commercially successful one at that, doesn't help his position among historians. But even more damning is the way he approached that role. His ever-smiling demeanor (see figure 1) and the subject matter of so many of his lyrics reflected a decidedly less urbane point of view than that of most bop devotees of his time. Jordan's biggest hits included such titles as "Beans and Cornbread," "Barnyard Boogie," "Ain't Nobody Here but Us Chickens," and "Saltpork, West Virginia," all of which depicted humorous scenes of black life in the rural South. When he wasn't playing the hick, Jordan could revert to some rather uncomfortable "jungle"-primitivist caricatures, as in his 1945 recording of "Mop! Mop!" with its plot tracing the roots of Swing rhythms to "Zulu" simpletons.[23]

Although such an Afrocentric story serves to undercut those who would promote Paul Whiteman and Benny Goodman as the "kings" of jazz and Swing, respectively, the song's location and action reinscribe derogatory notions of blacks as jungle-dwelling half-wits. Recent studies by scholars Krin Gabbard and Daniel Goldmark show that Louis Armstrong and Duke Ellington negotiated similar racial stereotypes in a variety of ways.[24] But again, both Armstrong and Ellington belonged to the jazz world before bop's emergence, while Louis Jordan's 1940s forays into primitivist imagery and quasi-minstrelsy would have embarrassed, even angered, those African-Americans striving to eradicate such racist depictions. At the same time, "Mop! Mop!" reached number 1 on what the music industry referred to at that time as the "race music" charts, which reveals that black attitudes and identities of the era were anything but monolithic.

Figure 1. Album cover, *Just Say MOE!: Mo' of the Best of Louis Jordan,* Louis Jordan. Courtesy of Rhino Records.

Given Jordan's light-hearted stage presence, his penchant for humorous and backward rural imagery, and his danceable, riff-based, blues-grounded musical approach, we can begin to understand the Tympany Five's absence in jazz history texts. For if we follow the evolutionary narrative constructed by many historians—that the complexity and seriousness of the bebop style demonstrates jazz's claim to art-music status—then Louis Jordan's seemingly frivolous approach must lie outside of that elite world.

Of course, this bop-centricism hits on the central point of our topic: that from Parker and Gillespie onward, historians' use of the term "jazz" would always denote a virtuosic, complex, and sophisticated music, one somehow separated from the commercial marketplace. In effect, most jazz historiography deals in what scholar and musician Georgina Born calls a modernist "antidiscourse," which she describes as the "envious denial or 'absenting' . . . of the existence of a rival discourse." For, just as with Born's description of the complete disavowal of popular culture that characterizes twentieth-century modernism, it is plain to see that jazz writers have ignored popular jazz styles and musicians in favor of the more arcane bop aesthetics.

This sort of narrative implies that bebop is not merely one stylistic branch of a larger genre called jazz but rather that bop literally equals jazz. Such a view ignores the historical reality that most audiences of the 1940s and 1950s—regardless of race—still revered Benny Goodman, Johnny Hodges, Artie Shaw, Woody Herman, and, yes, Louis Jordan, as the predominant jazz figures. In *Down Beat*'s 1946 readers' poll, for instance, Jordan finished behind only Nat Cole in the small combo category, well ahead of Gillespie, Art Tatum, and Ben Webster.[25]

I'm not the first to point out that a bop orientation has come to dominate the discourse surrounding jazz. Scott DeVeaux, for one, has shown the degree to which historians have framed their takes on early jazz history around bop-based aesthetics. And, as DeVeaux notes, once the goal of perceiving bop as autonomous art is accepted, "the whole narrative of jazz history must be adjusted accordingly. For if bebop is the juncture at which jazz becomes art music, then earlier styles are once again in a precarious position—unless it can be demonstrated that in some important sense they had always been art music, and that status was simply unacknowledged."[26]

But a shift in understandings of early jazz is not the only legacy of this sort of historiography. As Jordan's relegation to "mere" popular music status shows, what counts as jazz since the 1940s has also been affected. Yet we should see that despite such narratives, established jazz generations do not simply cease to exist once a new musical style comes into practice. Jazz critic Ira Gitler recalled that the first time he heard the music later known as bebop, he was listening to "Symphony

Figure 2: 1. Hilton Jefferson; 2. Benny Golson; 3. Art Farmer; 4. Wilbur Ware; 5. Art Blakey; 6. Chubby Jackson; 7. Johnny Griffin; 8. Dickie Wells; 9. Buck Clayton; 10. Taft Jordan; 11. Zutty Singleton; 12. Red Allen; 13. Tyree Glenn; 14. Miff Mole; 15. Sonny Greer; 16. Jay C. Higginbotham; 17. Jimmy Jones; 18. Charles Mingus; 19. Jo Jones; 20. Gene Krupa; 21. Max Kaminsky; 22. George Wettling; 23. Bud Freeman; 24. Pee Wee Russell; 25. Ernie Wilkins; 26. Buster Bailey; 27. Osie Johnson; 28. Gigi Gryce; 29. Hank Jones; 30. Eddie Locke; 31. Horace Silver; 32. Luckey Roberts; 33. Maxine Sullivan; 34. Jimmy Rushing; 35. Joe Thomas; 36. Scoville Browne; 37. Stuff Smith; 38. Bill Crump; 39. Coleman Hawkins; 40. Rudy Powell; 41. Oscar Pettiford; 42. Sahib Shihab; 43. Marian McPartland; 44. Sonny Rollins; 45. Lawrence Brown; 46. Mary Lou Williams; 47. Emmett Berry; 48. Thelonious Monk; 49. Vic Dickenson; 50. Milt Hinton; 51. Lester Young; 52. Rex Stewart; 53. J. C. Heard; 54. Gerry Mulligan; 55. Roy Eldridge; 56. Dizzy Gillespie; 57. Count Basie. "Harlem 1958." Photograph by Art Kane, copyright © Art Kane Estate. Courtesy of Art Kane Archives.

Sid" Torin's radio show in New York around 1948. Gitler remembers that Torin played the new sounds from Parker and Gillespie on radio station WHOM "between and among the Basies, Louis Jordans, Wynonie Harrises, and Billie Holidays."[27] Such circumstances reveal that when bebop clawed its way onto the scene, it did not completely displace the other jazz stylings any more than free jazz eradicated bop when that newer sound emerged in the late 1950s. Similarly, though the cultural meanings associated with earlier approaches never remain the same, neither do they disappear altogether.

This broadly conceived notion of jazz did not and does not merely circulate among audiences. Musicians from different stylistic orientations have always played and hung out together, and they continue to share concert and club stages. To take just one famous example, Art Kane's celebrated *Esquire* magazine photograph beautifully illustrated the diversity of jazz styles available in New York City at the end of the 1950s. Hardbopper Horace Silver stands behind stride stylist Luckey Roberts; Roy Eldridge clowns with protégé Dizzy Gillespie; Mary Lou Williams poses next to her former student, Thelonious Monk; and, in front of them all, the fifty-five-year-old Count Basie shares a seat on the sidewalk with a dozen Harlem youngsters (see figure 2, prior page).[28]

Meanwhile, the assumption in many texts that jazz requires extraordinary skills to both play and "appreciate" it disregards the fact that the vast majority of jazz musicians do not perform in regally appointed concert halls or in hip downtown New York performance spaces. Rather, most gigs occur in all manners of small-scale restaurants and bars. True, these less prestigious venues rarely offer cutting-edge styles. Still, on any given night one can find in every city a group competently going about the jazz business of swinging, improvising, and creating a pleasant mood for dining, romancing, and dancing. The musicians, patrons, and management at these establishments would be surprised indeed to hear from historians that the music they had just played, enjoyed, or paid for did not rise to an artistic level worthy of the jazz moniker.

Of course, if we accept that all musics that people have understood to be jazz are jazz, we must acknowledge that not only Louis Jordan but also Ray Charles, George Winston, and, perhaps most disturbing for some, John Tesh and Kenny G play jazz, too. As difficult as that is to swallow for loyal mainstream and avant-garde denizens, there is no reason why the above-named musicians should not count as jazz. Jazz never has been a pure domain, culturally or musically. To pretend otherwise is to engage in a sort of art-envious wishful thinking.

I do not mean for the preceding discussion to invalidate past jazz historiography. Each of the authors mentioned here has contributed enormously to our knowledge of the music, and I agree with all of them that jazz must have its stories told. Where we differ is in their shared belief—implicit or explicit—that jazz deserves coverage because it is somehow a dignified and wholly autonomous art form. I contend, instead, that we need to explore jazz because, longer than any other music in the twentieth century, it has mattered to people. Millions of individuals from a broad spectrum of communities the world over have played, listened to, fought over, and, in all manner of ways, identified with the wide variety of sounds and attitudes that have come to be called jazz. And it is for that reason that this consequential music demands our attention.

Scholars have rightly lauded Louis Jordan as a founding father of r&b and rock 'n' roll. But to leave it at that diminishes and overly simplifies jazz history, which, from the music's earliest days, has been a site of multiple, even contradictory, identities. Through his enormously entertaining bands, Jordan built a large and loyal following. That his music and stage persona fly in the face of a jazz-as-art narrative should be seen not as some kind of amusing yet ultimately embarrassing distant relative but rather as evidence of the richness of a complex musical and cultural tradition.

Three

REGENDERING JAZZ

Ornette Coleman and the New York Scene in the Late 1950s

*The construction of gender is the product and the
process of both representation and self-presentation.*

TERESA DE LAURETIS,
Technologies of Gender

*There was this thing when we played where there were
those who really loved it, the growth of it and the spirit of it.
And then there were those who didn't like it because they
felt it was jeopardizing their position in life.*

DON CHERRY on his 1959 New York appearances
with the Ornette Coleman Quartet,
quoted in Valerie Wilmer, *As Serious as Your Life*

THIS CHAPTER FOCUSES on gender codes in jazz. More specifically, it looks to the end of the 1950s as a moment of contestation between established notions of masculinity and a new approach embodied by Ornette Coleman. I should note at the outset that although I argue that Coleman's performances undermined accepted ideas of masculinity in jazz, I do not mean to suggest that his music is somehow "feminine." Musical practices, like all cultural practices, only "mean" in relation to other practices. If Coleman and his colleagues did serve to regender the music, it is only because jazz communities had already established tacit conceptions of the masculine.

Jazz historians routinely cite the 1959 appearance of Ornette Coleman's quartet at New York's Five Spot jazz club, as well as the coinciding release of Coleman's *The Shape of Jazz to Come* album, as turning points in the development of the genre. Most writers see these gigs and that recording as a significant moment in—if not the actual birth of—"free jazz" and all that went along with that movement.

Indeed, Coleman's music of that time quickly staked out the first serious battleground in jazz since the bebop versus Swing debates of fifteen years earlier.[1] Coleman biographer John Litweiler recounted the passionate responses that the quartet's first New York appearances inspired in musicians, critics, and fans. Describing the reaction of bop progenitor Max Roach to a live performance of the group at the Five Spot, Litweiler related that the drummer "punched Ornette in the mouth," and later showed up in front of Coleman's apartment threatening further physical violence.[2] By contrast, John Lewis, leader of the Modern Jazz Quartet and, like Roach, an early contributor to the bebop scene, heard Coleman's music as "exciting and different." Lewis described the music as "the only really new thing in jazz since the innovations in the mid-forties of Dizzy Gillespie, Charlie Parker, and those of Thelonious Monk."[3]

Historians attempting to explain this controversy typically describe the battle as one of contrasting musical approaches. For instance, Frank Tirro writes,

> The strength of the reaction, in retrospect, is somewhat amusing, for Coleman's music, by the standards of the classical avant-garde musicians of the day, was neither new nor shocking. The tone row, atonality, *musique concrete,* electronic music, computer music, random composition, prepared instruments, chance performance, happenings, and even silent music were but a few of the many forays into the possibilities of musical expression being mounted by Western classical composers before 1959. But the introduction of any of these concepts into jazz had never been accomplished with any security before the thirty-year-old Coleman took his stand.[4]

Tirro frames the Coleman controversy around musical style: Entrenched, old-guard bebop musicians and listeners reacted against new techniques, while forward-thinking partisans rallied to extol the sounds of the future. In the process, the writer's "amused" stance and lengthy enumeration of musical developments in the Euro-American classical music of the time seem to paint both the boppers and the emerging jazz avant garde as somewhat naive. To be sure, there are significant stylistic differences (and similarities) between Coleman's group and his mostly bebop adversaries. However, to explain negative reactions toward Coleman through musical style alone ignores the historical situation that gave rise to these stylistic changes in the first place.

I have discussed in the preceding chapters some of the questions of racial identity that have stirred in and around jazz. But modeling images of race is not the only cultural work that jazz accomplishes. Understandings of gender roles, too, have been influenced by the examples that jazz music and musicians have set. Though perceptions of the genre are changing, jazz has remained, since its earliest days, an overwhelmingly male domain. As such, it has served to create and recreate notions of manhood for its participants. Yet this gendering has not always presented a single, unified image of what it means to be a man in the jazz world. As Krin Gabbard, one of the few scholars to address the issue, writes, "Part of what has made jazz so intriguing is the number of alternatives it has offered to conventional notions of masculinity and male sexuality."[5] And as musicians and audiences have responded to changing social, historical, and cultural circumstances, they have questioned and refigured established roles, gender and otherwise.

Of course, gender constructions do not exist wholly apart from other issues. For instance, it is neither coincidental nor insignificant that jazz performance and heterosexual prowess remain two of the few areas of the popular imagination in which black males have been perceived to be superior to their white counterparts. Complex interrelationships such as this need to be spoken to. Therefore, this chapter, though concerned primarily with the gender-related dimensions of the Coleman/bebop confrontation, also touches on broader questions of identity in jazz, including the topic of race. In addition, I explore the implication of these questions as they relate to formalist attitudes toward and critiques of jazz. For now, it will help to review briefly certain attitudes and practices, both in and out of the jazz world, as they emerged and developed in New York after World War II and up to the time of Coleman's arrival in that city in 1959.

MASCULINITIES AND CRISES: JAZZ IN THE 1940S AND THE 1950S

In her important work *Male Subjectivity at the Margins,* feminist scholar Kaja Silverman traces a recurring theme running through many post–World War II American films: a crisis induced by the breakdown of traditional male social roles and responsibilities. Silverman recounts the physical and emotional scars that the war "hero"/ protagonist carries in movies such as *Pride of the Marines, Lost Weekend,* and *The Best Years of Our Lives.* She writes, "Sometimes the veteran . . . finds himself strangely superfluous to the society he ostensibly protected during the war; his functions have been assumed by other men, or—much more disturbingly—by women. These texts thus dramatize the vulnerability of conventional masculinity and the larger dominant fiction to what I will call 'historical trauma.'"[6]

Silverman coined the term "historical trauma" to describe a crisis in subjective identity effected by momentous events or trends in the broader social order. I raise her study here to suggest that the bebop/ Coleman conflict involved a similar sort of crisis. Although these ordeals differ significantly in terms of time periods, cultural domains, and dimensions of their effect, both stemmed from significant changes within a community, and both led to the breakdown of that community's prevalent gender codes.

To begin to understand the bop/Coleman situation, we should bear in mind that "the same" events can affect different communities differently. And in contrast to Silverman's depiction of white veterans in America, historian Eric Lott has demonstrated that the rise of bebop after World War II simultaneously represented and configured a new confidence and self-determination within many African-American communities.[7] As Lott points out, a subtext of "double victory" played out for many black Americans during the war: Success on the battlefields overseas might lead to respect from their white countrymen and women at home. Yet at the same time, other black communities felt that the conflict in Europe and the Pacific was simply "not our war." These Americans were not as heavily invested, financially or emotionally, in the war as their white counterparts were and thus did not experience the same sense of initial purpose or eventual alienation and disillusion that Silverman describes in the (all white) film characters and the real war veterans they mirror. After all, many blacks were not strangers to a feeling of "superfluousness" in prewar America.[8]

Thus in New York's emerging bop community, many African-American musicians and their audiences articulated a newly assertive stance through dress, language, posture, and music. Early boppers developed their own "mystery" language as a means of distancing themselves from unhip outsiders (white *and* black). Stage demeanor was "cooler," less "entertainer"-like, than that of many of their jazz predecessors. Meanwhile, jazz performances became increasingly virtuosic: Extremely fast tempos became commonplace, chord changes more complex, melodies longer, more intricate, and more angular than in the Swing era. As Lott describes this early scene, "At its hippest (and meanest), such a common language became a closed hermeneutic that had the undeniable effect of alienating the riff-raff and expressing a sense of felt isolation, all the while affirming a collective purpose—even at the expense of other musicians."[9]

The impervious enclosure surrounding the bebop movement relaxed steadily through the 1950s, however, as the style circulated more widely. Bop language became readily available to musicians all over the world via radio broadcasts, concert tours, and—most important—the distribution of recordings. Through this familiarity, a distinctly recognizable bebop performance style "solidified." It certainly was not easy to become a good jazz musician in the middle 1950s—excellence required countless hours of listening, practicing, and performing—but the bop world clearly was not the closed circle it had been during its earliest days.

This sedimentation of bop performance norms fortified the foundation of a distinctly competition-based jazz aesthetic. The ability to "run changes" (improvise over a preset harmonic progression) had long been held as the established measuring stick for jazz musicianship. Accordingly, chord-based soloing served as the basis for the "cutting contest," the principal means by which instrumentalists tested their virtuosity.[10] In these unofficial battles (which continue to this day in many circles), musicians attempted to play faster, higher, and louder while incorporating more intricate lines and complex harmonic substitutions than their adversaries did. For one night at least, the winner of a contest was viewed as "the king." As such, he received all the honor and glory befitting jazz royalty: the admiration of the crowd (including, perhaps, the amorous favors of one of its members), and, more important, the chance for a better gig the next night.

I do not mean to suggest that bebop-era musicians invented the cutting contest, or even that they were the first jazz musicians to associate instrumental virtuosity with manliness. Quite the contrary: As far back as the early New Orleans innovators, jazz musicians remained highly conscious of displaying a hearty and unambiguous heterosexual masculinity. Jelly Roll Morton, for instance, has described the ambivalence he felt toward taking up the piano as a youth because of the degree to which public perception of that instrument was linked to those of "questionable" tendencies.[11] However, the boppers carried the ideal of virtuosity and complexity into and through the period in question, and they were the ones who most connected instrumental proficiency with standards of excellence, power, and manhood.

Even jazz critics picked up on and reinforced these understandings, leading to highly gendered descriptions such as, "From the start of *Scrapple From The Apple,* the sheer strength, the virility of [Dexter] Gordon's horn is unquenchably evident. His tone is assertive but warm."[12] Or, more to the point, "Good jazz is hard masculine stuff with a whip to it."[13] And the bandstand and the jazz press were not the only locations in which musicians configured and demonstrated bop masculinity. Miles Davis, for example, frequently professed his love of boxing, that most "manly" of all sports (a famous photograph shows Davis sitting in the corner of a boxing ring, ostensibly during a sparring match).

Given these ideals of physical vigor, it may seem contradictory that heroin remained the drug of choice for many bop musicians. But while the insidious effects of addiction certainly took their physical toll on users, that drug did play an important role in reinforcing jazz gendering of the time. As Ben Sidran notes, heroin "was a shortcut to the presentation of a masculine 'front': the drug caused a 'drag' in the user's voice." Sidran describes the junkie demeanor as a "deceptive passivity," cloaking a "growing sense of community within the black culture around the notion of masculine assertion."[14] Thus, prevailing identities of the jazzman in the bop world were closely tied to notions of physical endurance and intellectual rigor (intricate lines, dense harmonic structures) and also to an implacable demeanor.[15] It was this attitude, essentially, that defined the bop style from the middle 1940s until the Coleman group's arrival in New York in 1959.[16]

BIRD FOOD

The Shape of Jazz to Come did not mark Coleman's recording debut as a leader (the Los Angeles–based Contemporary label had already released two Coleman-led dates), but it was the first that his band produced for New York's higher-profile Atlantic Records. More important, its release coincided with the group's controversial engagement at the Five Spot.[17]

Coleman spent his formative years playing in blues and r&b bands in the Southwest, and his flexible approach to pitch (about which more below) still reveals these roots. The musical contours of bebop, too, have always remained evident. An early recording of Coleman playing Charlie Parker's "Klactoveedsedsteen" clearly demonstrates the younger player's indebtedness to the bop innovator, and these influences can be heard throughout *The Shape of Jazz to Come*.[18] Specifically, the numerous sax and trumpet unison melodies evince a holdover from bop methods, while the twisting and turning eighth-note lines typifying Parker's compositional style are mirrored in many ways in the themes of "Eventually" and, especially, "Chronology."[19] Yet while the songform and melodic contours of Coleman's songs betray strong blues and bop roots, the realization of these forms in performance is another matter entirely. As LeRoi Jones (now Amiri Baraka) described it in 1961: "Ornette Coleman uses Parker only as a hypothesis; his (Coleman's) conclusions are quite separate and unique."[20] Still, perceiving this clear and deep connection of Coleman to earlier aspects of the jazz tradition is crucial to understanding the strong responses from his critics. If Coleman's music had been completely cut off from those established approaches, listeners would have viewed him as nothing more than an exotic oddity. It is when a jazz musician both did and did not hear a part of himself in Coleman's music that competing identities arose.

"LONELY WOMAN"

I have singled out "Lonely Woman" for a number of reasons. First, that track opens the album and so served as the initial exposure to this group for many listeners. Second, it has become one of Coleman's better-known tunes and the most widely covered of all of his nonblues compositions.[21] Last, the tune's title seems to connect to our topic of regendering by offering an alternative to many of the jazz compositions of that era. Certainly, Coleman's portrayal of a "lonely woman" presents a less objectifying stance toward females than do "Plain Jane" (Sonny Rollins), "Gertrude's Bounce" (Richie Powell), "The Rump Roller" (Lee Morgan), or any of the similarly titled tunes from the same period.[22]

With the bass/drum opening of "Lonely Woman," we find a conception of jazz playing previously unheard in the genre. This is no "throwaway" introduction such as one might suggest for a typical bebop blowing session ("give the drummer eight bars out front and the horns will come in with the head"). Instead, the preliminary rhythm-section passage—bassist Charlie Haden strumming a series of double-stops, followed by a brief D-minor modal melody over which Billy Higgins plays a fast ride-cymbal pattern—stands as one of the most distinctive introductions in the entire history of recorded jazz. Both players clearly share a basic pulse, but where exactly they have centered the groove cannot be pinned down. Is Haden playing a half-time feel?

Or is it, rather, that Higgins is implying double-time? The answer is, of course, "yes" to both questions, depending on how one hears it.

The barline-blurring implied pulse in jazz did not originate with this group. Charles Mingus, Lennie Tristano, and others had worked with similar conceptions for some time. But no one had explored this type of free-floating drone in quite this way before or for such an extended period. The dual nature of the groove lasts throughout the piece and represents a radical departure from the driving quarter-note, walking bass, and "two and four" hi-hat with steady ride-cymbal swing approach prevalent among the hard-bop rhythm sections of the day. That is, instead of the

$$1-\underline{2}-3-\underline{4}\ 1-\underline{2}-3-\underline{4}\ \cdots$$

emphasis propelling most jazz tunes (most African-American–derived musics, for that matter), one might more accurately represent the nonregimented feel underlying "Lonely Woman" as:

$$1-1-1-1-1-1-\ \cdots$$

Yet the absence of a backbeat does not cause the tune to feel cerebral or disembodied. Though it is not a "finger-popper" or a "toe-tapper" in the Horace Silver or Art Blakey sense, one can move one's body to this groove; one simply has to learn to move it differently.

After this extraordinary introduction, Coleman and Cherry enter with the song's theme. "Lonely Woman" often appears in musicians' "fake book" compilations as a tune consisting of four sections arranged AABA. But such a structural representation does not offer an accurate model of the way in which these musicians perform the piece. As with the "timeless" rhythmic pulse underlying "Lonely Woman," the phrasing of its melody unfolds in atypical fashion; it is as if the "head" consisted simply of a series of brief melodic fragments that follow one another according to the breaths taken by the horn players.[23]

The unique sound that Cherry and Coleman achieve in their unison statement enhances this impression. "Perfect intonation," in the sense of agreeing upon and maintaining a consistent location of a pitch center—a source of pride for "professional" musicians—is not the goal here. Martin Williams described it this way:

> Intonation is a matter of context and expression to Coleman. "You can play sharp in tune and you can play flat in tune," he has said, and a D in a context representing sadness should not sound like a D in a passage of joy. . . . This is not a matter of "good" intonation, and if there were any doubt about that, there are enough key notes and phrases in Coleman's solos on exact pitch to dispel that doubt.[24]

As Williams points out, to hear these horn players as "sloppy" or "out of tune," as many have, entirely misses the point of their music. The horn players' inclination to "scoop" or bend notes, sharpen or flatten pitches, serves to accentuate the rhetorical quality of their phrasing. Indeed, Coleman and Cherry enact a remarkably speechlike instrumental style, one of the closest to human vocal patterns that has ever been heard in jazz, comparable in this respect only to such pre-bop players as Johnny Dunn, Sidney Bechet, and the great Ellington "growlers," Bubber Miley, Joe Nanton, and Cootie Williams.[25]

The unusual instruments that these musicians selected also bear consideration. Coleman relied on a white plastic alto saxophone, while Cherry chose to play a pocket trumpet, an instrument that looks, and often sounds, like a mutilated version of "the real thing." That neither player used the typically sought-after expensive "axes" in their performances affected not only the sounds they produced but undoubtedly the reception of those sounds as well. Mention should be made, in particular, of Don Cherry's distinctive instrumental style. His tone—thin, pinched, wavering (all of which were only accentuated by his use of the smaller instrument)—was, by most standards, a "weak" one, the antithesis of traditional notions of the virile trumpet king. Yet many listeners found Cherry's unique playing attractive even as he resisted the established role of the trumpet as a signifier of masculine prowess, one that had been a part of the jazz tradition since the days of Buddy Bolden.[26]

Similar to bop-based practices in which individual improvisers follow each other in turn, Coleman takes a solo, but his is far from a standard statement. In the conventional bebop manner of improvising, soloists "blow" over a repeating harmonic structure borrowed, most commonly, from a Tin Pan Alley song or a twelve-bar blues. Coleman's quartet dispenses with this chord-based approach. Melody, rather than harmony, becomes the reference point from which the musician develops his improvised lines. This, of course, reveals the advantage of this group's piano-less lineup. By laying down tonally functional harmonic progressions, an unsympathetic pianist could constrict the quartet's melodic "free association," limiting each player's possibilities in terms of phrase length, note selection, and timbral manipulation. Coleman's group generally avoided functional bebop harmony, favoring instead an open-ended quasi-modality. The implications of the move toward this chordless style were profound.

As we have seen, the cutting contest stood as one of the most conspicuous (perhaps the most conspicuous) locations of masculine gendering in jazz performance. But all of this was undone, or at least thrown into question, by Coleman's approach. It simply makes no sense to stage a battle over a tune with a fluid form such as this one presents. There are no chord changes to run, nothing here to "conquer." By undermining this foundation of musical manhood, Coleman opened the door for a whole generation of players to find new criteria by which to understand themselves as jazz musicians.

Listen, for example, to Coleman's playing after what we may call "the bridge" of his solo (when Cherry reenters with chromatically ascending long tones similar to the "B section" of the melody, or approximately 2:40 into the performance). The exclamatory nature of his phrasing here is startling and singularly expressive. Coleman's saxophone work may be rooted firmly in the Southern blues of his upbringing, but the bends and cries evinced are not the lowdown, lascivious growls of the Texas roadhouse. His solo, while assertive, does not push to s(t)imulate carnal desire in the listener but seemingly to bear witness to—and for—the lonely woman.[27]

Proficiency with this voicelike style is exceedingly difficult for a musician to achieve, yet Coleman's playing does not draw attention to its skillfulness: There is no "grand-standing" or "chest-thumping" such as one might hear at that time from trumpeter Maynard Ferguson or saxophonist Eddie "Lockjaw" Davis. This assessment is echoed by an unnamed friend of Martin Williams in that author's landmark study, *The Jazz Tradition,* when he refers to Ornette Coleman as "the first jazz musician since King Oliver whose playing does not seem egocentric to me."[28] At the same time, however, the fact that Coleman opted to emphasize melodic considerations over harmonic progressions left him open to the charge that he "couldn't make the changes" or was, quite simply, "faking it," and both of these criticisms were indeed directed toward him and Cherry as well.

"Lonely Woman" closes with a restatement of the theme, played in an even more exclamatory manner than in the opening head. Following this impassioned plea is a brief coda, the last note of which Coleman holds out until all breath is gone. The openness characteristic of this tune continues to the end as the drums and bass slowly fade out while maintaining the same boiling feel with which they began the piece.

Again, one cannot overestimate the influence of innovative rhythm-section techniques on the overall affect of this recording. By challenging the hegemony of Tin Pan Alley songform, Coleman freed Charlie Haden and Billy Higgins to investigate new, less teleological strategies. No longer was it necessary for the rhythm section to outline cadences at eight-bar intervals, and Haden and Higgins worked together to invent a uniquely "floating" feel. While they demonstrate this interaction most clearly in the dual nature of the "Lonely Woman" groove, a cooperative spirit carries throughout their work together. The degree to which we can attribute this shift in rhythmic approach to Coleman's compositions and performance philosophy can be heard by comparing Higgins's playing on *The Shape of Jazz to Come* or *Change of the Century* with his more "straight-ahead" work as a sideman on the recordings of Dexter Gordon or Thelonious Monk from roughly the same time period.[29]

COLEMAN AS CULTURAL OUTSIDER

As with the offstage representations of jazz-musician-as-boxer masculinity exemplified by Miles Davis, Ornette Coleman's appearance and

demeanor amplified the regendering qualities of his music. The album cover of *The Shape of Jazz to Come,* for instance, offers an alternative to the prevailing images of jazz at that time. In the late 1950s
and early 1960s, many record covers portrayed jazz as a music for attractive people "on the move"; this was, after all, the era of *Playboy*
magazine and the new "swinging single." For example, the shapely
legs adorning the cover of Sonny Clark's popular *Cool Struttin'* album
from 1958 plainly reflect the desire by record companies to appeal to
a young, affluent, and predominantly heterosexual male segment of
society. By contrast, Coleman's demeanor on his album cover appears
completely unassuming, even stiff. He wears neither a "slick" suit nor
"jet set" casual attire, the look so often favored by Chet Baker, that
Golden Boy of jazz. Instead, Coleman dresses in a dark sweater under
which he appears to wear a fresh shirt and tie. If not for his white plastic saxophone, Ornette Coleman might be an earnest college student
selling encyclopedias door to door. In any case, he is certainly not the
model of hip male sexuality (see figures 3 and 4).[30]

Further, accounts of Coleman's personal experiences before, during,
and after the period in question offer insight into his attitude toward
traditional codes of male behavior in the jazz world. John Litweiler
writes of Coleman's early days in Texas: "Ornette appeared to be anything but a conventional nineteen-year-old musician. A skinny youth
with a long beard and straightened hair, he was a vegetarian with a
'Jesus-type image,' which in itself was enough to attract the attention
of racist cops."[31]

Even today, a "Jesus-type" man such as described above would not
pass unnoticed in many areas of the South. It almost goes without saying that in 1950 any male with long hair—particularly a black male—
was viewed with suspicion: For many in that place and time, long hair
was for "girls" and "faggots," or, in any case, undesirables. Coleman
described the situation this way:

> I was born in Texas and I was put in jail for having long hair, and I
> was called a homosexual, and I was going through so many things,
> and the only thing I was trying to do was find a way to have my
> own individual beliefs, freedom. I'd always go somewhere where I

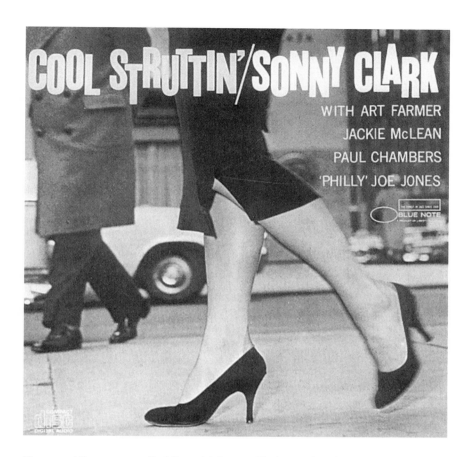

Figure 3. Album cover, *Cool Struttin',* Sonny Clark. Used with permission of Blue Note Records, a division of Capitol Records.

thought I'd be accepted, and found out I'd be kicked in the ass. . . . I was a vegetarian and everything, and I had hair down to my shoulders and a beard, and the cops took me to jail and cut my hair off, and I grew it back and went to California.[32]

Though deeply influenced by Charlie Parker and his bop contemporaries, Coleman never did spend any meaningful time in working jazz bands; he earned money, instead, touring with r&b groups or in day jobs. Stories abound of jazz musicians walking off the stage when Coleman approached to sit in with them. Such reactions support

Figure 4. Album cover, *The Shape of Jazz to Come,* Ornette Coleman. Courtesy of Rhino Entertainment Company.

LeRoi Jones's aforementioned assessment that Coleman wasn't consciously copying or patterning himself after Parker (as Jackie McLean, Art Pepper, Cannonball Adderley, Phil Woods, Frank Morgan, and so many others did). Instead, Coleman sought to explore and develop some of the melodic, rhythmic, and sonic implications of the earlier saxophonist's work.

With his sudden arrival on the New York scene, it must have appeared to some that Coleman had sprung fully formed from the head of a jazz Zeus.[33] He didn't, of course, but the fact that his reputation was not built by "paying dues" in the approved jazz circles certainly contributed to a perception that Coleman was "not one of us." That this outsider status stemmed at least partially from a conscious rejection of jazz identities on Coleman's part is reflected in his statement:

> I remember one night in a session where Clifford Brown and lots of guys were trying to play "Donna Lee," and I knew "Donna Lee" [forward and] backwards. So they asked me where I was from — because *I have never yet carried myself like a musician.* For some reason musicians always had this phony air about them like they had to have special attention, that they had to have a certain environment. I still don't like that image that people have of musicians — it's a very degrading human image of the way music and musicians have to identify what they do.[34]

By 1959, Coleman had cut the long hair that attracted so much animosity, but many still perceived him as "different." He did not dress like his bop contemporaries, and he remained a vegetarian in a time and place in which that practice could still raise eyebrows. He spoke differently too, decrying at times the sexuality surrounding jazz, a practice that marked him, at the very least, as someone who "didn't like to have chicks around."

> You don't know how many times I've come off the bandstand and had girls come up to me and hand me a note with their address on it. . . . Sometimes I say to myself "Well, shit, if this is what it's all about, we should all be standing up there with hard-ons, and everybody should come to the club naked, and the musicians should be standing up there naked. Then there wouldn't be any confusion about what's supposed to happen, and people wouldn't say they came to hear the music."[35]

The extreme degree of Coleman's aversion to the sexual overtones in the jazz environment was made clear when he inquired about the possibility of castration, an action that his doctor dissuaded him from pursuing.[36]

Given the excerpt above and the many others like it, it seems clear that
Coleman has given a great deal of thought to the complicated dynamics surrounding gender roles and sexuality in jazz.[37] He is not, however, the only jazz participant to take notice of the subject. Valerie
Wilmer devotes extensive space to the attitudes toward—and, refreshingly, of—female jazz fans and musicians in her outstanding
study, *As Serious as Your Life.* Wilmer's interview with one unnamed
(male) drummer is revealing and worth citing at length:

> I know a lot of musicians with a lot of women. . . . You got to have
> a lot of wives because one doesn't satisfy. But it's not that they have
> a lot of women, it's just like a one-night scene. I couldn't say that
> sex is the main force (behind playing). After it gets to the ultimate
> end state of music, you become the music, the music becomes you.
> So it has nothing to do with sex. The sex part of it comes when
> you're so much into the music and the music is so much a part of
> you, that you can project the feeling to someone. And usually it's a
> man up there doing it and it's a woman out there, and the woman
> feels that she must have this. The thing that he's projecting, it's
> coming from somewhere else but it comes through him and pro-
> jects to the woman out there. She feels that the spirit is strong but
> she can't collect that thing where it's coming from. And so she has
> to collect the person it's coming through![38]

The drummer in this passage opens his discussion by stating that
some musicians sleep with large numbers of women because "one
doesn't satisfy" but concludes by suggesting that male musicians have
little control over the situation. In the end, he characterizes female audience members as desirous of the "spirit," a transcendental state that
these listeners confuse with the man through whom it passes. He implies that when the women decide that they must "collect" this spirit/
person, males stand incapable of resisting.

That this drummer's characterization of both male jazz musicians
and their female listeners presents a complex view of jazz life is clear,
but other issues arise here as well. Most germane for this project is his

belief in a purely musical place, one that stands—for the performer at least—apart from all earthly matters. In this musician's world, the music and the musician become one, above the fray of the mundane.

The ideals expressed by both Wilmer's interviewee and Ornette Coleman imply the existence of a wholly and "holy" musical space in which the artist engages in unsullied music making. As attractive as those ideals may appear to some (but certainly not all) musicians, that pristine space never has existed in jazz, or in any other music, for that matter. Not that the "spiritual" or "mystical" are antithetical to jazz—the discourse that has built up around John Coltrane demonstrates that they most certainly do form a part of listeners' (and players') experiences. However, people compose, perform, and listen to music in specific cultural situations at specific historical moments, so that musical experiences (mystical, sensual, or otherwise) are always already based in a cultural matrix.[39] Musical meanings emerge not from some Hanslickian plane of disinterested contemplation, but from the interplay of listeners and performers as they realize, rethink, reinvigorate, recontextualize, and/or reveal the values of their respective cultural traditions.[40]

Trumpeter Cootie Williams presented a different perspective on the role of gender and sex in jazz when he said, "All great jazz musicians, every one of them, have had many loves and girls in their lives. People don't read about these things in books, but a girl *is* jazz music. They throw something into the mind to make you produce jazz."[41] The image of a woman "throwing something into the mind" certainly evokes the unfortunate stereotype of the femme fatale, but Williams's refusal to separate "the music" from its social and cultural situation is perceptive. Unlike Ornette Coleman, who wished to eliminate the sexual overtones of his performances, Cootie Williams understands that—for worse *and* for better—those relationships have long remained central to every jazz community's understanding of itself.

Try as he might, then, Ornette Coleman cannot erase the connections among jazz, masculinity, and sexuality that have existed since the earliest days of the genre.[42] His proposed castration, for example, would not even have solved the "sexual problem" for himself. As with the seventeenth-century castrato—where the very fact of the singer's emasculation (remasculation?) enhanced his rapture-inspiring "star power" for his audiences—a castrated Coleman would lose none of, and perhaps would even heighten, the eroticism that listeners may have attached to his playing. This is not to say, however, that understandings cannot change; individuals do reassess their roles and behaviors in light of developments in the social and cultural sphere. And it is not only Coleman's group and its fans that engaged in a refiguring of established jazz codes, for radical shifts in values and beliefs in one area of a social system transform the entire system, as individuals are forced to contend with competing models of identity.

JAZZ AND FORMALIST HISTORY

Having rehearsed briefly the development of bebop attitudes and the challenge to these posed by Ornette Coleman's group, I would like to return to Frank Tirro's comments concerning the Coleman controversy of the late 1950s. To restate briefly: Tirro expressed surprise and amusement at the degree to which some musicians and audiences attacked Coleman's music, given the fact that composers based in the European tradition had already explored similarly radical techniques. While it is true that all of the devices cited had entered the European art-music palette, such a critique implies that jazz musicians remained unaware of those developments, or of any music outside of their own genre. Yet jazz musicians have never limited their listening to those musics called "jazz." This assertion is easily demonstrable by browsing through transcriptions of interviews with jazz players from any period or style (bassist Charles Mingus: "Bird [Charlie Parker] called me on the phone one day and said: 'How does this sound?' and he was playing—ad libbing—to the 'Berceuse' or 'Lullaby' section of Stravinsky's *Firebird Suite!*").[43]

Again, Tirro's remarks seem to reflect an evolutionary model of the music's history, viewing increasing complexity or stylistic change as qualitative while suggesting that jazz hadn't quite "caught up" with classical practices. This sort of historiographical approach ignores the fact that the jazz and European music traditions differ in more ways than simply stylistically. Consequently, matters of race, ethnicity, nationality, gender, and social class—all of which contribute significantly to configuring a community's understanding of itself—get brushed aside.

As an alternative, I suggest that it would be more productive to question why some members of the mainstream jazz community rejected certain stylistic devices. We should see that musicians do not create, adopt, adapt, or reject techniques without compelling motivation to do so. Newly emergent technologies, shifting attitudes toward institutions, reassessment of established roles and values—all of these serve to modify the performance and reception of music. Techniques that may appear to be "the same," then, do not necessarily mean the same things in different contexts. In other words, jazz need not follow the narrative trajectory that many have constructed for "classical music." Clearly, Ornette Coleman was not satisfied with reproducing the musical world configured by bebop approaches, and he sought new ways of understanding himself as a jazz musician. For historians to place the musical developments in the European avant garde next to the musical developments in the jazz avant garde without consideration for the social and cultural perceptions of each tradition creates a kind of "blind" formalism. In the end, such an approach works to conceal rather than to reveal the meanings and values of both music communities.

Issues of meaning and identity always involve more than simple binary opposites of black/white or masculine/feminine. They consist, instead, of extremely complex and fluid relationships among cultural values, understandings, and practices. As was demonstrated so forcefully in Jacques Attali's provocative work *Noise,* music can offer the historian unique glimpses into the transformation of these relationships. If we listen, we can hear the Ornette Coleman Quartet as more than simply the first "free jazz" group. Indeed, their music can be heard as a foresounding of many of the contesting models of identity that arose in the decades that followed.

And it is here that we can again see the relevance of Kaja Silverman's depictions of postwar film characters to our topic of jazz and gender. Some jazz musicians certainly experienced their own "historical trauma" of identity when confronted by Ornette Coleman's methods, musical and otherwise (though in a time and place different from those of the veterans whom Silverman describes). As we've seen, Coleman presented an alternative model of the male jazz musician. His music and demeanor worked to downplay the prevalent phallocentric aspects of jazz performance, destabilizing positions of masculinity and prestige in the jazz community, particularly among black musicians. The pain and resentment caused by the myth of the "black stud" need not be rehashed here. Still, the reality remains that as long as phallic power went hand in hand with musical virtuosity, the black bebop musician could be seen as one of the most potent of all American males. In this light, the fact that some bop musicians resisted Coleman's new approach appears more understandable: So many of those attitudes and practices that had served as markers of jazz/male identity were held up as questionable, even worthless. For some jazzmen faced with the new style, the crisis went beyond simply not knowing what to play, engaging the very real dilemma of who to be. And given the extreme marginalization of the African-American male during the 1950s, it should come as no surprise that some musicians would be reluctant to let go of one of their few domains of perceived power.[44]

Almost a half century has passed since the first rumblings of this controversy, and *The Shape of Jazz to Come* might sound surprisingly tame to our ears, especially when compared to the "free jazz" and "New Thing" that emerged in the decade that followed.[45] But even if the furor surrounding Coleman and his band no longer makes sense to us musically, reconsidering the controversy this group sparked can offer us some perspectives on the changes occurring during that period, both in and out of the musical world. For despite the trauma experienced by some jazz participants, many others found the new model compelling. And in this regard, Ornette Coleman can be seen to foreshadow the sexual and political questioning that marked the 1960s and 1970s. As evidenced by the broad range of musical styles and contentious debates surrounding jazz at the start of the twenty-first century, the challenges posed by Coleman have remained far from resolved to this day.

Four

BODY AND SOUL

Performing Deep Jazz

*Father said, "Watch him closely and reverently, look into his
face and hear the music of the ages. Don't pay too much attention
to the sounds—for if you do, you may miss the music.
You won't get a wild ride to heaven on pretty little sounds."*

CHARLES IVES,
Charles Ives' Memos

THIS CHAPTER CONCERNS the relationship between musical sound
and the physical performance of it: the ways that musicians' bodily
gestures reinforce certain possible meanings for their audiences while
delimiting contrasting interpretations. I focus particular attention on
the presentation of expressive "depth" in jazz through two highly regarded and influential post–bop-era pianists, Bill Evans (1929–1980)
and Keith Jarrett (born in 1945). We'll see that both of these players
communicate a sense of artistic and personal depth (profundity, sensitivity, seriousness) to audiences through a variety of means, not the
least of which is their physical demeanor while performing.[1]

The chapter's subtitle derives from an essay called "Deep Jazz: Notes
on Interiority, Race, and Criticism," in which Robert Walser argues
against the many forms of music criticism that would present jazz as
a purely subjective expression of a musician's "inner being":

> Evocations of an inner emotional realm seem natural to us because
> they have so powerfully shaped our lives. They produce an individ-
> ualized image of the self, an "inside" not only defined against the

outside, but imagined as somehow autonomous from it. They ask us to accept an intangible inner life as the essence of a person: truer than behavior, deeper than one's closest relationships. They offer psychological explanations of an identity which is made to seem free-floating, detached from social experiences of class, race, ethnicity, and gender. They paint the social world as a shallow backdrop to the mysterious wellsprings of subjectivity.[2]

Walser's essay reminds us of the socially, culturally, and historically dependent nature of subjectivity, that one's sense of an "inner self" is very much bound up with one's interactions in the "outer world."

While Walser highlights the written discourse surrounding jazz, we can see as well that the notion of deep jazz has come to play an important role in shaping understandings of artistry, prestige, and purpose of the jazz performance itself. As I suggested in chapter 2, professional survival in a commercially marginalized genre such as jazz often hinges on a musician's ability to present him- or herself as an "artist": uniquely gifted, incorruptible, and spiritually attuned. This chapter, then, builds on Walser's work to trace some of the ways in which certain performance practices may signal to audiences the presence and extraordinary intensity of a jazz musician's "inner life."

I do not mean to suggest that audiences who hear these players as "deep" are misguided or that either of these players is "insincere." Neither do I mean to imply that the types of depth expressed by Evans and Jarrett are alike; indeed, as we will see, I hold quite the opposite view. What I do want to emphasize is the pivotal role that the body—its posture, movement, and even shape—plays for both of these musicians in communicating the distinctive types and degrees of depth upon which their formidable reputations are founded.

Until quite recently, musicologists had largely ignored this nexus of sound, body, and meaning. Instead, the Central-European orientation of historical musicology tended to esteem the written score as the embodiment of "the music." Such a bias implies that musical performance—the physical act of playing and singing—can achieve only a greater or lesser, but never "perfect," realization of what amounts to a Platonic ideal rendered on the page. This score-based scholarly emphasis has even worked its way into the hearts of many present-day "classical" performers whose unfortunate goal in many cases is simply not to mess up.[3]

Almost by necessity, critiques of non- or minimally texted musics, traditionally the domain of ethnomusicologists, have centered on the sounding of music. Recordings (either from "the field" or, as with this project, commercially produced and distributed) play a prominent role in all such studies. As welcome as this inclusion of sound into critical discussions of music undoubtedly is, we should recognize that sound does not "mean" in and of itself any more than does a score. Aurally transmitted meaning (whether musical or linguistic) always remains culturally based. To communicate verbally, speakers and listeners engage a common (though never wholly stable) semantic field, one that includes facial and bodily gestures and the context and venue of discourse, as well as words and the ways in which these are inflected.[4] In music, performers, composers, and listeners engage in an ongoing (if usually subconscious) mediation as to which sounds signify "music" and "not music," and the range within which those sounds deemed "music" are understood to represent (or not represent, or challenge) certain attitudes, beliefs, and/or emotional affects. These, too, are dependent upon nonsonic gestures.

For example, in other essays Walser has traced rock and heavy-metal guitarists' use of sonic feedback—long viewed by musicians and audiences from nonrock-based music cultures as unwanted noise—to represent and enact a sense of power.[5] But people not only hear music, they also see it, and musical meanings such as Walser describes are always intimately bound up with the physical enactment of the sound. To continue with the feedback example: An important clue for rock audiences that the piercing shriek of feedback was actually the musician's intended aural effect was the ability to see someone such as the Who's Pete Townshend (in person, on television, or through concert films) deliberately face his guitar toward the amplifier. This action invariably produces a high-pitched squeal and/or low-frequency hum (assuming the volume settings are high enough). And with his arms outstretched and head thrown back, reveling in the moment, Townshend's apparent welcoming of this sonic onslaught displayed an unmistakable defiance toward previous codes of polite musicking in America and Britain. Meanwhile, his message of the 1960s came across loud and clear: "My Generation" is not my parents'.

The arrival of MTV in 1981 brought increasing recognition that the popularity of a musical performer correlates in large measure to that performer's appearance. Could Madonna, for instance, ever have achieved such widespread fame on the strength of her singing alone? Pop singer Pat Boone discovered the extent to which audiences connect meanings to visual and musical presentations when he walked on stage at the 1996 MTV Music Awards to the "crunch" of heavy metal guitar riffs. Boone, clad in studded, black-leather pants and vest—apparel widely associated with motorcycle gangs and alternative sexual lifestyles—was engaging in a good-natured skewering of his own squeaky-clean image. But the joke backfired as conservative groups, longtime Boone supporters, condemned his action and called for a boycott of his recordings, concerts, and television appearances. Their denunciations served notice that "nice people" neither look nor sound like *that.* Of course, the marriage of the visual and the musical in rock 'n' roll occurred long before the launching of music video networks. The decision by the *Ed Sullivan Show*'s producers to present Elvis Presley from the waist up illustrates only one of the more memorable instances of sound and the body coming together to extraordinary social and cultural consequences.[6] Indeed, it was only in this century that a sight/sound split was even made possible. Modern technology and our own listening habits cause us to forget sometimes that before the advent of recording, virtually all music was simultaneously seen and heard![7]

To be sure, the overt theatricality of much pop and rock foregrounds the interrelationships among sound, its physical enactment before an audience, and the meanings surrounding these. But these same relationships function just as deeply, if not as openly, in the seemingly more staid world of jazz. When Wynton Marsalis started out as a sideman with drummer Art Blakey in the late 1970s, the trumpeter often wore workman's overalls (as did the sixty-year-old Blakey). What a very different reputation—even sound—Marsalis and the rest of the jazz world might have carried through the 1980s and 1990s had the powers that be at CBS Records not seen fit to insist on a new wardrobe for the label's promising upstart.[8]

No scholar has done more to trace these connections between the visual aspects of musicking and the social and cultural meanings they both represent and structure than Richard Leppert. In *The Sight of Sound: Music, Representation, and the History of the Body,* Leppert studies painted images of musicking in Europe from the seventeenth century to the twentieth, noting:

> When people hear a musical performance, they see it as an embodied activity. While they hear, they also witness: how the performers look and gesture, how they are costumed, how they interact with their instruments and with one another, how they regard the audience, how other listeners heed the performers. Thus the musical event is perceived as a socialized activity.[9]

Leppert's work illustrates how "music" always entails more than just organized sounds and silences. Although driven by sound, this cultural activity encompasses a much larger domain, integrating an array of sensuous experiences. With this in mind, I wish to turn now to the ways in which the "embodied activity" of musical performance resulted in the founding of two very different deep-jazz identities.

BILL EVANS: THE JAZZ INTELLECTUAL AND SENSITIVE MALE INTERIORITY

I think jazz is the purest tradition in music this country has had. It has never bent to strictly commercial considerations, and so it has made music for its own sake. That's why I'm proud to be part of it.

BILL EVANS,
in Len Lyons, *The Great Jazz Pianists*

The pianist has remained a fixture of the jazz world since the genre's earliest days. Jelly Roll Morton, Fats Waller, Albert Ammons, Earl Hines, Duke Ellington, and Teddy Wilson represent only a few of the many musicians who carried a rich keyboard tradition through the first four decades of the twentieth century. Somewhat later, Art Tatum and Bud Powell brought astonishing technical facility and harmonic complexity to the music, helping to usher in the jazz movement that eventually became known as bebop.

The piano's expansive polyphonic capabilities played a vital role in enabling it to become one of the very few instruments capable of sustaining solo performances acceptable to public taste. This quality, along with the fact that pianists, unlike horn players, could sing and play at the same time, also opened the door for keyboardists to step into the widest variety of professional situations. From Morton and Waller to Nat "King" Cole and Sarah Vaughan, jazz pianists before bebop often served a dual function as singers. This practice essentially allowed nightclub owners to hire two musicians for the price of one, while patrons enjoyed the chance to hear their favorite lyrics as well as their favorite melodies.

But as the distinction between "jazz" and "popular music" sharpened with and after the emergence of bebop, fewer jazz pianists seemed willing to accept this double role. In recent decades, those who have both played and sung—Ben Sidran, Mose Allison, Harry Connick Jr.—have been widely dismissed by instrumentalists and journalists (but not necessarily audiences) as mere "singers who play," "lounge acts," or simply "commercial." Clearly, many circles have equated the singing instrumentalist with "selling out"; the jazz musician of today is seen as an "artist" and is expected to act and play accordingly. And no pianist has both created and fulfilled that expectation more completely than Bill Evans.

It would not be a stretch to suggest that since the late 1950s Evans has exerted a stronger influence on jazz pianists than any other keyboardist. His rich harmonic palette, fluid rhythmic conception, and crystalline sound have served as the stylistic basis for two succeeding generations of players, among them Herbie Hancock, Chick Corea, Alan Broadbent, Kenny Kirkland, Geri Allen, and, most recently, Brad Mehldau. More important for our purposes, Bill Evans is not merely understood by his followers as a great jazz virtuoso; he is also always seen as a "serious musician," somehow outside of or above the fray of the entertainment side of the music world. And the high regard paid to Evans during his lifetime has not diminished since his passing in 1980. In fact, as with so many deceased jazz pianists (Bud Powell, Herbie Nichols, Thelonious Monk), Evans's successes—most notably the trio recordings with Paul Motian and Scott LaFaro from the very late 1950s and early 1960s—are offered as evidence of the musician's genius. At the same time, his fans generally downplay or ignore altogether his lesser work (and even his staunchest supporters must agree that few of his recordings after 1961 match the brilliance of the early sides).[10]

Even at the height of his professional career, Bill Evans seemed to eschew the public spotlight. The thin, pale face, greasy hair, and black-framed eyeglasses reproduced on dozens of album covers and magazine photographs lent him an inconspicuous, even dour, look (see figure 5).

But if Evans's visage appeared more reminiscent of a "nerdy" eighth-grade science teacher than of a professional musician, the seriousness of his endeavors remained unquestionable. It seemed as if a private world deep inside him housed both a profound intellectuality and an exquisite loneliness. Historians have rarely failed to take note of this semblance. For instance, Frank Tirro writes that

> Bill Evans . . . acquired, through his presence and personality, the aspect of a guru—thoughtful, gentle, introspective, caring. When he played, especially as a soloist, he almost seemed to become one with the instrument. The image of his body, curved over the keyboard, listening intently to every aspect of the sound his fingers released from the strings of the piano, became a symbol to many jazz artists seeking beauty in a Romantic but completely unpretentious quest.[11]

Mark Gridley echoes Tirro's assessments, noting, "'Introspective' is the adjective most frequently applied to [Evans's] music."[12]

In the original liner notes to the 1961 Bill Evans Trio recording *Sunday at the Village Vanguard,* the record's producer, Orrin Keepnews, wrote:

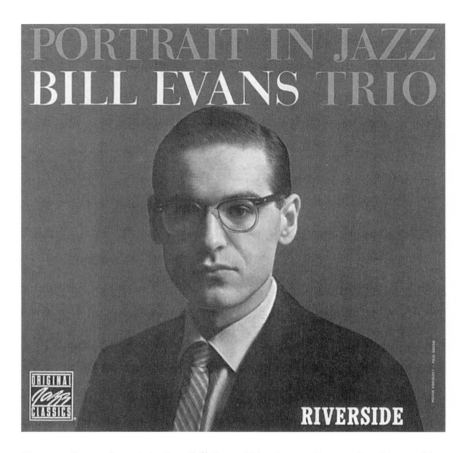

Figure 5. Cover, *Portrait in Jazz,* Bill Evans Trio. © 1987 Fantasy, Inc. Licensed by Fantasy, Inc. All Rights Reserved.

> Anyone who has experienced the playing of Bill Evans is aware of his deep feelings and the great clarity with which he communicates them. . . . In listening to the present album, I find myself so absorbed that consciousness of my body disappears and I become as one large ear, equipped only with a psyche. I am not aware of the act of listening. I am suffused by the music and become one with the music.[13]

All of the above commentaries raise a number of points germane to our present topic of jazz identities and the body. Most obviously, the suggestion that anyone familiar with Bill Evans's music is aware of the pianist's introspective "deep feelings" raises some questions: How do we become aware of his feelings, and how does Evans seem to communicate these so clearly? Also relevant here are Tirro's description of Evans's posture, as well as Keepnews's depiction of his own mode of listening wherein his body "disappears." To begin to address these issues, I turn to Bill Evans's piano style, through which we can see how performance posture, stage demeanor, and other factors help to determine the meanings associated with the sounds.

The Sound

Evans's playing style, aspects of which have been imitated in various ways by almost every subsequent pianist, remains instantly recognizable. In general, he used a clear, "developing variation" approach to linear improvisation wherein a solo line seemed to generate itself naturally out of the previous line. He grounded the apparent logic of the flow of his phrases—at times bordering almost on a sense of inevitability—in short, melody- or arpeggio-derived motives that move sequentially through the chord changes. Evans avoided over-predictability and tediousness through skillful rhythmic displacement of motives (about which more below).

Evans's harmonic conception, too, remains distinctive and was quite unusual for its time. Though still based in functional, tertian harmony, he was one of the first to experiment with quartal sonorities; his "So What" chords on Miles Davis's *Kind of Blue* served as the foundation from which McCoy Tyner built his entire harmonic approach. Evans also spurred the now-prevalent use of "rootless voicings" in which pianists relinquish the lower registers of the instrument to the bass player. Working predominantly in the middle range of the piano, Evans replaced the root-7 left-hand voicings of most bop-schooled players with richer, closely voiced sonorities, typically "rubbing together" the root and 7th, 9th and 3rd, or 13th and 7th of a chord.

Evans's various approaches to harmonic voicing often evoked affects and sonic colors reminiscent of the French Impressionist composers, and his conception was, in fact, heard as one of the most "European"—

to be read, as it was in the early 1960s, as "sophisticated"—of his time. Indeed, when asked in a 1959 questionnaire sent by Leonard Feather to provide any information that the readers of Feather's *Encyclopedia Yearbook of Jazz* might find interesting, Evans described himself in the third person: "Very 'advanced' cat, this one." [14]

Perhaps the most recognizable aspect of Evans's musical personality remains his innovative rhythmic conception. He once remarked:

> I don't really understand why the basic four-four has to be pounded out year after year when other things which are more subtle can be projected, as long as it is within you. In other words you don't have to mark it out continually. It's sort of like shadow lettering in which you don't actually draw the letters, but rather the shadow of the letters, yet you see the letters and not the shadows. [15]

He approached swing without the deep-in-the pocket, "funky" feel of Horace Silver; the refined, yet bluesy, inflections of Oscar Peterson; the relentless "burn" of McCoy Tyner; or the sharply arrhythmic stylings of Cecil Taylor. Though a consistent pulse underlies Evans's work, the strong, insistent groove felt in all of the above-mentioned players (except Taylor) remains conspicuously absent. Rather than a given, rhythm for Bill Evans was another parameter—like harmonic sonority or thematic development—for him and his band mates to manipulate. Miles Davis described the difference between Evans and Evans's more overtly swinging predecessor in Davis's band, Red Garland, this way: "Red's playing had carried the rhythm but Bill underplayed it." [16] Another way of saying it would be that Evans generally played *with* the time, while Garland and the others played *within* it.

Evans's rhythm-a-ning (to borrow a term from Thelonious Monk) distanced the music from its "entertainment" roots in the world of the professional dance band. His was a decidedly more fluid conception. To be sure, other players had tugged at the time as Evans did (Charles Mingus, Ornette Coleman, and Sonny Rollins stand as conspicuous examples) but normally over and against the steady beat of the rhythm section. In Bill Evans's most heralded groups, each player contributed freely and equally to the rhythmic interplay, and this was, in fact, the oft-stated goal of the trio. As Lewis Porter and Michael Ullman note, "It is usually clear who is playing lead in the Bill Evans Trio, but it's never clear for how long he'll be doing it." [17]

Even the interplay between Evans's hands was unusual rhythmically. He deployed his left-hand "comps" (a jazz abbreviation for "accompaniment") either in tandem with and to accentuate the rhythmic displacement of his right-hand lines or to evoke a "back and forth" effect against the right hand. This comping style contrasts markedly with the regular left-hand punctuations of most of Evans's predecessors and contemporaries, punctuations that "solidified," rather than destabilized, the time feel. The opening measures of Evans's "solo" on "Alice in Wonderland" from 1961 can serve as an example of many of this group's stylistic trademarks. Evident here are both the rootless left-hand voicings and the multilayered rhythmic play. The unusual starting and ending points of Evans's phrases sound logical because of the recurring five-note melodic figures. The rhythm section of Motian and LaFaro begins in a straightforward manner, but both players pick up on Evans's "open" downbeats in bar 4, setting the stage for what will become near-constant rhythmic interplay between the three musicians. From bar 3 on, LaFaro avoids the typical "walking bass" function, and, as Porter and Ullman have suggested, his instrument acts as often as a second melodic line to Evans's right hand as it does a traditional accompaniment. [18]

James Lincoln Collier has rightly observed that Evans "sometimes goes for long stretches without touching the piano with his left hand at all, and plays long strings of notes only with the right hand." [19] This is surely one of the traits that proved most influential on subsequent pianists. Players such as Herbie Hancock, Chick Corea, and Keith Jarrett frequently resorted to such unaccompanied single-note lines. But Collier's conclusion that Evans "is less concerned with rhythm than most pianists had been hitherto" seems to miss the very point of Evans's style, for the pianist is precisely "concerned with rhythm," as he and his group explore various possibilities of rhythmic manipulation within a jazz context. [20] The absence of his left hand evokes a more open texture, one in which the musicians less explicitly define and articulate the usual eight-bar cadences of the Tin Pan Alley songform.

Adding to this effect, Evans's melodic contours always parallel grad-ual, but constant, dynamic fluctuations, occasionally punctuated by sharply accentuated notes. These rhythmic/dynamic waves remain clear stylistic markers of Evans's playing, if not his innovation; as Scott DeVeaux has pointed out, Charlie Parker devised similar strategies in the early to mid-1940s.[21] But Evans used this technique differently. He smoothed out the flow of the lines, removing all traces of the "bounce" of Parker's blues roots. In doing so, he achieved a much more subdued, almost "breathy" quality on the piano.[22]

We can also discern Evans's interest in rhythmic exploration in his propensity for material in 3/4 time, a meter that seemed to allow the pianist and his groups to engage in even freer rhythmic variation. At the same time, that less common groove also pulled the music still fur-ther from its foundation in dance. Even beyond the fact that the waltz no longer enjoyed the popularity it once had (reduced to the role of quaint material among "society bands"), the degree to which Evans and his sidemen played with the time, coupled with tempos often leaning toward the fast or "up" side, rendered all of his waltzes, for the most part, undanceable. His groups only exacerbated this rhythmic instability by their tendency to shift from 3/4 to 4/4 in many of their "waltzes," including two of their more famous vehicles, "Someday My Prince Will Come" and Evans's own "Waltz for Debby."

Finally, a distinctly bell-like sound permeates Bill Evans's playing, a trait he shares with many of the other former Miles Davis pianists from the mid-1950s to the late 1960s: Red Garland, Wynton Kelly, Herbie Hancock. But that sound differs greatly from the "punchier" or "dirtier" sounds of the period, particularly those of Thelonious Monk, Horace Silver, Sonny Clark, or Bobby Timmons. This sense of purity heard in Evans's tone was intensified by the quiet volume at which he and his trio played; as the voices and tinkling glasses cap-tured on their live recordings reveal, the group's decibel level reached only slightly higher than that of "background music."

In his liner notes to the Evans Trio's *Waltz for Debby* album, Joe Goldberg alludes to this subdued quality and describes the evolution of Evans's playing from Evans's days as a sideman with Miles Davis and George Russell to his work as leader this way:

Evans . . . abandons, to a great extent, the muscular excellence of [the Davis and Russell] performances when he is leading his own trio, and gives expression to the more romantic side of his nature. He reveals himself as an Impressionist; and the man who wrote the brief and lovely "Epilogue" . . . must have been influenced by the English pastoral composers. In some respects, Evans shares identity with the Modern Jazz Quartet: both groups could probably play all night long, and a drunken listener would never know that he had heard anything more than quiet, pleasant cocktail music.[23]

Goldberg's use of the term "muscular" is instructive. It denotes, quite literally, a solid, healthy, and "manly" body. Yet he implies that Evans's trio shuns these brawny qualities. He allies Evans with the British pastoralists and the French Impressionists, with their very delicate sonorities, while he omits any allusion to the hustle and bustle of urban America, the soundscape so closely associated with jazz. While Goldberg's allusion to the "romantic" seems to have as much to do with everyday notions of the word (i.e., wedding-anniversary-remembering, flower-sending) than with nineteenth-century aesthetics, the connotations remain parallel to the serene worlds of both Claude Debussy and Ralph Vaughan Williams. In this regard, it is pertinent that Evans rarely played the blues, the African-American-rooted staple of so many jazz groups of the day. Instead, his repertoire consisted overwhelmingly of Tin Pan Alley standards augmented by a handful of original pieces composed by himself or bassist Scott LaFaro, neither of whom incorporated blues textures into his compositions. LaFaro remarked in an interview held shortly before his death, "I am not a city man. . . . I've never been through that 'blues' thing."[24] This absence of blues earthiness, as well as the quietness and convoluted rhythmic approach of his music, distanced Evans from the "good times" identity presented by or projected onto the harder-swinging musicians of that period.

The endorsements adorning the cover of the 1959 release *Everybody Digs Bill Evans* attest that many of Evans's contemporaries heard him as both "original" and "tasteful."[25] But not "everybody" was impressed. As Miles Davis observed, "a lot of people were saying he didn't play fast enough and hard enough for them, that he was too delicate."[26] This was, after all, the height of the hard-bop period, exemplified by the groups of Art Blakey and Horace Silver, as well as the time in which John Coltrane's groups were developing a freer and more forceful style. In fact, Coltrane's now-legendary first series of Village Vanguard recordings followed Evans's sessions at that club by only five months.

Given Evans's musical approach, we can begin to understand Orrin Keepnews's aforementioned "disembodied" listening experience. As record producer of such unmistakably earthy players as Cannonball Adderley, Thelonious Monk, and Johnny Griffin, Keepnews had grown accustomed to "hearing" jazz as much in his feet and, through the more forceful volumes at which these groups played, even his torso, as in his ears. With Evans, as with Ornette Coleman around the same time, there is an absence of an obvious toe-tapping element, and the remarkably low volume at which the Evans trio played only lessened the viscerality of their music. I've discussed in chapter 3 the notions of masculinity prevalent in the late 1950s. In many ways, Bill Evans, like Ornette Coleman, can be seen as another musician uncomfortable with those established codes of jazz manhood, even despite his obviously formidable technique. This is "thinking man's jazz": music for contemplative listening (or dining, or reading, or romancing), but certainly not for grooving.

Yet as I have noted, sound alone does not tell the whole tale. The jazz identity configured by Bill Evans and the related meanings accrued around his work depend upon the interplay of both the sounds he produced and the audience's witnessing of the manner in which he produced them—the "sight of sound." And we can turn now to the ways in which Evans's performances reinforced understandings of him and his music as "deep."

Portrait in Jazz

Bill Evans's attitude at the piano illustrates yet another approach nurtured by the pronounced shift in jazz ideals and understandings in the wake of bebop. Not only did he refrain from leaning toward and smiling at his audiences while playing (an amiable practice employed by dozens of pre-bop pianists including Ellington, Waller, Count Basie, and Nat Cole, and now by that highly talented yet seemingly anachronistic actor/player/singer, Harry Connick Jr.), Evans usually refused to recognize that an audience existed at all. He neither announced song titles nor introduced his fellow musicians, two widely used stage tactics among musicians across genre boundaries in both Europe and the Americas, with the notable and very pertinent exception of the European classical tradition, a connection to which I return below.

His earliest recordings evince an affinity for bop inflections: angular melodic lines punctuated by short, left-hand comps. It is a style firmly rooted in the playing of Bud Powell. Yet the softer volumes and different breed of rhythm favored by Evans suggested an emotional reserve in sharp contrast to Powell's expressive fire. In this regard, Evans may be seen to empathize with the "cool" style typified by Lennie Tristano. But while influences of both Tristano and Powell clearly manifest themselves here, it would be a mistake to characterize Evans simply as an amalgam of these two. For though neither Powell nor Tristano belonged to the "entertainer" school of pre-bop pianists, neither did these players display the sorts of mannerisms that Evans did.

For instance, both Powell and Tristano maintained relatively erect postures at the piano: the blind Tristano alert to the contrapuntal interplay of which he was the center; the more aggressive Powell staring seemingly distractedly across the piano or around the room. As opposed to these upright postures, Evans remained nearly always hunched over the piano, almost "fetal." At times it looked as if he was hiding behind the instrument, unwilling or unable to face either his patrons or even his fellow musicians. With his eyes closed, head bent down to the keyboard, Evans appeared to be in retreat from or at least in quiet battle with the unwanted and unseemly distractions of the "real world" of noisy audiences and cash register bells. This position became so associated with Bill Evans that it was incorporated into the logo of a quarterly newsletter dedicated to him (see figure 6).

What did this physical attitude convey to his audiences? Images from the world of secular and religious painting and sculpture have led us to see the bowed posture as representing variously a sense of

Figure 6. Logo for *Letter from Evans* newsletter.

deep thought, profound piety, or heartfelt sadness. Works such as Rodin's *The Thinker,* J. L. David's *The Death of Socrates,* or Mary in any of the pietàs from the fifteenth century onward all display the bowed head and stooped shoulder as expressing the qualities of grief, solitude, or pensiveness.[27] In contrast, one would be hard pressed to locate a similarly positioned body that was meant to represent elation or humor.

It is no surprise, then, to find that audiences saw and heard Evans as both "intelligent" and "sensitive." Even beyond his bowed posture, he looked "brainy." His owlish glasses and unkempt appearance seemed incongruous with the streetwise hipster image of jazz musicians presented in the film and print of the time. Many interviews noted his propensity for philosophy and European literature, a trait that strengthened impressions of him as bookish.[28] But Evans was far from the only book-smart jazz musician of his generation. Charlie Parker was widely respected by his peers for his far-reaching knowledge, and Charles Mingus, Max Roach, and others also read broadly. However, the discourse surrounding Parker and these other black boppers generally ignores their "literary" side, replaced by lurid tales of drug-induced excesses and bizarre behavior. While these stories are not without basis in fact, it is equally true that Evans was just as deeply entrenched in drug abuse as was Charlie Parker, a point that seems to get passed over or dismissed as "personal problems."

It seems beyond question that Evans's "whiteness" accentuated the perceived intellectuality of his musicianship. The simplistic binary relationships "white = intellectual versus black = physical" are clearly in play here, both in the way that the listening public, long accustomed to such assumptions, viewed Evans and in the way that articles and history narratives continue to depict him today. Even Evans's body shape served to amplify these understandings. His skinny arms and concave chest, undoubtedly exacerbated by years of serious involvement with heroin and cocaine, only highlighted the "disembodiedness" of his music. In many photos, it appears as if Evans is all glasses, hair, ears, and hands; a decidedly unhip suit hangs limply on whatever body remains. Had he possessed a more robust physical stature, such as that of Fats Waller, say, or Count Basie, Art Tatum, or Oscar Peterson, Evans would almost certainly have been perceived differently.

In this light, Ian Carr's assertion that "in Bill Evans, Miles [Davis] had with his group a pianist with the same inward-looking and self-examining approach as himself" appears slightly off the mark.[29] While both musicians abstained from stage announcements and the like, Evans's physical presentation and musical aesthetic were not the same types as Davis's. The sharply dressed Davis, like that white proponent of "cool" Chet Baker, played off a sense of aloof, almost callous, worldliness, a persona akin to that presented by film stars Marlon Brando and James Dean. Evans, by contrast, seemed too sensitive for and out of place in the world, set apart from the crude sexual and commercial transactions of the jazz marketplace. Davis himself reinforces this point when he remarks that "Bill was a very sensitive person and it didn't take very much to set him off."[30] No one ever accused Miles Davis of hypersensitivity.

This "sensitive intellectual" jazz identity displayed by Bill Evans must be viewed against that pianist's historical location within the spectrum of American music in the late 1950s and early 1960s; that is, against the steady rise of rock 'n' roll as America's popular music. Robert Walser has shown that "interiority is anything but private" because it involves "a strategy of disengagement that depends on naturalizing the values and desires of some people as 'deeper' and thus more prestigious than others."[31] With this in mind, Evans's position (both at and away from the piano) becomes easier to understand: For a musician dependent upon public support, Evans's professional existence, like that of most other jazz musicians of the time, necessitated some sort of response to rock's ascent. One could either move toward rock styles and hope to attract those audiences (as did Cannonball Adderley, Wes Montgomery, Miles Davis) or distance oneself from the rising tide of rock's popularity. Whether due to a refusal to "sell out," a discomfort with rock sounds, volumes, and rhythms, or a self-perception that he would not be able to play and move convincingly within rock performance aesthetics, Evans maintained a jazz identity that was to be perceived as apart from—and ideally better than—the one then beginning to generate significant attention. He cultivated allegiances with a genre already established as "good" and "sophisticated," that is, with "classical music," an aspect of Evans's musical upbringing emphasized in so many of his interviews. His statement suggesting the noncommercialized "purity" of the jazz tradition in America can be seen as another example of his stance, as is his belief, stated in a 1974 interview, that a "personal sound . . . [has] been lost in much of the rock and pop music. That big electric sound. It worries me. It seems desperate. The elements are coarse. There's no element of greatness. It makes me worry about the state of the world. What qualifies for greatness now is whatever sells the most records."[32] In presenting his music as he did, Bill Evans represented not only the jazzman whose artistry, though financially supported by nightclub owners and record-buying patrons, would not be altered to suit the public but also a sensitive, lonely, alienated (and seemingly alienating) individual who was, paradoxically, attractive to many.

Evans's influence can still be witnessed today, particularly among but by no means limited to white, male pianists. Not surprisingly, it is in the slower-tempo pieces ("ballads" in the jazz vernacular) that contemporary pianists most closely follow Evans's example: eyes closed, head down to the keyboard, playing "Some Other Time" or "When I Fall in Love" or "My Foolish Heart." On such songs, with their lush harmonies, poignant melodies, and, if a listener is aware of them, heart-breaking lyrics, a player can display both his/her grace-ful negotiation of complex musical materials and the deep emotional scars of long-remembered loves lost. This "sensitive intellectual" pre-sentation stands as Bill Evans's legacy just as surely as his influential approaches to rhythm, harmony, and sound do. As I have noted, how-ever, there is more than one mode of interiority, more than one way of displaying profundity, and Keith Jarrett represents one such differ-ent brand of deep jazz.

KEITH JARRETT: THE PIANIST AS MYSTIC

The virtuoso was a troublesome paradox: at once,
the embodiment of extreme individuality but one that ran the
risk of exceeding the demands of bourgeois decorum, reserve,
and respectability. . . . For some—those carried away—the
sublime was experienced vicariously; others, of course, were
convinced that they were simply being taken to the cleaners.

RICHARD LEPPERT,
"The Virtuoso as Fetish"

Keith Jarrett first rose to prominence during the middle 1960s as a sideman in groups led by Art Blakey, Charles Lloyd, and (like Bill Evans) Miles Davis. Since leaving Davis's group in 1971, Jarrett's activities have covered a broad spectrum of musical situations. He has founded a number of commercially and critically successful small jazz ensembles. More recently, he has released a series of piano and harp-sichord recordings of pieces by Bach, Mozart, Shostakovich, and others from various eras of the European classical tradition. Jarrett has also worked away from the keyboard, composing both large- and small-scale works in the manner of European art music and perform-ing and recording on an array of other instruments including soprano saxophone, tabla, flutes, and guitar. There is no question, however, that his formidable reputation is based primarily upon his first series of solo piano concerts, performed between 1972 and 1984.

Keith Jarrett did not invent the concept of solo jazz piano—a majestic lineage of unaccompanied keyboardists dates back to the earliest days of the genre—but it would not be exaggerating to suggest that he radically reinvented the concept. For, instead of the typical jazz performance comprising individual songs (usually Tin Pan Alley standards, as in the case of Bill Evans), Jarrett's performances were utterly spontaneous improvisations, completely free of precomposed structures.

That someone would possess the courage (some say arrogance) and skills required to improvise for two hours, ostensibly using no preconceived forms whatsoever, in front of a paying audience would be ground enough to attract notice. But it is the aura that surrounded these concerts that led, ultimately, to Jarrett's considerable acclaim throughout the world. And it is this same aura that connects us to the topics of jazz depth and the body, configuring, in Jarrett's case, a type of sensual-sacred music ritual.

Solo Music

While Jarrett's solo concerts were promoted as wholly unique and spontaneous musical events, it's plain to hear that sections of these concerts tended to fall into a few distinct categories. In general, his stylistic palette included a seamless blend of quasi-Romantic rhapsodies, diatonic folklike passages, "free" counterpoint, angular atonality, extended techniques (plucking or strumming the piano strings, striking the frame, etc.), and protracted ostinatos. To suggest that one can readily discern such tendencies is not a qualitative critique of Jarrett's abilities; quite the contrary, the fact that he continually discovered fresh-sounding material from within these "bags" is, to say the very least, quite impressive.

Of all these devices, writers most frequently associate the pianist's solo work with the ostinato passages. Jarrett structures these sections around highly rhythmic patterns, typically emphasizing a single tone in the lower register of the instrument while remaining harmonically ambiguous enough to allow his right-hand lines to move readily in and out of various modes. More than any of his other standard devices, it is through his extensive use of these "mantra grooves" that some circles have likened Jarrett's work to that of pianist George Winston and other "New Age" musicians.[33] While Jarrett does not wear this association gladly (claiming, quite rightly, that the ostinatos represent only one part of his musical world), he is not unaware of the effectiveness of this device: "Any kind of a groove that gets into *itself* is everything, while it's going on. It isn't just, 'Hey, that's a groove and now we'll leave.' You can't leave when something's happening like that. So . . . at least I [knew] that no one was gonna leave . . . during the section, and I would enjoy . . . those grooves, too."[34]

In addition, much of the potency of Jarrett's improvisations can be traced to his manipulation of rhythm. He rarely locks into a swing pulse of the type associated with bop-type improvisers. As with Bill Evans, Jarrett continually pushes, pulls, or otherwise plays with the rhythmic motion, often achieving a feeling of being at once "in time" and "above" it. The structural formlessness of his concerts accentuates this sensation: Jarrett would blunt the open-endedness so crucial to these performances were he to resort to the traditional "standards" orientation of his jazz-keyboard predecessors or even of his own trio.[35] The harmonic resolutions built into the cyclical Tin Pan Alley song-form structure time very differently from the solo concerts' less teleological approach.[36]

In a similar vein, his melodic construction entails a perpetual modal ebb and flow. Jarrett's lines don't resolve; they continually mutate. Small motivic cells develop into longer and longer phrases: An "exotic" Middle Eastern inflection melts into a gospel-soaked passage, which transforms into an angular post-Coltrane type of linearity. Also like Evans's music, Jarrett's lines achieve a breathy quality through constant dynamic fluctuation. This combination of "endless melody," rhythmic play, and dynamic flow s(t)imulates a sense of a sensual, yet mystically tinged, musical yearning or desire analogous to some European musics, such as the sultry affect achieved by Richard Wagner in *Tristan und Isolde,* or some of the seventeenth-century Italian compositional strategies as characterized in the works of musicologists Susan McClary or Andrew Dell'Antonio.[37]

The Sun Bear

Few reviews of Jarrett's solo concerts fail to address the manner in which he plays the piano. It is in fact almost impossible not to notice a performance style so radically different from orthodox instrumental technique. As one account describes him, Jarrett

> doesn't just play the piano, he performs an intricate ballet (some would say a primitive primal rite) with it. He stands in a half-crouch, his posterior a foot above the bench, writhing and stamping his foot. His hands, far from being relaxed in the approved efficient fashion, stab down at the keys, every tendon straining. He uses vibrato on the keys. He arches his back. He rocks his shoulders. He crouches under the piano, so that his eyes are level with the keys. . . . The overwhelming impression one gets is that an electrical current is surging through him, and that only the contact of his hands on the keys, the one constant in this storm of motion, serves to anchor or ground him. Without that contact, one feels, he would fly across the stage in a series of chaotic and involuntary, if not entirely graceless, spasms.[38]

To the unsuspecting audience member watching Jarrett for the first time, the effect of these gyrations can be more than a little unnerving. But for those initiated into Jarrett's world, the movements are accepted as an integral part of the musical experience. Drummer Jack DeJohnette has said that Jarrett's technique reflects an expression of the pianist's "love affair with the piano."[39] Others have used less decorous language to describe the patently amatory motion of Jarrett's hips thrusting toward and away from the keyboard. John Litweiler, for instance, has labeled Jarrett's technique "autoerotic," a critique to which I return below.[40]

Beyond the movements, the other most frequently cited aspect of the pianist approach is his vocalizations. Jarrett's penchant for vocal exclamations goes well beyond the Glenn Gould model of "singing-along," as Jarrett accompanies his playing with a near nonstop litany of moans, groans, grunts, and sighs that epitomizes a sort of spiritualized eroticism. All of these wailings remain clearly audible on his recordings and provide his record-buying public with some sense of the effort exerted in these concerts, even if the listener is unable to attend one.

Significantly, these physical and vocal histrionics occur only in Jarrett's improvisational performances. Indeed, his series of recordings covering the European art-music tradition have been cited for their conspicuous absence of these mannerisms, to which Jarrett has responded: "Playing Mozart standing up is a contradiction in language."[41] Clearly, then, Jarrett brings a different set of expectations and goals to improvising than to his interpretations of some of the European repertoire. For Jarrett, Mozart and Handel do not speak the "language" of ecstasy, at least not of an excruciatingly sensual type, whereas it seems to be the very purpose of the solo improvisations to s(t)imulate an ecstatic experience.

I have suggested that European musicians and audiences of previous centuries were not strangers to performances drenched in a type of sensual sacrality. Here is an eyewitness account of a baroque-era Italian violin concert: "A symphony of furies shakes the soul; it undermines and overthrows it in spite of all its care; the artist himself, whilst he is performing it, is seized with an unavoidable agony; he tortures his violin; he racks his body; he is no longer master of himself, but is agitated like one possessed with an irresistible motion."[42]

If one were to replace the term "violin" with "piano," this description would appear remarkably similar to typical depictions of Jarrett's concerts. Meanwhile, C. P. E. Bach made clear in his eighteenth-century performance-practice guides that a musician's facial expressions and bodily gestures are oftentimes—and should be—conscious choices, inseparable from "the music." As Bach noted, "fitting expressions help the listener to understand our meaning."[43] Richard Leppert's recent work on Franz Liszt explores many of these same issues in the context of nineteenth-century European audiences. Explaining the importance of seeing the virtuoso at work, Leppert writes, "Liszt's entire body reads the music to the audience at the same time as his fingers, so to speak, realize the notes. Liszt's 'inspiration,' more than aurally evident, is available in two complementary ways, one sonoric, the other visual, which together overdetermine the preferred reading of the performance situation."[44]

By no means do I wish to suggest that all of these musical genres and historical situations configure identical meanings for their audiences. However, their similarities do help to emphasize the point that musical meanings remain very much bound up with performance and that a type of eroticism (being the most widely experienced bodily form of ecstasy) offers musicians a way of communicating to listeners an inkling of their "profound inner being." Just as Franz Liszt and the unnamed seventeenth-century violinist made sure that their listeners were aware of the seriousness of their respective endeavors and the agonizing virtuosity necessary to withstand the burdens of this activity, Keith Jarrett shows his audiences that the jazz improviser's task goes beyond mere sound production. His beatified/agonized movements and equally wrenching/ecstatic vocalizations make it clear to even the casual observer that he is not on stage simply to play the piano. Jarrett leaves us little doubt that he is reaching for, and perhaps achieving, something beyond the typical jazz concert. As I have noted, all of this effort does not go unnoticed in the reviews and other discourse surrounding these solo events.

Circulated Discourse

Much has been made in the press about this mysterious vacuum out of which Jarrett's improvisations are spun. The general impression, which he carefully fosters, is that everything is completely spontaneous, of the moment, the mystical outgrowth of his total involvement with the audience, the piano, the acoustics of the hall, and the Great Beyond.

JIM AIKEN,
"Keith Jarrett: Redefining the Solo Piano in Jazz and Beyond"

Many of Jarrett's followers are aware that something extraordinary might happen at a solo concert, not just to the musician onstage but to themselves and everyone else in the hall. They remain alert to this possibility because they have been "briefed" ahead of time that something is supposed to happen at a Keith Jarrett concert. Published concert reviews serve to enhance public perceptions of Jarrett as a kind of shaman: "Jarrett does not quote from history, he conjures with it. He is not a mannerist interpreter, he brings into being. He practices magic."[45] Frank Conroy called him "Mr. Epiphany," while Edward Strickland raised the stakes on the concerts, claiming that "the improvisations . . . have a mythic dimension; being the closest compositional approximation of the *creatio ex nihilo* of Genesis, with further hints, in their execution, of the Passion."[46]

Performing a musical equivalent of Genesis or the Passion would seem to loom as a somewhat daunting task for most piano players. But Jarrett apparently accepts, even cultivates, that responsibility in radio and print interviews. In many ways, he has taken on the mantle of a modern spiritual guide, a not-so-reluctant artist-priest in a cultural climate marked by distrust in spiritual institutions. He admits as much when he says, "In an age when there's no real father figure—there's no church saying 'this is right and this is wrong,' and if they did no one would believe it anyway—and when there's no faith in teachers or a path that everyone would agree, 'Here's a wise man . . . ,' all that's left is the arts. There's nothing else."[47]

Jarrett implies, of course, that—like Wagner and other nineteenth-century Romantics—his concerts deliver "the arts" as our contemporary "church." Or consider this example:

> If there was something that could come through [in the solo concerts] that hadn't been remembered, you know, something about music, something about the way music *is* that could actually be produced in front of an audience, they would have to hear it. They might not hear *what* it was. But they'd have to hear it as a physical thing. . . . I mean, in a way, it's like I'm taking some sort of pulse as I walk on stage. And, it would be like, not necessarily prescribing this. But usually when something is out of balance, you're missing something, you know.[48]

Jarrett's claim that he is "not necessarily prescribing this" rings a little empty here. On the contrary, he seems to be precisely "prescribing" something. What it is or how it corrects imbalances remains somewhat unclear, but it presumably involves a type of sacrality, one that he mentions in almost all of his interviews:

> All through each day, every day, I am aware of that place. It's like a place, a state. And I would say that it's the only state from which to make music of any value to you or anyone else. But, because I know of it, I also know it's a gift. I mean, it isn't as though we'd have to have this available to us. And I would never have been able to invent it. *I consider it a sacred thing,* not to be fooled with, or played with, you know. So, the strange thing is that luckily, if I say I'll do a concert, that concert is already set long in advance. Which means that I'm not "playing" when it gets to be eight o'clock. It is serious at this point. You know. That state is requested of me, because I have set a precedent for being in it, at least for myself.[49]

Jarrett places a mystical or sacred spin on his music through his choice of album and song titles. Though he doesn't title his solo concert recordings (he calls them simply *The Vienna Concert, The Paris Concert, The Lausanne Concert,* etc., perhaps to emphasize the uniqueness of each event), Jarrett's other releases often suggest religious themes.[50] Examples of these include the albums *Mysteries, Hymns and Spheres, Invocations, Spirits,* and tunes such as "Prayer," "Ritual," and "Processional." He perpetuates and strengthens this impression in interviews:

> If I could call everything I did *Hymn,* it would be appropriate, because that's what they are when they're correct. . . . If [the music] does not connect with a greater . . . power, and if I do not surrender to it, nothing happens. In that sense everything feels like a hymn, because I don't have access to this just by the fact of being Keith Jarrett and having recorded all this time. There's no reason why I should have this experience *ever.* Every time it's a gift. So if I want to acknowledge this gift, I would have to call it a hymn. *Ritual* was, in a way, just another word about something perhaps surrounding a state of prayer.[51]

We can see that the discourse surrounding Jarrett's music helps to turn each solo performance into a type of sacred event. But we should also note that Jarrett's interviews and many of his reviews emphasize that he intends this spiritual transcendence for both himself and for his audiences, a stance reflective of the 1960s "counterculture" milieu from which he and many of his listeners emerged. Edward Strickland has remarked, "There is something gladiatorial as well as priestlike in Jarrett's opening and closing bows to the audience, characteristically delivered with hands joined at the chest. A submission to fate—the 'Divine Will' in the artist's own terminology. With respect to the audience moreover, it is a gesture of just that—respect."[52] Jarrett remains notorious for interrupting his concerts to admonish inattentive audiences. On the surface, these tantrums may strike casual observers as the acts of a prima donna. But on closer examination, this severity is not inconsistent with the goal he sets for each performance, which appears to be nothing short of a type of *collective* unitive experience. He has said:

> I've been considered—what's the word?—a typically touchy artist. You know: fussy and grumpy. But people don't understand that I'm almost playing on the audience, instead of the piano. I mean, the audience is in the room and it's vibrating. Sometimes the most silent audience can be the most annoying, because you know they're being silent because they're not sure whether they should relax.[53]

Ben Sidran has referred to the Jarrett solo concert as a "mass seance," a fitting description in that it recognizes both the communal and ritual aspects of these events.[54] For this reason I find John Litweiler's charge of autoeroticism to be slightly misplaced. While the pianist's mysticism is certainly erotically charged, Jarrett and his audiences seek a shared sacred space, not simply a voyeuristic/exhibitionist example of musical masturbation.

In this regard, Jarrett's approach to performance also illustrates a rare exception to Albert Murray's rule of thumb that blues/jazz musicians artfully engage in artifice. In his *Stompin' the Blues,* Murray argues that musicians who play the blues do not necessarily have the various spiritual, psychological, or economic manifestations associated with the blues; rather, they perform as if they were subject to those conditions. But Jarrett remains a product of a different time from the musicians portrayed by Murray.[55] And, true to his 1960s roots, with that period's penchant for things mystical, Keith Jarrett seeks to enter a state of inner being that is simultaneously reflected in and shaped by the manner in which he plays.

Keith Jarrett's pianistic musical/sensual "enthusiasm"—to be understood in the ancient Greek sense of being "filled with god"—stands in marked contrast to Bill Evans's withdrawn demeanor. It is clear through their almost diametrically opposed approaches to the piano that both musicians presented a very different sense of both jazz and self. Yet these two also share much common ground. Most notably, they each view the jazz musician as "artist," unsullied by commercialism. They promote such a stance even while they both also enjoyed the fruits of unusually lucrative careers (Len Lyons remarks that the tremendous sales of Jarrett's *Köln Concert* album established the viability of ECM Records and "revived confidence in the commercial potential of the piano in jazz").[56] Their detached, even dismissive attitude toward "entertainment" helped to place them above the marketplace at the same time that they made their very comfortable livings from and within it.

There is another peculiarly related arena in which these two can be seen to be in accord, one that demonstrates a pronounced shift in historical understandings through the twentieth century: the use by both of the acoustic piano to convey a sense of artistic integrity. Richard Leppert's discussion of Liszt's professional demeanor and the nineteenth-century social milieu within which it made sense also notes that audiences at that time saw the piano as an extraordinarily "modern" instrument, an engineering marvel unmatched as a feat of technological splendor. Since the end of World War II, however, we have lived in an age dominated in sound by amplifiers, synthesizers, and "effects processors" (not to mention the nonmusical technologies ranging from the television set and the Chevrolet Corvette to Mars rovers, "stealth" bombers, portable computers, and microwave popcorn). With such marvels it is plain that the earlier understandings of the piano no longer hold, that that instrument no longer represents the cutting edge of human innovation. Rather, both Evans's and Jarrett's deep jazz identities very much depend upon understandings of the piano as "old," even "timeless." Although both of these players flirted briefly with electric instruments such as the Fender Rhodes and the Hammond organ, neither one moved decisively toward those instruments (unlike a number of their colleagues, including Joe Zawinul, Herbie Hancock, Chick Corea, and Bob James). Jarrett, especially, insisted on the "purity" of the grand piano, waging a war of sorts on the "evils" of electronic technology. Such shifts in historical understanding should serve to remind us that while artifacts (books, scores, musical instruments) may endure from the past, their meanings do not, and those things that may appear to remain the same never do so.

I have not raised these issues here to "debunk" the deep-jazz performance styles of Keith Jarrett and Bill Evans. Rather, I have hoped to show that an "inner life"—our own or others'—not only is formed by the "outside" but in many ways gets displayed there and continually shapes the way we understand ourselves and our world.

Five

JAZZ 'TRANING

John Coltrane and the Conservatory

*Literate society often turns a deaf ear
to the implications of an oral culture.*

BEN SIDRAN,
Black Talk

OVER THE PAST THIRTY years, college music departments have emerged
as among the most powerful forces shaping understandings of jazz in
this country. The profusion of jazz history classes, performance ensembles, improvisation courses, and visiting-artist series presented under the auspices of America's most esteemed educational institutions
has unquestionably and drastically altered public perceptions of the
genre. As late as the 1960s, popular depictions of jazz suggested a dis-
reputable "underground" music played by African-American or white
outsiders (in the early sitcom *Dobie Gillis,* it wasn't the clean-cut, fair-
haired Gillis who "dug" Thelonious Monk but rather his misanthropic
beatnik friend, Maynard G. Krebs). But college programs and events
such as the annual Notre Dame Intercollegiate Jazz Festival gradually
shifted understandings by celebrating jazz as a technically demanding
but fun "All-American" music.[1] As we will see, however, the very
arena that served to elevate jazz to the level of "good music" also
served to marginalize some of the musics played as jazz in the outside
world—that is, beyond the academy walls.

This chapter seeks to illuminate the effects wrought on perceptions
of jazz through the seemingly innocuous collegiate setting. It touches
on a variety of issues pertaining to college-level jazz history and per-

formance courses but focuses its view of this topic on one of the music's most highly regarded figures, John Coltrane (1926–1967). Although that saxophonist holds an exalted position within the jazz-education canon of "great masters," he enjoyed an extraordinarily prolific—and, more important for this project, diverse—career, spawning radically differing viewpoints on him and his music. This essay investigates which "Coltranes" count within the academy and which "Coltranes" do not (here I mean both the aspects of his musical styles chosen for emphasis and the types of stories told about him). We will see that in spite of the seemingly unblemished reputation that John Coltrane's name carries today, certain musical and extramusical aspects of his work challenge the guidelines of "good music" set by most schools. Consequently, these aspects get brushed aside as aberrations or ignored altogether in college jazz ensembles and improvisation classes. Such institutional biases carry repercussions: they affect what kinds of music jazz students value as they make their way into the world as players, listeners, and teachers, ultimately influencing what they and others hear as "good jazz" and even what counts as "jazz" at all. Before turning to the specific question of John Coltrane and his position vis-à-vis jazz pedagogy, I will trace very briefly the development and prevailing methodologies of jazz education in America.

PART I: JAZZ GOES TO COLLEGE

Until well into the 1970s, only a very few accredited music programs in this country offered students jazz in any form, the vast majority of schools remaining staunchly dedicated to providing instruction in the Western classical tradition. Some of the more prestigious conservatories not only omitted the genre but also actually forbade the playing of jazz in the school's practice rooms, with transgressions possibly leading in extreme cases to students' expulsion from the institution.[2]

Even in less prim surroundings, school big bands (sometimes called "lab" or "stage" bands) frequently defined the sole jazz outlet, and these were usually offered only as extracurricular activities, with few students earning college credit for their participation. Conservatory-trained directors led most institutional big bands of this period, even as their main responsibilities typically included the concert or marching band (but not the more prestigious symphony orchestra). Not surprisingly, these jazz-band directors generally stressed the same musical concepts valued in their other ensembles—centered and stable intonation, correct note reading, section balance—while improvisation often went overlooked. As models toward which their students should strive, directors recommended the very "clean" and "professional" recordings of Thad Jones / Mel Lewis, Maynard Ferguson, Stan Kenton, and Woody Herman (in fact, all of these musicians augmented their incomes through college and high school master classes). Eventually, even the charts (notated big-band scores) and albums of other college big bands, most notably those of North Texas State University, provided material and role models.

Writing of Midwestern music schools as recently as the 1990s, ethnomusicologist Bruno Nettl noticed that "the large jazz band, a miniature of the concert band, plays from scores a substantial amount of music that may lack improvisation. This kind of big-band has a very modest role in the outside world of jazz, but the school nevertheless selects it to be the exemplar of jazz within its walls."[3] As Nettl suggests, discussions of soloing concepts in big-band rehearsals remain minimal. Exceptions aside, directors possess little or no insight into improvisational skills, an absence reflecting their training in contemporary European-rooted ensemble practices. To satisfy the demand for nonprofessional-level jazz material, a growing cottage industry of school-oriented big-band composers and arrangers has emerged, and these writers, mindful that most ensemble directors view improvisation as a somewhat mysterious world ("you either have it or you don't"), write performers' solos into their charts. Directors often encourage players to rely on these notated passages rather than to improvise, avoiding precarious moments in school concerts or in the annual competitions and festivals held at Notre Dame and elsewhere. Recent articles in the *Jazz Educators Journal* (published by the International Association of Jazz Educators) entitled "The Improvised Jazz Solo: An Endangered Species" and "Don't Neglect Improvisation" demonstrate the degree to which this trend continues to this day in many schools.[4]

Answering calls for a more "relevant" and diverse cultural landscape within the academy, college-level jazz-studies programs have appeared with increasing frequency since the 1970s. In 1972, only fifteen colleges or universities in America offered degrees in jazz studies.[5] By September 1998, the Music Educators National Conference listed sixty-seven undergraduate and thirty graduate programs specifically devoted to jazz. In addition, dozens of other schools now offer a "jazz emphasis" or "jazz track" under the umbrella of their music performance, composition, or education degrees. In all, almost two thousand applied music faculty in North American colleges teach jazz improvisation or applied jazz lessons of some kind, while over fifteen hundred direct jazz ensembles.[6] At the same time, jazz-history classes now constitute some of the largest enrollments among the "general education" courses offered by music or fine arts departments.

In order to justify their continued existence, jazz programs need to entice new students. An early solution to this problem sought to foster a reputation through local high school recruiting or appearances at festivals. Eventually, the schools hoped, one of their "products" would find commercial or critical success, engendering word of mouth distinction for the institution.

A more recent trend involves the hiring of "name" teachers, that is, individuals with impressive credentials as professional performers and recording artists. Richard Davis, Steve Coleman, Charlie Haden, Kenny Burrell, Harold Land, Billy Higgins, Max Roach, and Anthony Braxton are only a few of the well-known jazz musicians who have found that academia can provide a stable and, for some, quite lucrative adjunct to performing and recording. Academic positions appear particularly attractive to performers in light of the medical coverage and retirement benefits available through school employment, especially given the uncertain future hanging over so many jazz performance venues and record labels. This new generation of musician-teachers belies the adage that "those who can, do; others teach," as jazz musicians—young and old—increasingly consider the university or conservatory, rather than "the street," to be the prime training ground for beginners.[7]

One significant consequence of the increase in jazz programs is the development of smaller performance ensembles (three to eight players) coexisting alongside the ubiquitous big bands. In turn, the increased soloing responsibilities inherent in the small-group format have necessitated the creation of classes devoted to improving students' improvisational skills. For reasons both practical and accreditational, clear-cut methods and standards of teaching and adjudicating these skills require development, and instructors, administrators, and textbook authors have set about devising guidelines. Music departments and accreditation boards seek to answer a few basic questions: What does an aspiring jazz player need to know in order to be considered a "good musician"? How does a teacher best go about conveying that information, and how does one test a student's knowledge and understanding of these principles? Should every student be required to study "classical music"? What is the optimal and practical balance among private lessons, ensembles, and classroom instruction (both musical and general)?[8]

Responses to these questions have varied according to each music department's size and financial resources. But a less conspicuous factor enters as well: that is, the values and concerns of a department's faculty members. Yet as we will see, even with the hiring of experienced performers and a new small-group emphasis, jazz programs and published educational materials have tended to valorize the same musical parameters and skills as those stressed earlier by the band directors. That is to say, jazz pedagogy remains decidedly classically based.

We hardly need to mention, for example, that harmony enjoys an exalted place in the European art-music tradition, and it stands to reason that conservatories emphasize harmony- (and score-) centered musical instruction in their discussions of Mozart, Haydn, and Beethoven. It is less clear, however, why harmonic theory should predominate to the virtual exclusion of all else in jazz improvisation courses or why written materials should hold such a privileged position in college-level jazz pedagogy. These are crucial points and I will return to them, but I wish to consider first some of the vital elements of improvisation neglected in most conservatory environments.

To begin, it may seem unthinkable, given the frequency with which swing appears as a "necessary ingredient" in defining jazz, that rhythmic conception remains largely ignored in improvisation courses and manuals.[9] But this situation persists, and one explanation for it may lie in the difficulty of notating the many different kinds of rhythmic "feels" employed by jazz musicians (should a transcription of "swing eighth notes" played by Chick Corea look the same as those played by Wynton Kelly?).

Yet this deemphasis of rhythm goes beyond mere notational difficulties. The European musical tradition has long downplayed rhythmic elements, both in its compositions and the theoretical and historical studies of those works (which perhaps explains why systems to notate rhythmic feels more precisely were never widely adopted). Reviews and commentaries from the turn of the twentieth century display attitudes toward rhythm, and syncopation in particular, which were frequently condescending and often overtly malicious. For instance, musicologist Charles Hamm has shown the degree to which ragtime — a music now heard as charming and quaint — was reviled by a segment of America's respected musical "leaders," some of whom aired their views in music education journals. Hamm recounted the turn-of-the-century critics who wrote in the *Musical Courier, Etude,* and the *Musical Observer* of ragtime's "pernicious influence." These writers repeatedly characterized rhythmic elements as "primitive" or "primeval"; the veil concealing their racism was thin or nonexistent.[10]

A pair of somewhat later excerpts concerning early jazz and Swing reveals further widespread mistrust of rhythmic potency. The first excerpt appeared in a 1921 *Ladies Home Journal* article called "Does Jazz Put the Sin in Syncopation?" The second was published in a 1940s textbook on teaching music in high schools.

> Jazz originally was the accompaniment of the voodoo dancer, stimulating the half-crazed barbarian to the vilest deeds. The weird chant, accompanied by the syncopated rhythm of the voodoo invokers, has also been employed by other barbaric people to stimulate brutality and sensuality. That it has a demoralizing effect upon the human brain has been demonstrated by many scientists.[11]

> Swing music — which is merely a highly emotionalized style of playing jazz, and to which we are in no sense objecting to as a legitimate type of human experience — is primarily physical. It induces

violent physical movement—note the *jitterbug*. It is "fleshly" in its conception. It does not lead toward the spiritual. It is "good fun" at the time, but it does not yield abiding satisfaction. To use such music in the school as a substitute for serious music is to cheat youth of a highly important experience which has the possibility of assisting in the development of spiritual resources.[12]

Both of these passages contrast jazz's rhythmic vitality with values regarded as somehow stable and refined, either by invoking science or the idea of "serious music." Jazz, they suggest, results in a regression to the "fleshly," by which they mean either a sexually charged, "African"-inflected primitiveness or a spiritually bankrupt immaturity. Like the responses to ragtime before it (and rock 'n' roll and rap after it), writings such as these betray fears of cultural and physical miscegenation at the same time that they reinscribe the centuries-old hierarchical relationship between "the mind" and "the body."

Ironically, American-studies scholar Sieglinde Lemke has shown the extent to which many within the European music cultures of the 1920s welcomed the arrival of jazz to their continent. Lemke points out that jazz rhythms helped to revitalize the European music scene (as evidenced by the works of Milhaud, Stravinsky, Ravel, and others) while they dismantled the strictly "one way," East-to-West musical-cultural exchange between Europe and America prevalent since the New World was first colonized.[13] She notes a *New York Times* article from 1928, which bears the rather foreboding title "Jazz Bitterly Opposed in Germany" but cites the director of the Frankfurt Conservatory as asserting, "the teaching of jazz is not only the right but the duty of every up-to-date musical institution." The conservatory director claimed that "an infusion of negro blood can do no harm. It will help to develop a wholesome sense of rhythm, which after all constitutes the life element of music."[14] While the director's remarks may seem to lean toward some of the same racial stereotypes as the North American views noted above, his observations regarding jazz's rhythmic vitality reflect a decidedly less contemptuous stance. Meanwhile, the fact that the *New York Times*'s editors selected such a clearly negative title for the article reveals that American newspaper's conservative position on this issue, one that, as Lawrence W. Levine's work has shown, remained deeply entrenched.[15]

This new "real world" relationship notwithstanding, the same hierarchy of musical values persisted (and persists) within many music schools on this side of the Atlantic. In order that jazz receive the institutional respect and financial support that its adherents covet, many teachers and authors have resorted to a "jazz has all of the things that classical music has" approach. For example, Robert Walser has shown that some early and influential critical studies of jazz are based in nineteenth-century European aesthetics that valued "organic unity," "motivic development," and harmonic complexity.[16] In this way, by demonstrating that certain solos or compositions worked "just like the classics," music departments could rest assured that they were still teaching their students "serious music." Clearly, such efforts have served to elevate the status of jazz. But in the process, these ideals also brush aside much outstanding jazz that counters conservatory-based measures of excellence.

To be sure, the privileged position jazz now enjoys in such an august institution as Lincoln Center demonstrates that a steady swing feel, like ragtime syncopation, no longer denotes the primitive. Quite the contrary: coupled regularly in television advertisements with images of fine wines, stylish clothing, and expensive automobiles, a swing feel now suggests classy and sophisticated, if occasionally "retro." This shift in understandings reminds us that musical works, styles, and procedures are not "timeless." Their use or omission by composers, performers, and even advertising agencies reflects the values that those musics hold in a particular place, time, and culture.[17]

Besides rhythm, other musical elements less commonly considered in jazz pedagogy include sonority-based aspects such as timbre and intonation. Music teachers or ensemble directors may raise these issues as they relate to creating a "good sound," usually thought of as a stable ideal. But discussion of timbral manipulation—employing a variety of tone colors within a musical performance or, for that matter, on one note—seldom arises. The European orientation of most teachers returns here, for traditional conservatory training provides students with the tools necessary to work within a large ensemble setting (soloist prodigies excepted). Players win and keep orchestra jobs by realizing as cleanly and consistently as possible the notes set down on the printed page in a manner dictated by the conductor. As many very fine musicians have discovered, it can lead to disastrous musical and professional results for a player in such a setting to alter radically his or her sound during a performance.[18]

Jazz education programs reinforce these ideals, setting norms for tone, vibrato, and pitch center. This pedagogical approach appears somewhat understandable where big bands are concerned, with that larger ensemble's increased possibility of chaos, but less so in small-group settings, where so many important jazz musicians earned their reputations through distinctive, flexible, and oftentimes quite unorthodox "sounds." Lester Bowie, Dewey Redman, Sidney Bechet, Ornette Coleman, Cootie Williams, Joe "Tricky Sam" Nanton, Miles Davis, and Bill Frisell represent only a few of the many instrumentalists who made their mark through their unique manipulations of timbre.

Harmony and the Jazz Program's *Gradus ad Parnassum*

To Music Building society, the concept of musical notation is enormously important. Having perhaps forgotten that they learned their first songs by hearing them, many of the denizens cannot conceive of a music culture that does not use notation. . . . Music to Music Building society is notated music.

BRUNO NETTL,
Heartland Excursions

Given that the written score is the document with which most conservatory-trained music teachers and department administrators are familiar, it seems almost inevitable that the focal points of "note choice" and harmony would carry over into jazz education. Notation and harmony-based improvisational theory suit classroom use: notes, chords, and harmonic progressions translate easily to paper, blackboard, and textbooks. And teachers can measure the students' grasp of the materials "objectively" through written exams.

By contrast, concepts of rhythmic feel or timbral manipulation necessitate more one-on-one guidance. Though most music departments provide private lessons, these remain the least cost-effective means of education for colleges, and many schools simply cannot afford to provide a teacher on every instrument. Where private instructors are used, departmental hiring policies favor "legit" (European-oriented) instructors over jazz-based (illegitimate?) teachers by a wide margin. For example, the College Music Society lists approximately twenty-one hundred oboe and bassoon teachers in U.S. and Canadian colleges and conservatories, more than their entire listing for all jazz instructors. In fact, the society doesn't even provide subcategories such as "jazz piano" or "jazz saxophone," though they do offer listings for "harpsichord," "recorder," and even "timpani." [19] It goes almost without saying that those private instructors schooled in the European traditions encourage, if not require, their students to adopt the same ideals of sound and technique in which they were themselves trained. Although predating the widespread emergence of jazz programs, Max Roach's brief experience in a conservatory reveals attitudes and practices that persist in many schools:

> Some years ago in the '40s, I had been playing on 52nd Street and had a little loot. So I enrolled in a conservatory, with a percussion major. I went the first day to my percussion teacher and he asked me to play something for him. Well, the first thing he said to me was *that I held the sticks wrong.* Now I was on 52nd Street working with Charlie Parker, Coleman Hawkins, making more money than he was making. He said, "You are holding the sticks wrong." Well, his point of reference was how to drum in a symphony orchestra. Whereas, my thing was down close to everything, settled into the drums so that any of them could be reached instantly. So I said, "Man, if I change the way I hold the sticks and everything, I wouldn't be able to pay tuition to this place." [20]

Jazz-education pioneer David Baker also laments the tacit Eurocentrism of most conservatories. In his handbook, *Jazz Pedagogy: A Com-*

prehensive Method of Jazz Education for Student and Teacher, Baker objects to the reinscription of classical ideals on jazz students. But even he reinforces these aesthetics to a large degree. The sample course syllabi he provides for prospective jazz improvisation teachers deal overwhelmingly with memorization of songs and jazz-related harmonic theory. Baker does stress some ear training, but the mock exams he includes test students only on their ability to notate chord symbols and write out scales; one finds no material in his syllabi that relates to either rhythmic or timbral approaches. Baker lays particular emphasis on students' ability to convert basic chord progressions into "Coltrane changes," a harmonic device to which I return below.[21]

Getting the Notes Right: The Chord-Scale System

David Baker's emphasis on scale writing reflects his preference for the "chord-scale system." He is not alone, as this is the most widespread pedagogical approach in jazz education. This system enables students to identify quickly a scale or mode that will offer the fewest "wrong notes" against a given harmonic structure. While most college jazz programs advocate some form of this system, saxophonist, publisher, and jazz educator Jamey Aebersold stands as that method's most widely influential proponent, as well as its chief codifier. His enormously popular summer camps and even more popular mail-order "music-minus-one"-type recordings and books have served as the foundation for two generations of beginning improvisers, and as primary materials for college improvisation classes.

Aebersold's ever-expanding "Play-a-Long" series features rhythm section–only renditions of standard songs, typical jazz chord progressions, and canonic jazz compositions.[22] The cornerstone of the system is the "Scale Syllabus" printed in each volume. Here Aebersold provides a list of chords commonly found in big-band charts and jazz "fake books" along with a series of scale possibilities for each chord. As he notes:

> This SCALE SYLLABUS is intended to give the improvisor a variety of scale choices which can be used over any chord. . . . The scales are arranged according to the degree of dissonance they produce in re-

lation to the basic chord sound. . . . Each player is urged to start with the scales at the top and with practice and experimentation gradually work his way down the list to the more dissonant or tension producing scales. [See table 2.]

Aebersold's chart illustrates quite clearly that this improvisational approach encourages a concept of "note choice": the student sees a chord and plays a corresponding series of pitches. Meanwhile, the underlying idea that students should aspire to higher degrees of dissonance as they acquire more technical control over their instrument has affected improvisational concepts dramatically since the 1970s, and I return to this subject below.

Teachers advocating this method encourage their students to recognize chord-scale relationships through all keys and may test them on their ability to memorize these. Beyond familiarity with the typical chord progressions and their concomitant note-choice possibilities, persistent practicing of this system also builds technical facility, the ability to "run" scales and arpeggios in all ranges of the instrument. Yet while this pedagogical approach does succeed for the most part in reducing "clams" (notes heard as mistakes) and building "chops" (virtuosity), it presents a number of major and related drawbacks as beginners strive to play idiomatically within various jazz contexts. Most obviously, this approach ignores the sonic and rhythmic conceptions discussed above, but it also overlooks other important aspects such as musical interplay among players. Although I return to these ideas, I wish to begin by looking briefly at that aspect that the chord-scale method purports to offer, namely "correct" note choice.

First, by dividing the twelve possible pitches of the Western scale into a binary of "right notes" and "wrong notes," this system precludes the nonscale tones that characterize so much bop and freer playing, as well as the "in between" sounds characteristic of the blues. Such a categorization also ignores the fact that even within the list of acceptable pitches, each note always achieves a different effect: Playing the flatted 7th scale degree on the last beat of a dominant chord does not function the same as playing the root of that chord in that same place.

TABLE 2 Aebersold Scale Syllabus

Chord/Scale Symbol	Scale Name
1. B♭ or B♭Δ	Major (Ionian)
2. B♭7	Dominant 7th (Mixolydian)
3. B♭-	Minor (Dorian)
4. B♭Ø	Half-diminished (Locrian)
5. B♭°	Diminished (8-tone scale)
Five basic categories	

Major Scale Choices	Scale Name
1. B♭Δ (can be written B♭)	Major (don't emphasize the 4th)
2. B♭Δ +4	Lydian (major scale with + 4)
3. B♭Δ ♭6	Harmonic major
4. B♭Δ +5+4	Lydian augmented
5. B♭	Augmented
6. B♭	Blues scale
7. B♭	Major pentatonic

Dominant 7th Scale Choices	Scale Name
1. B♭7	Dominant 7th (Mixolydian)
2. B♭7+4	Lydian dominant
3. B♭7♭6	Hindu
4. B♭7+ (has +4 and +5)	Whole tone (6-tone scale)
5. B♭7♭9 (also has +9 and +4)	Diminished (begin with H step)
6. B♭7+9 (also has ♭9, +4, +5)	Diminished whole tone
7. B♭7	Blues scale

Minor Scale Choices	Scale Name
1. B♭-	Minor (Dorian)
2. B♭-Δ (major 7th)	Melodic (ascending)
3. B♭-	Blues scale
4. B♭-	Minor pentatonic
5. B♭-Δ (♭6 and maj. 7th)	Harmonic
6. B♭-	Phrygian
7. B♭-	Major Phrygian (8-tone scale)
8. B♭-	Diminished (begin with W step)
9. B♭-♭6	Pure or natural minor

Half-Diminished Scale Choices	Scale Name
1. B♭Ø	Half-diminished (Locrian)
2. B♭Ø #2	Half-diminished #2 (Locrian #2)

Diminished Scale Choice	Scale Name
1. B♭°	Diminished (8-tone scale; begin with W step)

Dominant 7th Suspended 4th	Scale Name
1. B♭7 sus 4 (could also be written F−/B♭)	Dom. 7th scale (don't emphasize the 3rd)

Whole and Half Step Construction	Scale in Key of B♭	Basic Chord in Key of B♭
W W H W W W H	B♭ C D E♭ F G A B♭	B♭ D F A C
W W H W W H W	B♭ C D E♭ F G A♭ B♭	B♭ D F A♭ C
W H W W W H W	B♭ C D♭ E♭ F G A♭ B♭	B♭ D♭ F A♭ C
H W W H W W W	B♭ C♭ D♭ E♭ F♭ G♭ A♭ B♭	B♭ D♭ F♭ A♭
W H W H W H W H	B♭ C D♭ E♭ E F♯ G A B♭	B♭ D♭ E G

W and H Construction	Scale in Key of B♭	Chord in B♭
W W H W W W H	B♭ C D E♭ F G A B♭	B♭ D F A C
W W W H W W H	B♭ C D E F G A B♭	B♭ D F A C
W W H W H -3 H	B♭ C D E♭ F G♭ A B♭	B♭ D F A C
W W W W H W H	B♭ C D E F♯ G A B♭	B♭ D F♯ A C
-3 H -3 H -3 H	B♭ C♯ D F G♭ A B♭	B♭ D F A C
-3 W H H -3 W	B♭ D♭ E♭ E F A♭ B♭	B♭ D F A C
W W -3 W -3	B♭ C D F G B♭	B♭ D F A C

W and H Construction	Scale in Key of B♭	Chord in B♭
W W H W W H W	B♭ C D♭ E♭ F G A♭ B♭	B♭ D F A♭ C
W W W H W H W	B♭ C D E F G A♭ B♭	B♭ D F A♭ C
W W H W H W W	B♭ C D E♭ F G♭ A♭ B♭	B♭ D F A♭ C
W W W W W W	B♭ C D E F♯ A♭ B♭	B♭ D F♯ A♭ C
H W H W H W H W	B♭ C♭ C♯ D E F G A♭ B♭	B♭ D F A♭ C♭(C♯)
H W H W W W W	B♭ C♭ C♯ D E F♯ A♭ B♭	B♭ D F♯ A♭ C♯(C♭)
-3 W H H -3 W	B♭ D♭ E♭ E F A♭ B♭	B♭ D F A♭ C(C♯)

W and H Construction	Scale in Key of B♭	Chord in B♭
W H W W W H W	B♭ C D♭ E♭ F G A♭ B♭	B♭ D♭ F A♭ C E♭
W H W W W W H	B♭ C D♭ E♭ F G A B♭	B♭ D♭ F A C E♭
-3 W H H -3 W	B♭ D♭ E♭ E F A♭ B♭	B♭ D♭ F A♭ C(E♭)
-3 W W -3 W	B♭ D♭ E♭ F A♭ B♭	B♭ D♭ F A♭ C(E♭)
W H W W W H -3 H	B♭ C D♭ E♭ F G♭ A B♭	B♭ D♭ F A C(E♭)
H W W W H W W	B♭ C♭ D♭ E♭ F G♭ A♭ B♭	B♭ D♭ F A♭
H W H H W H W W	B♭ B C♯ D E♭ F G♭ A♭ B♭	B♭ B D♯ F A♭
W H W H W H W H	B♭ C D♭ E♭ E F♯ G A B♭	B♭ D♭ F A (C E♭)
W H W W H W W	B♭ C D♭ E♭ F G♭ A♭ B♭	B♭ D♭ F A♭ C E♭

W and H Construction	Scale in Key of B♭	Chord in B♭
H W W H W W W	B♭ C♭ C♯ D♯ E F♯ A♭ B♭	B♭ D♭ E(F♭) A♭
W H W H W W W	B♭ C D♭ E♭ F♭ G♭ A♭ B♭	B♭ D♭ E(F♭) A♭ C

W and H Construction	Scale in Key of B♭	Chord in B♭
W H W H W H W H	B♭ C D♭ E♭ E F♯ G A B♭	B♭ D♭ E(F♭) G

W and H Construction	Scale in Key of B♭	Chord in B♭
W -3 W W H W	B♭ C E♭ F G A♭ B♭	B♭ E♭ F A♭ C

SOURCE: From Jamey Aebersold, *John Coltrane: Eight Jazz Originals* Play-a-Long, vol. 27 (New Albany, Ind.: Jamey Aebersold, 1983), p. 33.

Second, the chord-scale method's "vertical" approach teaches players to outline chord structure rather than harmonic progression. In this way, the chord-scale system is "static," offering little assistance in generating musical direction through the movement of chords. But we should recognize that Swing- and bop-era songforms operate teleologically with regard to harmony. Highly regarded soloists in those styles typically imply the movement of chords (thus the term "chord *changes*") either by creating lines that voice-lead smoothly from one chord to another or by confounding the harmonic pull through anticipating or delaying harmonic resolution. Skilled linear improvisers such as Sonny Rollins, Clifford Brown, Sonny Stitt, and Johnny Griffin require no rhythm section to "lay down the changes" for them. Indeed, the penchant of these and similarly skilled players for spontaneous reharmonization coupled with a meticulous attention to voice-leading sometimes works best when pianists "lay out" (don't play).

Even casual listening to Charlie Parker's recordings reveals that that bebop innovator was not simply playing the "correct modes" up and down his horn. Passing tones, appoggiatura, and "blue notes" constitute a significant percentage of Parker's note selections, and this is to say nothing of that saxophonist's extraordinary manipulation of rhythm, phrase shape and length, dynamics, and tone color.

Close listening to the shape and length of students' phrases can reveal those who devote the lion's share of their practice time memorizing and playing chord-scale relationships. Students of that method tend to play highly symmetrical lines that correspond predictably with the downbeat of each chord's arrival. Again, these players learn to play "on" chords rather than "through" them. While the disadvantages of this system may become clear when students begin to question why their own playing does not sound like any of the "linear" players named above (let alone some of the "free" stylists discussed below), this method presents fewer problems over less harmonically functional forms.

With this background in mind, we can return to John Coltrane and his position within jazz education. We will see that the chord-scale system works exceptionally well for certain of Coltrane's styles and that jazz educators have stressed these styles to the virtual exclusion of many of the saxophonist's other works.

PART II: "COLTRANES"

Since his death in 1967, John Coltrane's name, music, and likeness have appeared in contexts well beyond those typically associated with jazz. He has been commemorated and acclaimed through a United States postage stamp, two official State of North Carolina proclamations,[23] an ever-increasing list of biographies,[24] and a range of Hollywood films. In differing ways, each of these instances evokes this musician to represent a sense of human integrity, technical mastery, and even spirituality.

In Hollywood, for example, Coltrane's "Psalm," from *A Love Supreme,* played under the closing credits to Spike Lee's *Mo' Better Blues.* In fact, Lee originally wanted to title that film *A Love Supreme,* but the saxophonist's widow, Alice, rejected his proposal, feeling that the film's graphic situations were inconsistent with Coltrane's ideals.[25] In the film *Mr. Holland's Opus,* Richard Dreyfus plays the title character, a frustrated high school music teacher who yearns for a life as an "artistic" composer. Mr. Holland names his son Coltrane, in honor of one of his two heroes (Beethoven is the other), and hangs posters of the saxophonist throughout his classrooms. Coltrane's music goes unheard in the movie—Michael Kamen's soundtrack relies on traditional orchestral fare—however, the use of John Coltrane's name and photographic likeness purport to convey to audiences a sense of the pure, unflinching creator whom, "deep down," Holland feels himself to be. Hollywood has also invoked Coltrane briefly, but with reverence, in such big-budget productions as *Malcolm X, The Fabulous Baker Boys, Jerry McGuire,* and *The Doors.*[26]

Nothing illustrates this musician's extraordinary position within American culture more clearly than the existence of Saint John Coltrane African Orthodox Church in San Francisco. Again, the saint in that church's name does not refer to John the Baptist or the apostle

John but to John Coltrane—the "Divine Sound Baptist"—whom worshipers there regard as a messenger from God. A painted icon of Coltrane (complete with halo) hangs above the altar, and church congregants venerate the saxophonist's recordings, particularly his works from *A Love Supreme* (1964) onward, as both that musician's own spiritual declarations and as aural sacraments for them to receive.[27]

As evidenced by its appearances in these various settings, the name "John Coltrane" has come to take on a kind of life of its own. It serves as a "shorthand" for a variety of musical, ethical, and spiritual attributes that may or may not correspond to all or even part of "the real" John Coltrane. This is much the same phenomenon that Michel Foucault explored in his essay "What Is an Author?" when he wrote that "the author's name is not . . . just a proper name . . . [or] simply an element in discourse (capable of being either subject or object, of being replaced by a pronoun, and the like); it performs a certain role with regard to narrative discourse, assuring a classificatory function."[28]

Foucault's work demonstrates that proper names can come to represent a variety of qualities, values, or ideas to which the actual experiences or ideals of their bearers may relate only partially. Further, an artist's name may shape not only understandings of that artist's own works but also the larger cultural milieus from which these emerged and in which they are engaged. In this way we can see that the name "Karl Marx" has taken on meanings well beyond "the German author of *Das Kapital* who lived from 1818 to 1883." Similarly, "John Kennedy" refers to more than an "author of *Profiles in Courage* and heir to a wealthy Massachusetts estate who was assassinated in 1963 during his term as the thirty-fifth president of the United States." Obviously, the name and likeness of both Marx and Kennedy have represented and bred a vast array of meanings and discourses, from "a liberator of the people" to "the Evil Empire," from "Camelot" and "the New Frontier" to "sexual indiscretion."

Thirty years ago it would have seemed a stretch, even absurd, to place Coltrane alongside the two aforementioned figures (and, of course, one could go on: Freud, Einstein, Darwin, Beethoven, Mohammed, Jesus, or, as Foucault himself mentions, Shakespeare or Aristotle). But clearly Coltrane has become a remarkably powerful figure in a relatively short time. Even beyond Saint John's Church, an aura of "purity" has come to surround this musician and encompasses a large portion of the ways in which listeners understand him and his approaches to jazz. And while any of these understandings of John Coltrane's name and music would make ideal subjects for extended study, I will direct the remaining portion of this chapter toward the ways in which John Coltrane has come to be revered—and ignored— within the world of college-level jazz pedagogy.

Coltrane in College: Harmonic Complexity and the Woodshed

As I have suggested, Coltrane's musical output over the last decade of his life covered an extraordinarily broad stylistic range. From conventional bop and blues stylings in the early 1950s, Coltrane devised a "vertical" approach to improvisation, and the complicated harmonic substitutions implied in his approach were reflected more and more in his own compositions as that decade drew to a close. There followed in the early 1960s "modal" and, beginning around 1965, "freer" stylings. Of the dozens of tunes Coltrane composed during this span, two—"Giant Steps" and "Impressions"—have risen to special significance in jazz pedagogy. And it bears investigating why these particular pieces, and not other Coltrane works, have formed the basis for most understandings of him and his music in the academy.

"Giant Steps"   This piece stands as the best known of Coltrane's compositional explorations into non-functional harmonization. Indeed, it is safe to say that no piece enjoys as much prestige or overall "aura" in all of jazz education as this one does. Just as Tolstoy's *War and Peace* has worked its way into general cultural discourse to represent any long or "heavy" book, "Giant Steps" has spawned a body of meanings in jazz pedagogy involving notions of virtuosity, complexity, and "hipness." Writing in the introduction to Jamey Aebersold's *John Coltrane* Play-a-Long volume, saxophonist David Liebman notes that

> "Giant Steps" was the title tune of that ground-breaking album in
> which Trane improvised on the cycle of a minor third up, down

a fifth, alternating dominant and major chord qualities. *The speed at which he did this showed great practice and diligence on what was, and still is, an extremely difficult challenge. Again, the ability to navigate these changes is a must for all improvisors after Coltrane.*[29]

As Liebman's commentary suggests, Coltrane composed the piece as a sixteen-bar exercise in atypical root movements and harmonic resolutions (see table 3). This tune is not really *in* any particular key. There are few moments of real harmonic stability here, and it feels instead as if the form "falls into itself." Typical ii–V–I progressions appear in the last eight bars, but the symmetrical relationships among the three predominant centers (B, E♭, and G) preclude strong gravity toward a single tonality. For players accustomed to Tin Pan Alley–based progressions, the piece can feel awkward, as the composer purposely thwarted the usual paths toward harmonic resolution.[30]

Despite its peculiarities, "Giant Steps" does offer a short, steady and, once one becomes accustomed to it, predictable series of chords *on* which to play, and this provides a key to jazz pedagogy's fascination with the song. Unlike boplike material, skilled voice-leading is not prerequisite to sounding idiomatically correct on this tune. And while getting lost in this harmonic minefield can lead to embarrassing results, obeying the precepts of chord-scale theory will lead to an acceptable solo.[31] Even Coltrane himself took a "vertical" approach to this song (as was his propensity throughout much of the late 1950s), relying on arpeggios and simple four-note patterns (mostly emphasizing scale degrees 1–2–3–5) on each successive chord.[32]

The chord-scale method works perfectly on "Giant Steps." The harmonic structure of the tune, as well as the customary manner in which musicians have come to approach it, requires that players have to confront neither the highly chromatic challenges involved in bebop voice-leading nor the sort of musical-rhetorical gestures that mark many "New Thing" stylists.[33] Instrumentalists may easily work out phrases and even entire solos ahead of time, for—unlike in a freer or, for that matter, New Orleans–style context—interplay among musicians is not a priority here. Moreover, contrasting with Ornette Coleman's

TABLE 3   "Giant Steps" Harmonic Structure

II:	BΔ	D7	I	GΔ	Bb7	I	EbΔ	I	a-7	D7	I
I	GΔ	Bb7	I	EbΔ	F#7	I	BΔ	I	f-7	Bb7	I
I	EbΔ		I	a-7	D7	I	GΔ	I	c#-7	F#7	I
I	BΔ		I	f-7	Bb7	I	EbΔ	I	c#-7	F#7	:II

compositional/improvisational approach of the time, the minimalistic melody of "Giant Steps" provides little inspiration for alternative soloing possibilities. In fact, Tommy Flanagan recalled of the original lead sheet of the tune that, "I don't think there was any melody, just the chord sequence, which spells out the melody practically."[34] With "Giant Steps," a player is simply expected to "burn," that is, to outline assertively each succeeding chord at a brisk tempo and through several choruses of the form.

Given its general harmonic nonfunctionality, it comes as no surprise that "Giant Steps" ranks as a favorite in classroom instruction as well as at jam sessions among intermediate-level student players. By "spelling out" each chord just as Coltrane had, musicians can readily demonstrate their technical adroitness on a tune with a reputation of being "hard." Rather than sounding idiomatically awkward, as this vertical approach would in some other jazz styles, nascent improvisers can sound "hip." Meanwhile, the tune offers music teachers a clear sense of each student's ability to recognize the proper successive chord-scale relationships, either on paper or with an instrument. One can't fake one's way through this piece; typical blues licks or other riff figures will sound blatantly wrong if carried through an entire chorus. In this way, a teacher can identify quickly and easily which students have done their homework and which have not.

Coltrane's near mythological reputation as an incessant practicer also plays into the position of "Giant Steps" within the jazz academy. As is reiterated in articles, books, and liner notes and by music teachers, Coltrane constantly worked on scales and worked to improve his facility on the horn. Stories circulate of him playing marathon-length sets with his band (single songs routinely lasted for thirty minutes or more) only to retire to the club's "green room" to resume his musical-exercise regimen during the ensuing break.

Coltrane biographer J. C. Thomas narrates it this way:

> John Coltrane is practicing. . . . His embouchure is as tight as
> the mouthpiece and reed connections. But he feels the occasional,
> sometimes frequent, stabbing pain in his increasingly disintegrating
> molars. More bridgework is now there, but the pain still continues,
> digging like a dentist's drill into his nerves. But he does not stop;
> nothing short of nuclear war can stop his incessant, compulsive
> practice sessions. . . . The music goes round and round inside John
> Coltrane's head, pouring forth from his horn as he continues his
> creative explorations, the only way any artist must if he is to be
> worthy of the name.
>
>   Alone.[35]

Stories such as this one—elevated to the status of gospel among jazz students—paint Coltrane, and by extension any other "great" jazz musician, as a master soloist, the beauty and power of his playing unconnected to the players that surrounded him. To be sure, Coltrane achieved astounding technical virtuosity through thousands of hours of practicing, but equally important to his success was his commitment to playing with Elvin Jones, McCoy Tyner, and his other fellow musicians. As Tyner told interviewer David Wild,

> It's a funny thing, the John Coltrane Quartet was actually four elements. We had one guy who led the whole team, but it was really a compounding of personalities, like four personalities contributing. Whenever any of us were missing . . . when Roy [Haines] was with the band it was interesting, but when Elvin [Jones] came back it was a glorious situation. . . . One time, when my son was born, I took a couple of weeks off, Eric Dolphy was with the band, and John didn't hire a piano player for those weeks—he played without a piano player.[36]

John Coltrane's interest in musical interplay and interdependence only deepened in his later years as he moved toward more "open"

TABLE 4   "Impressions" Formal Structure

II:	d dorian (8 bars)	I	d dorian (8 bars)	I
I	e♭ dorian (8 bars)	I	d dorian (8 bars)	:II

forms, yet this aspect of his musicianship gets widely overlooked. Even at the time he recorded "Giant Steps," Coltrane expressed concern about the effectiveness of his approach, remarking, "I'm worried that sometimes what I'm doing sounds like just academic exercises, and I'm trying more and more to make it sound prettier."[37]

In fact, Coltrane dropped "Giant Steps" from his performance repertoire almost immediately after recording it, in favor of more flexible forms. But jazz-education manuals present the tune and others like it as the cornerstone of Coltrane's music. That sort of narrative supports both a discourse of complexity and the legend of the jazz musician as a solitary hero, reinforcing an already prevalent "practice-room aesthetic" in the academy and often rendering rhythm sections little more than living versions of Aebersold's Play-a-Long records.

"Impressions"   "Impressions," which is a reworking of Miles Davis's "So What," stands as the other predominant Coltrane composition within jazz-education programs. As with so much bebop-rooted material, Coltrane wrote "Impressions" in a thirty-two bar, AABA form. But instead of being based on chord progressions, this tune was among the first that he based on modes, in this case the dorian mode (see table 4). In many ways, "Impressions," first recorded in 1961, can be seen as a direct reaction against the harmonic complexity that Coltrane had worked out in "Giant Steps" and his other late-1950s explorations ("Countdown," "Satellite," "26–2"). For Miles Davis, Coltrane, and like-minded players, the practice of reharmonizing standards or composing their own complex pieces had grown tiresome. The new modal format allowed these players the chance to "take their time." Even at a fast tempo, the music seemed less hectic than before, and this approach allowed for a greater use of "space."

In the classroom, teachers rely on "Impressions" as another practical application of the chord-scale concept. As on "Giant Steps," voice-leading concepts become irrelevant, as there are no harmonic progressions as such to negotiate. The static sonic field, frequently rendered even more stable by bass and piano pedal points, also enables players to move "outside" into alternative modal juxtapositions without sounding wrong.

For this reason, "Impressions" and the other modal tunes like it have spawned an entire generation of "pattern" players among college-educated musicians, most notably among saxophonists. Recall Jamey Aebersold's scale syllabus, down which students are encouraged to progress methodically, gradually "earning" increasingly dissonant scales. Augmenting this chart, Aebersold's company markets a number of other manuals offering students a selection of "hip" scale-based patterns for use over modal material.

Saxophonists David Liebman, Steve Grossman, Bob Mintzer, and Michael Brecker seem to embody the results of such work. These players have not only built successful performing careers by devising complex patterns off the more "remote" scales; they have also served as powerful role models for a generation of students who have been taught to esteem virtuosic displays of these sorts of arcane constructions.[38] Workbooks, recordings, and interviews that feature these musicians serve to strengthen understandings that equate "the great Coltrane" with (and only with) a pattern-based approach to jazz.

To be sure, Coltrane's music from the late 1950s to the early 1960s was often pattern oriented. Lewis Porter observed, "It would be as if pianists who studied Hanon's sequential exercises in their youth went on to invent or write music based on Hanon. That generally doesn't happen. Yet in Coltrane's case it did—quite literally."[39] But this approach describes only a certain period of Coltrane's life, not his entire output, for recordings from his last years evince an entirely different style of playing.

Coltrane's Late Works

Damn the rules, it's the feeling that counts.

JOHN COLTRANE,
quoted in Joe Goldberg, *Jazz Masters of the Fifties*

The year 1965 proved to be an exceptionally fruitful and creative one for Coltrane and his group as they embarked on U.S. and European tours in the wake of their highly successful *A Love Supreme* album. That year also marked the beginning of what could be considered Coltrane's final stylistic period. His music from that point to the end of his life showed him at his most "expressionistic," clearly influenced by the approaches opened up by Ornette Coleman, as well as the younger Coleman (and Coltrane) protégés Archie Shepp, Albert Ayler, and Pharoah Sanders. Contrasting with chord-based pieces such as "Giant Steps," songs from the last phase of Coltrane's career entailed a decisive turning away from the harmonic complexity, pattern playing, and other traditional shows of individual virtuosity that had marked much of his earlier work.

Coltrane's extraordinary commercial success (by jazz standards) and trusting working relationship with producer Bob Thiele at Impulse Records afforded him the creative freedom to record whatever and whenever he desired. Coltrane and his colleagues returned to the studio on a number of occasions to document the various new approaches they were exploring. Their 1965 recording dates resulted eventually in the albums *Sun Ship, The John Coltrane Quartet Plays, Ascension* (released in two different editions), *Om, Meditations,* and *Kulu Se Mama.* MCA/Impulse reissued many of these later recordings (all of *Ascension, Om,* and *Kulu Se Mama*) in 1992 as a two-CD package entitled *The Major Works of John Coltrane.* The title of this set underscores the scope of these sessions—none of the cuts lasts less than fifteen minutes—while helping to evoke a sense of the importance and seriousness of the music: these aren't simply "tunes," the packaging implies, they are "works." By contrast, Atlantic entitled its seven-disc reissue of Coltrane's earlier work *The Heavyweight Cham-*

pion, reflecting the lingering "change-running," "cutting-contest" aesthetic prevalent during the late bop era.

As I've noted, Ornette Coleman left a profound influence on the later sessions. In a 1963 interview with a French journalist, Coltrane remarked of Coleman:

> I love him. I'm following his lead. He's done a lot to open my eyes to what can be done. . . . I feel indebted to him, myself. Because, actually, when he came along, I was so far into this thing ["Giant Steps" chords], I didn't know where I was going next. And I don't know if I would have thought about just abandoning the chord system or not. I probably wouldn't have thought of that at all. And he came along doing it, and I heard it, I said, "Well, that must be the answer."[40]

Indeed, as far back as the early 1960s, Coltrane began to test some of Coleman's ideas for himself. The 1960 sessions that would produce Coltrane's *The Avant Garde* album, for instance, featured Ornette Coleman's compositions as well as performances from the altoist's longtime collaborators Don Cherry, Charlie Haden, and Ed Blackwell. But while this recording marked one of Coltrane's first recorded forays into some of the "freer" settings that Coleman had marked out, the sonic and rhythmic implications of this new approach didn't become fully manifest until the middle of the 1960s.[41]

1965: Recordings Full of Sound and Fury Signifying Something

Coltrane won numerous awards in 1965, but critical and popular opinion of his music remained decidedly mixed.[42] Responses had, in fact, become increasingly polarized since at least the "anti-jazz" debate instigated by John Tynan in 1961.[43] Even some of those who had followed Coltrane's playing from his hard-bop days and "sheets of sound" period through his early modal recordings found some of the new music puzzling at the very least.[44] A review of *John Coltrane Quartet Plays* begins, "This recording from 1965 finds Coltrane well advanced down the path of ugliness which he started to tread in 1961.

Perhaps surprisingly, I find the one soprano [saxophone] track (Chim Chim Cheree) the most acceptable, which will probably make it the least acceptable to Coltrane enthusiasts!"[45]

Yet as this negative review hints, many listeners did find Coltrane's later work rewarding, sometimes extraordinarily so. Stories abound of individuals who experienced a fundamental transformation through Coltrane's music of this time. Indeed, these last sessions are often regarded as his most "spiritual" and led more than any others to the literal canonization of this musician.

Again, J. C. Thomas's commentary hints at the degree to which—as well as some of the discourse through which—Coltrane's reputation in some circles had evolved toward the saintly:

> John Coltrane was more mystic than musician.
>
> This is the only logical explanation for the effects his music had on many members of his audience; in fact, many of them knew nothing whatsoever about any kind of music, including jazz, yet they were mesmerized, entranced, and quite often . . . had their lives changed from continuous exposure to Coltrane's music. There had to be something else *besides* music there; in reality there was a force beyond music that was communicating with Trane's audience on quite a different, higher level of meaning.
>
> Call it Universal Consciousness, Supreme Being, Nature, God. Call this force by any name you like, but it was there, and its presence was so powerfully felt by most people that it was almost palpable.
>
> John Coltrane was a mystic, somehow attuned, as are all mystics, to the Ultimate Reality.
>
> And the Ultimate Reality is Death.[46]

Thomas's take on Coltrane and his music may seem rather extravagant, but his melodramatic prose was based in at least some shared experience. For instance, it was at a live appearance of Coltrane's group shortly before the saxophonist's death that Bishop Franzo King experienced his own epiphanal and transformative sonic "baptism" leading to his foundation of Saint John's Church.

Sound as Structure

It's difficult to pin down the reasons for Coltrane's greatness, but for me, I'd say his "Sound" was the most outstanding quality. It was so much him. And his expressivity was so heartfelt. One thing we can take comfort in is the fact that whatever he was searching for, he just about achieved. . . . I think the sense of freedom with his own group—as compared to what he was saying with Miles [Davis]—put him on another level which he once described as a "religious awakening."

HAROLD LAND,
quoted in "Tributes to John Coltrane," *Down Beat*

While many jazz-history texts include notated transcriptions of at least a portion of Coltrane's "Giant Steps" solo, few devote extensive space (and fewer still reproduce musical examples) of Coltrane's later works. Such an observation is not meant as a criticism. The authors' choices merely exemplify the gulf separating the saxophonist's early and later approaches and confirm that musical notation can reveal only certain aspects of certain kinds of music. Neither "Ascension" nor most of the other post–*A Love Supreme* pieces are structured in such a way as to readily accommodate written representations. Even Andrew White, who has built a successful and widely respected career by transcribing and marketing hundreds of Coltrane solos, has passed over *Om, Ascension,* and portions of many of the other later recordings. White describes Coltrane's playing on these discs as "effectual saxophonics," instrument-specific gestures irreducible to the page. Those things that notation can readily symbolize—chiefly discrete pitch and harmonic progression—play a decidedly subservient role in the later music. White notes too that the densely collective aspects of these recordings sometimes even render player recognition difficult.[47]

In diametrical opposition to the complex harmonic schemes that Coltrane had devised in the late 1950s, the later albums feature open-ended pieces organized around "energy," interplay, and sonic gesture.

Even the modality such as found on "Impressions" is largely attenuated. One can descry modal or at least modal-like sections in many of these pieces, but the Tin Pan Alley framework that organizes "Impressions" does not organize the later works. Due to their less regular rhythmic conceptions, these go beyond even Coltrane's early-1960s composition "India," which he based on an open-ended G-mixolydian modality but which maintains a steady pulse.[48]

In "Ascension," for example, we don't find the traditional eight-, twelve-, sixteen-, or thirty-two-bar "touchstones" that structured earlier jazz styles. This is not to say that the piece lacks form. As with Ornette Coleman's "Free Jazz" of 1960, Coltrane organized "Ascension" around alternating sections of soloist and large ensemble (he expanded his usual quartet to include eleven musicians for this recording). However, as Ekkehard Jost has pointed out, the two musicians approached their senses of large-scale freedom differently. Unlike Coleman's conception of interplay, Jost notes that "the central idea [of 'Ascension'] is not to produce a network of interwoven independent melodic lines, but dense sound complexes."[49]

Tenor saxophonist Archie Shepp, one of the "New Thing's" most outspoken proponents and a contributor to the *Ascension* recordings, described the session this way: "The emphasis was on textures rather than the making of an organizational unity. There was unity, but it was a unity of sounds and textures rather than, like, an A [A] B A approach. You can hear, in the saxophones especially, a reaching for sound and an exploration of the possibilities of sound."[50]

Some criticisms leveled against the freer saxophone approaches of Shepp, Sanders, and other players comment to the effect that their playing "doesn't sound like a saxophone at all." True, many of the "cries" and "squeals" audible on *Ascension* and similar discs do not sound like the saxophone playing of Lester Young or Coleman Hawkins (much less that of classical performers and teachers). However, they do "sound like a saxophone." Indeed, these gestures—Andrew White's "effectual saxophonics"—are the most instrument-specific. What they do not do is reinscribe the established ideals of tone as set forth by the European tradition or, for that matter, by the big-band and other jazz musicians who adopted some or all of those ideals.

Equally important to the freer styles of this period are the more "open" rhythm-section approaches. On tunes in which the drummer and bass player followed traditional accompaniment roles, a soloist could create sections of teleologia. But Coltrane's rhythm-section members of this time (Elvin Jones, Jimmy Garrison, Art Davis, McCoy Tyner, and, later, Rashied Ali and Alice Coltrane) began to explore looser rhythmic strategies. "Ascension," like most of the later works, is "gestural" music, and these players concern themselves more with providing sonic color than with maintaining a steady background for soloists. Jones, Garrison, and Davis occasionally fall into a steady quarter-note, walking feel, but these instances are generally short-lived: the unrestrained playing of the horn players almost demands a like-minded response of dramatic intensity. This seems especially true during the collective portions of the recording, where a more boplike rhythmic feel would undermine the sense of cooperative transcendence, that feeling of "ascension."

Signifying What?: Sound as Search

Even among those audience members who found this freer music deeply satisfying, there was disagreement as to what the approach signified. In general, many players and listeners associated the extreme gestures of the 1960s jazz avant-garde with a musical "search." A search for what exactly—peace, war, civil rights, God—was sometimes unclear and in any case was understood differently by different players and listeners. For some, the widespread upheaval in social and cultural values, and particularly the emergence of a more confrontational search for racial justice, seemed to find voice in this tumultuous sonic assault. Frank Kofsky hinted at this sort of meaning when he dedicated his *Black Nationalism and the Revolution in Music* "to the memory of John Coltrane and Malcolm X."[51] Kofsky's comments in his interview with Coltrane published in that book even suggest a rather concerted effort to elicit some sort of "angry black man" response from the saxophonist. But Coltrane, unlike some of his protégés (Archie Shepp most notably), never allied himself publicly with the more militant factions of the civil rights movement, and his oft-stated goal remained one of peace.[52]

For another faction of Coltrane's followers, the saxophonist's sound came to signify a striving for some type of spiritual transcendence. Reviewing the 1966 performance later released as *Coltrane Live at the Village Vanguard Again!* Pete Welding wrote, "Coltrane's is music of total engagement, of relentless questing, a music that is more than anything else the chronicle of a journey to the center of the self, a dissection—often painful—of the psyche in which every nerve is laid bare, every feeling, impulse, and reaction probed mercilessly for what it will reveal. It is not easy or comfortable music by any means."[53] As Welding's review shows, Coltrane's later style came to symbolize a kind of anguished/ecstatic journey or transcendental "dissolution of the self." That Coltrane's very aggressive musical onslaught would come to be understood as "mystical" rather than "angry" has much to do with the discourse surrounding his music. With song and album titles including *Om, Meditations,* "Compassion," "Amen," and "Ascent," Coltrane (and, after his death, his widow and his record company) wrapped the later music in a panreligious sacrality. Clearly, the song titles, solemn photographs, liner notes, and prayers accompanying the recordings from *A Love Supreme* onward lean much more toward the spiritual than do his earlier, bop-inspired Atlantic- and Blue Note–period tunes such as "Big Nick," "Lazy Bird," or "Like Sonny."[54]

Of course, song titles alone cannot account for the reverence in which listeners held these later works; significant musical factors played into this reception as well. Ethnomusicologist and saxophonist David Borgo has explored the connection between "extended" musical techniques and certain ecstatic states engendered in some players and listeners. Borgo's list of musical devices used by "freer"-minded saxophonists includes exaggerated vibrato and articulations, harmonics, extremes in range, multiphonics, vocalizing effects, "kinetic shapes," circular breathing, and recitation tones. Borgo notes quite rightly that "there is nothing inherent in the nature of extended saxophone techniques that triggers ecstatic states in musicians and listeners."[55] But contrasting with a smooth, reassuring sound of, say, Stan Getz's bossa nova recordings of the time (or, more recently, Kenny G.'s stylings), the sonic extremes and oftentimes precarious execution that accompany these techniques can lend a "striving" quality to the musician's playing. The perceived musical searching is mapped by those listeners and performers so inclined onto a type of mystical search for the transcendent.

The New Thing and the Classroom

As I've noted, the extended techniques that Coltrane and the other musicians engaged on the later recordings are not in themselves mysterious; they can be taught. Yet for a teacher and student to begin the process of exploring such devices, both must recognize these as useful, that is to say, "musical," skills to develop. And to music instructors who prize a clear, clean, stable tone, the seemingly otherworldly shrieks, screams, honks, clucks, and clicks produced by the "New Thing" saxophonists must sound like sheer incompetent caterwauling.

Even beyond the question of sonority, other issues come into play when we discuss the marginalization of Coltrane's later styles in the academy. For one, though the quest for the Infinite was not an uncommon one in the heady days of the middle 1960s, these sorts of goals have proven less acceptable in the very rational worlds of the music conservatory (and render grading rather difficult). More to the point, however: to the denizens of music institutions, encouraging students to play "like that" might undermine the authority of—even the necessity of—instrument teachers. Schools run on the tacit understanding that their instructors possess specialized knowledge that they can pass on to their pupils. Instances of jazz freedom—such as the time when Ornette Coleman recorded *The Empty Foxhole* with his ten-year-old son, Denardo, on drums (who, though refreshingly devoid of cliches, was not a child prodigy)—throw into question the assumption that individuals require extensive training to earn the title of "musician." Teachers who exhort their students to "just play, man" might soon find themselves out of work. Meanwhile, parents footing the bill for this sometimes very expensive conservatory training might wonder just what sort of school it is that would encourage that type of "noise" and whether their son or daughter might not get a better education elsewhere.

In addition to these aspects, the increasing collectivity of Coltrane's later music raises problems for a jazz-conservatory system that, somewhat paradoxically, pushes for standardized performance norms at the same time that it extols individual improvisers. We have seen that jazz educators—whether through workbooks, private lessons, or in-class improvisation courses—orient their students to esteem the soloist. I've remarked on Coltrane's reputation as a practicer, but those stories only reinforce the many other "woodshedding" legends that circulate around bop-era soloists. The tale of Charlie Parker's early humiliation at the hands of drummer Jo Jones and the saxophonist's subsequent retreat into the country for extensive solitary practicing may or may not be apocryphal. But beyond question is the fact that the idea of Parker's experiences has evolved into jazz lore. Certainly Clint Eastwood presented this episode as defining for Parker in the director's darkly romanticized bio-pic, *Bird*. Sonny Rollins's well-documented withdrawal to the bridges of Kings County further supports this myth of the isolated jazz hero. These sorts of stories work to reinforce perceptions of jazz as a music of great soloists, and only soloists. Teachers encourage young musicians to aspire to join this majestic lineage. Consequently, students learn to hear recordings of New Orleans/ Chicago-style polyphony as quaint reminders of what jazz was like in its "primitive," pre-bop stages and to view more recent collective performances as a type of musical deception, cloaking the players' soloing inadequacies.

As schools have a mandate to turn out competent, professional musicians, structuring individual displays of versatility and virtuosity offers one way for jazz programs to ensure that that they are producing hirable players capable of "making it" (to the extent that jazz musicians can in an era when rock, rap, and country stand as America's truly popular musics). At the same time, avoiding freer styles of play decreases the possibility that a student may be "faking it" and makes the grading process much more "objective." Even for a young player inclined toward collective playing, obstacles are encountered at every turn. It is virtually impossible to practice group improvisation by oneself. With so many lessons, assignments, and even practice rooms geared toward the honing of individual skills, little if any time or space remains for the development of the very different musical tools necessary to improvise successful collective jazz.

To be sure, much can be gained by fostering professional individual skills in jazz students as they prepare for life as working musicians. Yet by ignoring the collective musics of Coltrane and the other avant-gardists (as well as the early New Orleans players), jazz pedagogy marginalizes other skills and traditions that have circulated in various guises since the genre's earliest days, resulting in a skewed view of jazz history, practices, and ideals.

Ultimately, the issue boils down to knowledge: what sorts of knowledge will be esteemed in a given setting, how will that knowledge be transmitted, by whom, and to whom? In many instances, tests and grades measure only a student's ability to reproduce, rather than apply, a given knowledge system. Saxophonist Branford Marsalis's experiences at the Berklee College of Music in Boston indicate this sense of reproduction: "Berklee has its own system of doing things, the Berklee way, the Berklee method. They basically say that when you write things that are theoretically against the Berklee method, then they're incorrect. Even if they sound great. Musically they sound great, but theoretically it's wrong, so it's wrong. Which is not the purpose of music. Music theories are just theories."[56] Marsalis points out the difference between the actual sounding of jazz, which involves a type of practical knowledge, and the production of a theoretical type of knowledge about jazz. These knowledges—musical practice and the codifications of those practices in the academy—do not always overlap completely. I do not mean for these discussions of conservatory-based teaching to demean either music teachers or the European classical tradition that they studied and promulgate but rather to emphasize that ideals are not universal. What one musical tradition values highly another may not value at all. Although genres evolve and influences move back and forth between jazz and European musics (and blues, and country, and rock), an improvisation-based genre does require different skills than does a score-based genre.

Younger musicians who are encouraged to emulate those musics that are deemed "important works" in the jazz canon will, of course, tend to replicate or at least build on those works. In the case of John Coltrane, music teachers who hold to aesthetic models formed for another musical tradition serve to marginalize a significant portion of his recorded output and one of the primary reasons for his virtually god-like status among some listeners. This is not to say that the saxophonist's works from 1965 onward reveal the "true" Coltrane any more than "Giant Steps" does. But to ignore the later musics results in a type of musical "half truth" passed on from teacher and institution to student.

To be sure, jazz is not an isolated genre, and European models have always helped to shape its aesthetics, structures, and ideology. Yet it is not wholly European, and jazz pedagogy's classical biases result not only in an incomplete view of John Coltrane's contributions as a musician but, more important, in a narrower understanding of what counts as "jazz" in America today.[57]

Six

[The word] "tradition" survives in English as a description of a general process of handing down, but there is a very strong and even predominant sense of this entailing respect and duty.

RAYMOND WILLIAMS,
Keywords

IN 1991, COLUMBIA RECORDS released the second of trumpeter Wynton Marsalis's ongoing *Standard Time* series of recordings, this one subtitled *Intimacy Calling.* As the title suggests, "standards," generally considered the enduring repertoire from America's popular-song composers, make up the majority of the recordings' selections. *Standard Time Vol. 2* features the familiar jazz instrumentation of trumpet, saxophone, piano, acoustic bass, and drums. Two years after Marsalis's release, guitarist Bill Frisell recorded *Have a Little Faith* for Elektra Records. Like *Standard Time,* the Frisell album also features works from American composers, but those represented here include Muddy Waters, Charles Ives, Madonna, Stephen Foster, and John Philip Sousa. Despite the broad range of compositions and the fact that the album's instrumentation includes electric guitar, accordion, clarinet, electric bass, and drums, record stores and print media present *Have a Little Faith* as a jazz album.

This chapter explores these two recordings as they relate to and help to configure jazz identities at the start of the twenty-first century. Though both Marsalis and Frisell appropriate a distinctly American repertoire, they do so in widely divergent ways, and their very differ-

146

ent musical texts raise significant questions beyond the simple delimitation of jazz-genre boundaries. We will see that the particular choices these musicians make with respect to their material reflect both competing claims to jazz "authenticity" and contested views on the cultural and musical legacy of the music.

Three principal questions directed the selection of these particular albums for study: 1) who plays the music? 2) what tunes do they play? and 3) how do they choose to play them? With regard to the first question, Wynton Marsalis has been called "the spokesman for an entire generation of young musicians," his prestige extending well beyond the circles of contemporary jazz performers and listeners.[1] Featured regularly in *Down Beat* and other jazz periodicals, Marsalis has also appeared on the cover of numerous mass-market magazines, including *GQ* and *Time,* and on a wide range of PBS television productions. As a performer, Marsalis stands as the only musician to receive Grammy Awards in both the jazz and classical categories during the same year (1983). His compositions have also been honored: his 1997 *Blood on the Fields* won the Pulitzer Prize. Not the least of his many accomplishments have been his roles as the musical director of the prestigious Jazz at Lincoln Center program since its inception and senior creative consultant for Ken Burns's ten-part PBS documentary, *Jazz.* Wynton Marsalis—currently "jazz's most visible symbol"—presents a clear choice for study as a musical "standard bearer."[2]

Bill Frisell, though considerably less well known than Marsalis in the broader public sphere, has nonetheless achieved significant stature within the genre. A quotation from the *Seattle Times* included with one of Frisell's more recent releases proclaimed that "Frisell is without a doubt the single most important guitarist in jazz."[3] In particular, Frisell receives frequent mention in the jazz press as one of the leading figures to emerge from the Knitting Factory scene of lower Manhattan.[4] He also enjoyed a certain amount of widespread attention for composing and performing music for the re-released silent movies of Buster Keaton and for *Nashville,* his recording of country-flavored material.

Regarding the question of repertoire: scholars may explore the formation, preservation, and/or evolution of musical genres through any recording or live performance. But both *Have a Little Faith* and *Standard Time* draw upon compositions that originate in and are associated with a wide variety of historical figures and musical traditions—the performances of which are all presented under the "jazz" rubric. For those reasons, these recordings offer particularly rich possibilities for investigations into contemporary jazz identities.

Finally, the manner in which the musicians approach this material—the sounds, textures, and rhythmic feels that make for recognizable variations in and between musical genres; in a word, their *style*—reveals a great deal about how musicians locate themselves in relation to their own time and, in a broader context, to a sense of a jazz tradition. Performing style not only hints at these musicians' listening habits but also suggests how each has incorporated that listening into his playing, in light of his surroundings, ideals, and experiences. Ethnomusicologist Charles Keil virtually equates musical style with cultural identity when he remarks that "style tells you who your home folks are and gives you that rock-solid reference point."[5] A discussion of musical styles presented on these recordings is crucial, then, to an understanding of where these various contemporary jazzes are "coming from" and to whom they may be speaking.

JAZZ AND REPERTOIRE

"Tiger Rag" was transformed into jazz by me, from an old French Quadrille, that was played in many tempos. I also transformed many light operas such as Sextet, Melody in F, Humoresque, *etc., and* After the Ball, Back Home in Indiana, *etc., and all standards that I saw fit.*

JELLY ROLL MORTON,
"I Discovered Jazz in 1902"

Jazz musicians have always looked to other genres for source material. Jelly Roll Morton and other early New Orleans musicians borrowed from European art music, as has every generation since. Stan Getz, Pat Metheny, and Wayne Shorter found rich resources in Brazil's vast musical heritages. Herbie Hancock even appropriated the sounds of the Pygmies of central Africa (listen to the introduction to Hancock's "Watermelon Man").[6] But while all compositional forms have served as fair game for the improviser in search of a tune that may inspire him or her to "say something," some tunes have proven to be particularly durable, functioning as vehicles for generations of players.

Compositions based on the twelve-bar blues form, for instance, have remained favorites of musicians since the earliest days of jazz and are likely heard, in one style or another, at least once during any given performance. Selections from vaudeville revues and Broadway and Hollywood musicals have also passed into general use among jazz musicians. These songs make up the core of the repertoire referred to as "standards." Jazz musicians are expected to memorize dozens, even hundreds, of standards,[7] as—after the blues—these make up the most frequently played fare at gigs, jam sessions, and recording dates. For many musicians, such tunes (particularly Ray Noble's "Cherokee," George Gershwin's "I Got Rhythm," and Jerome Kern's "All the Things You Are") still form the core repertoire, even seventy or more years after their initial publication.

While the "mainstream" jazz repertoire consists mainly of blues tunes and standards, one should not attribute the longevity of a particular song solely to the structure or even to the "quality" of a specific piece. Rather, we must also consider the ways and places in which the composition has been recorded, published, or written about in the past. For instance, one may ascribe the durability of some songs published in the *Real Book* (a particular "fake book" consisting of lead sheets to hundreds of songs) merely to the fact that that songbook remains the most widely used among beginning jazz students. Of course, that the *Real Book*'s editors included a composition in the first place suggests that it may have already circulated for some time, but the publication of a tune in that book certainly encourages its continued use.[8]

That jazz musicians frequently base their performances of a tune on a previously recorded version of that song also illustrates that "structure" alone does not dictate repertoire. For example, when players perform "If I Were a Bell," they often draw their stylistic orientation from Miles Davis's famous 1956 version of that tune. In such instances, a trumpeter may recall Davis's "sound," while a pianist may approximate Red Garland's light touch and buoyant swing feel or use Garland's "Westminster Chimes" introduction. Similarly, if a group plays the song "My Favorite Things," its stylistic orientation typically refers, not to the famous Julie Andrews version, but to the John Coltrane recording from 1960. Here the saxophonist may display his or her "Trane-isms" (sounds and stylistic devices associated with Coltrane), while the pianist switches to quartal-based voicings à la McCoy Tyner. Although this propensity to look to earlier styles and musicians holds especially true for nascent players, it is not exclusive to them. Experienced musicians, even those possessing a discernible "voice" in the genre, also recognize the associations they and audiences make with individual pieces; witness the many tribute albums on which various artists perform songs affiliated with the tributee.

We can see then that when a musician performs a song, he or she not only plays a melody and a set of chord changes but also plays with and in some ways "comments" on earlier versions of that song. Robert Walser's essay "Out of Notes: Signification, Interpretation, and the Problem of Miles Davis" helps to illuminate this intertextual nature of jazz performance. Modeled on Henry Louis Gates's theory of signification in African-American literature, Walser's article explores the relationship between Davis's 1964 rendition of the standard "My Funny Valentine" and an earlier recording of the same tune by vocalist Tony Bennett:

> "My Funny Valentine" was composed by Rodgers and Hart in 1937. By the time of Bennett's recording, Davis had already recorded the song twice himself, in 1956 and 1958; his live recording was made five years after Bennett's. Now can we say that Davis is signifyin' on—commenting on, in dialog with, deconstructing—Bennett's version? The question is made complex by the idea that as a performer, Davis is signifyin' on all of the versions of the song he has heard, but for his audience, Davis is signifyin' on all the versions each listener has heard. What is played is played up against Davis' intertextual experience, and what is heard is heard up against the listeners' experiences.[9]

Walser's thought-provoking work foregrounds the frequently over-looked fact that previous versions of a composition ground all under-standings of and reactions to subsequent performances of that piece. In this way, the shared jazz repertoire carries an evolving "effective his-tory"[10] influenced by past musicians, styles, eras, places, recordings, and discourse. Of course, these principles apply equally to composi-tions from outside the genre. Jazz musicians and their audiences do not limit their listening to those musics called "jazz." In a time when music is virtually ubiquitous in public spaces, it is almost impossible not to acquaint oneself with a wide range of musical styles. This point comes to the fore as we consider contemporary visions of the jazz tradition.

STANDARDS AND TRADITION IN THE 1990S

A plethora of jazz record releases featuring Tin Pan Alley composi-tions entered the market in the 1980s and 1990s, and this phenome-non both reflected and helped shape new meanings of the term "stan-dards." Beyond describing simply the popular-song-based repertoire of many musicians, "standards" in jazz also began to imply a state-ment—revealing an awareness of and reverence for a legacy handed down by the music's forebears. Over the course of those two decades, the understanding emerged that a musician's relationship to "the tra-dition" explicitly and consciously related to the history of the compo-sitions he/she chose to play.[11]

A number of factors played into this standards–tradition correla-tion, but business concerns clearly contributed. Guitarist Kevin Eu-banks, musical director of NBC's Tonight Show band and former Blue Note record label recording artist, contended in 1994 that an ex-cessively profit-conscious, musically conservative, corporate mindset drove the trend:

> The pressure is from the labels and the media that you're not a
> ["young lion"] unless you're doing standards. You have to question
> this whole generation of musicians who are pursuing tradition as a
> future, because that makes the musicians interchangeable. To have

to sound like Wes Montgomery just to bring attention to myself as a deserving guitarist is an unacceptable position.[12]

Record companies exist in order to sell products, and they will drop from their roster any artist—no matter how "brilliant"—who does not move an expected number of units. By encouraging (or requiring) musicians, especially lesser-known ones, to play familiar material, record producers can increase the chances that their albums "sound like jazz." As Eubanks has suggested, companies continually sign new faces billed as "keepers of the flame," "torch-bearers," or "young lions," decreasing the need for busy consumers to reconsider their understandings of the genre.

As pervasive as corporate influence remains, it cannot account for this pattern alone. How we understand the present of any cultural activity depends on how we interpret the past, and the standards-as-tradition phenomenon has also served as a powerful tool for those musicians, critics, and scholars who seek to offer a particular narrative of jazz history.

LINER NOTES: "SPINNING" STANDARDS

Although a musician or record company executive may select a song based on its perceived jazz lineage, the broad effective history of so many standards dictates that not all audience members will hear a particular piece as a jazz song. If, for example, a musician plays "The Surrey with the Fringe on Top," that musician may find (to his or her dismay?) that a given listener connects the performance to Gordon MacRae's version in the film *Oklahoma* rather than to any distinctly jazz lineage. Indeed, the first jazz performances of that song did refer (with amusement, condescension, and/or affection) to *Oklahoma*. Not until Sonny Rollins and Miles Davis released their respective jazz renditions did audiences hear "Surrey with the Fringe on Top" as anything but a Broadway/Hollywood-musical number.

Yet subsequent jazz meanings have emerged in the wake of those recordings, and, depending upon the way in which a musician sets up a

TABLE 5   Album Selections, Wynton Marsalis,
Standard Time Vol. 2: Intimacy Calling

Composition	Composer and Year
1. When It's Sleepytime Down South	Rene/Rene/Muse (1931)
2. You Don't Know What Love Is	G. DePaul/D. Raye (1941)
3. Indelible and Nocturnal	W. Marsalis (late 1980s?)
4. I'll Remember April	Raye/DePaul/Johnson (1941)
5. Embraceable You	Gershwin/Gershwin (1928)
6. Crepuscule with Nellie	T. Monk (1957)
7. What Is This Thing Called Love?	C. Porter (1929)
8. The End of a Love Affair	E. C. Redding (1950)
9. East of the Sun (West of the Moon)	B. Bowman (1934)
10. Lover	R. Rodgers/L. Hart (1933)
11. Yesterdays	J. Kern/O. Harbach (1933)
12. Bourbon Street Parade	P. Barbarin (1952)

performance, these expectations, understandings, and ideals can be engaged. In live performance, for instance, a player may place a spin on his or her work through stage introductions. That is, if a musician announces, "we would now like to perform a song made famous by saxophone great Sonny Rollins, 'The Surrey . . . ,'" he or she locates the ensuing performance within a specifically jazz context. Conversely, a musician would open up a very different set of meanings and expectations if he or she announced, "we would now like to play 'The Surrey with the Fringe on Top' from the great Rodgers and Hammerstein musical, *Oklahoma*."

In recordings, liner notes play a role similar to that of stage patter, and the booklet accompanying *Standard Time* features just such a written commentary. As shown in table 5, the repertoire on *Standard Time* consists predominantly of songs composed between the 1920s and the early 1950s, the "Golden Age" of Tin Pan Alley (see table 5).

All but a few of these compositions derive originally from shows or films and only later passed into common use by jazz musicians. However, Stanley Crouch's liner notes for *Standard Time* never refer to the nonjazz histories of the tunes; instead, they invoke specific jazz performers and their recordings.[13] For example, Crouch writes, "'What Is This Thing Called Love?' is another song that Clifford Brown and Max Roach recorded."[14] Yet he omits to mention that that particular

Cole Porter composition first appeared in the 1929 Broadway show *Wake Up and Dream,* resurfaced in the movie *Night and Day,* and has remained a favorite of cabaret acts and "lounge lizards" ever since.

Similarly, Marsalis states in those same notes that "'East of the Sun' . . . is a feature for [pianist] Marcus Roberts. . . . This song got on the record because he and I first heard it on Louis Armstrong's *The Silver Collection,* which we listened to day and night." [15] Marsalis offers some history of the tune (the Armstrong version), but "East of the Sun" first appeared in a 1934 Princeton University Triangle Club Revue called *Stags at Bay,* and these "roots" go without notice. Likewise, though Marsalis remarks of "Embraceable You" that it "is a melodic challenge and its lyrics combine with the music to make it what I consider one of the greatest in American popular music," he never names George Gershwin as composer, though Gershwin remains one of American music's luminary figures. [16] This sort of discourse is not entirely unusual, as many jazz musicians have come to understand their repertoire in this manner; Ornette Coleman, an important composer in his own right, called jazz the "art of the improviser." But Crouch does choose to mention two composers by name: Thelonious Monk and Wynton Marsalis.

The inclusion of Monk's relatively obscure ballad "Crepuscule with Nellie" broadens the scope of required knowledge implied by the term "standard." But with widely covered pieces to his credit such as "Round Midnight," "Blue Monk," and "Straight, No Chaser," he certainly deserves recognition as a canonical composer. Wynton Marsalis as "standards composer," however, provides a somewhat more intriguing twist. Few outside of that musician's immediate circle could have possibly recognized his "Indelible and Nocturnal" before the release of this album. Yet its presence between the oft-recorded "You Don't Know What Love Is" and "I'll Remember April" in the album's sequence helps to situate Marsalis and his tune among the enduring figures and pieces in American music.

Crouch makes this arrangement explicit when he writes, "What Marsalis seeks is a place for himself within every aspect of the entire sweep of jazz, from New Orleans music to Ornette Coleman and John

Coltrane."[17] Here the writer not only declares the trumpeter's goals in relation to a perceived lineage but also unambiguously delimits the cultural realm of that lineage—"the entire sweep of jazz." Crouch begins with New Orleans, the city widely acknowledged as the birthplace of jazz and the one that produced most of the music's earliest luminaries. Wynton Marsalis, too, hails from that city, and Crouch and Marsalis emphasize these roots, strengthening the trumpeter's claims to jazz legitimacy. Louis Armstrong, now an undisputed and exalted member of the jazz pantheon, receives mention nine times in the album's liner notes, and one finds numerous references to New Orleans and "the South" in general. On his selection of "When It's Sleepytime Down South" to open his album, Marsalis says, "I wanted to interpret 'Sleepytime . . .' for two reasons: one is that it was Louis Armstrong's theme song, and it also represents my attitude toward the South, which is, of course, something I share with Pops [Armstrong]."[18]

Similarly, Crouch tells us that, "We . . . hear the sort of development [in Marsalis's playing] that can easily be attributed to an ease with his influences—Clifford Brown, Freddie Hubbard, Clark Terry, Miles Davis (before rock and roll), Don Cherry, Dizzy Gillespie, Fats Navarro, Woody Shaw, and Louis Armstrong."[19] Here he positions Marsalis within a fraternity of great jazz (but not rock) trumpeters. In this way, the compositions selected for *Standard Time,* together with Stanley Crouch's liner notes, help to ensure that a reader/listener understands Wynton Marsalis as a logical extension of a rich jazz ancestry while they ignore any other historical or cultural understandings that these tunes may carry for listeners.

We should bear in mind that this type of discourse affects understandings not only of Marsalis vis-à-vis a jazz tradition but also of all the other musicians listed as well. As seemingly unassailable as Armstrong's position in the canon now appears, the jazz world did not always regard him so highly. Many bop-era players, for instance, saw "Satchmo's" cheerful music and smiling countenance as a sign of "Tomming," and they distanced themselves from that sort of musical and social presentation.[20] Thus, Marsalis's and Crouch's comments also help to resuscitate Armstrong's reputation.

Musical instruments not only produce sound; they also articulate cultures. One needs no more illustration of this assertion beyond the fact that the mere possession of the Highland bagpipes in eighteenth-century Great Britain was punishable by death.[21] Even in less severe circumstances, the look and sounds of instruments remind us every day of who we are and, just as clearly, who "others" are as well. Film composers utilize the cultural associations of specific instrumental sounds to tell viewers how to feel about a movie's characters or location. If a U.S.-produced film is set overseas, we can tell a great deal about America's current political relationship to the selected country by the manner in which the soundtrack composer manipulates "exotic" instruments and sonorities to achieve the film's narrative designs. Instruments can place us in time, too: a heavily distorted electric guitar backing a "period" film such as Merchant and Ivory's *A Room with a View* or Kenneth Branagh's *Henry V* would certainly strike us as incongruous. Yet that sonority effectively took the Clare Danes–and Leonardo DiCaprio–starring version of *Romeo and Juliet* out of Renaissance-era Verona and re-placed it in late twentieth-century Miami Beach.

In jazz, the trumpet and saxophone most signal the genre. Images abound on posters, in movies, and in magazine and television advertisements of the "man with the horn." In these instances, horns represent sexiness (much to this piano player's dismay), evoking a sultry, smoky, late-night underground.[22] Jazz scholar Barry Kernfeld places the trumpet at the very top of his jazz "instrumentarium," which he describes as "a tightly circumscribed body of instruments."[23] He notes that while violinists, vibraphonists, and other musicians contributed significantly to the genre, most jazz players, at least during the music's first half century, limited themselves to exploring the sonic possibilities of a limited set of instruments.

Marsalis upholds this custom, as his *Standard Time* band consists of trumpet and tenor saxophone accompanied by a rhythm section of piano, bass, and drums. One finds no synthesizers or electric basses here, no effects-laden guitars or programmed drum machines, and no "foreign" instruments, all of which emerged in jazz since the late 1960s, drastically altering the sound and even look of the genre.[24] To be sure, Marsalis's traditional lineup does not dictate that his musicians must necessarily play in a traditional style—radically new approaches have emerged from that format. But this instrumentation connects securely to Swing and bop-type musicking and, like song selection, works as a marker of genre "purity" for many contemporary jazz musicians and listeners.[25]

The Performances: Marsalis

The opening track of *Standard Time,* "When It's Sleepytime Down South," shapes much of the stylistic palette to follow. Marsalis's bucket-muted trumpet and concise melodic ideas lend "Sleepytime" a gentle quality that hearkens back to the sounds of the 1930s and early 1940s. The rhythm section supports this laid-back feel throughout: Drummer Herlin Riley relies solely on brushes, while Reginald Veal provides an unobtrusive, steady quarter-note, walking bass line. Pianist Marcus Roberts's brief solo lingers in the upper register, displaying a light, elegant style reminiscent of Teddy Wilson or Nat Cole.

The Marsalis group demonstrates their "classic" conception just as clearly on their rendition of Rodgers and Hart's "Lover." In this performance, Roberts plays the melody in an unadorned fashion, freeing Marsalis to solo over the top. "Lover" displays all of the earmarks of the bebop style of the mid-to-late 1940s: a fast tempo, a single soloist playing long streams of chromatically inflected eighth-note lines, walking bass, and a drummer providing a stable "2" and "4" on the hi-hat along with a rhythmic wash of brushes on the snare drum. In an example of musical quotation, Marsalis subtly hints at another standard, "The Way You Look Tonight," near the end of the second A section. Crouch writes of this performance, "[Marsalis] is . . . such a virtuoso that the whirlwind lyricism bebop brought to jazz is executed [here] with Olympian ease," reflecting a particular attitude toward virtuosity to which I'll return below.[26]

To close the album, Marsalis chooses "Bourbon Street Parade." The pianist and saxophonist "stroll" for this cut, leaving the trumpeter supported by only bass and drums.[27] The trio's approach reaches back even further here, exploring New Orleans "second line" parade music. The cut opens with a lone buglelike trumpet figure—a "call"— suggestive of the early decades of the twentieth century when horn men Buddy Bolden, Joe Oliver, Freddie Keppard, and Louis Armstrong reigned as the "kings" of jazz. Though much less raucous than the marching bands they salute, Marsalis's rhythm-section tandem of Reginald Veal and Herlin Riley captures the joyous lilt of a parade. Riley lays down "swing-march" snare-drum figures rather than ridecymbal patterns, while Veal's bass maintains a relaxed but steady twobeat feel, reminiscent of a marching-band tuba. The group employs a series of stop-time figures in the third chorus, a common device in early jazz.[28]

The placement of this track as the album's finale signals a homecoming of sorts: the record opened with the gentle "When It's Sleepytime Down South" and now closes with a march down Bourbon Street. These two performances affirm Marsalis's connections to early jazz suggested by Stanley Crouch (though one aspect of early New Orleans jazz is absent from these Crescent City-inflected pieces: polyphonic, collective improvisation; the improvisational passages throughout the entire album involve only individual soloists).

But if Marsalis has succeeded in establishing a "place for himself" among a New Orleans lineage of jazz trumpeters, Crouch's assertion that Marsalis's music ranges as far as the stylings of Don Cherry, Ornette Coleman, and John Coltrane seems less supportable. *Standard Time* elicits a decidedly more controlled feel than the works of those exploratory musicians, eschewing the edgier aspects of its alleged influences in favor of a disciplined, understated approach. Cherry's and Coleman's irreverent "blues connotations," especially, remain indiscernible in these cuts. And though one might detect a connection between *Standard Time*'s "intimacy" and Coltrane's more subdued Impulse recordings such as *Ballads* or his recording with Johnny Hartman, one hears very little of the ecstatic expressionism displayed on Coltrane's famous Herculean performances from the 1960s. Instead (and with the exception of "Bourbon Street Parade"), the Marsalis performances recall the musical idioms of pre-"New Thing," mid-

1940s to mid-1950s boplike approaches. The band even bases its introduction to "I'll Remember April" on the Clifford Brown and Max Roach Group version from the 1956 *Brown and Roach at Basin Street* album.[29]

As Crouch suggests, the musicians in Marsalis's group leave no doubt that they each possess a high degree of instrumental skill. Clearly, technical control of one's instrument (Crouch calls it "domination" on page 2 of his notes), honed through years of individual effort, remains an aesthetic ideal of this band. He writes of the expressive abilities of these players that "emotion is personal, but expression is objective. Though even the most untalented are capable of emoting, only those who have been called by talent and chosen by their own will are in command of expression. Expression transcends the personal and allows us to recognize the objective—actually, communal—fact of heroic individuality."[30]

To be sure, Crouch reminds us that improvisation generally entails not so much expressing one's "inner being" as it does an act of skillful ingenuity, a position echoing the principal theme of Albert Murray's insightful *Stomping the Blues.*[31] But Crouch's comments also seek to elevate Marsalis's brand of virtuosity to the status of objective greatness while suggesting that Marsalis and like-minded musicians personify "heroes," uniquely possessed of both extraordinary talent and tremendous will. And while not a wholly original position—"music appreciation" classes and jazz education programs promote much the same ideal—we'll see that this is not the only manner in which contemporary jazz musicians understand themselves or their craft.[32]

Images (Part I): "Intimacy Calling"

Just as liner notes can shape some of the potential attitudes and ideals surrounding a recording, an album's photographic images present ways of understanding the music. As I've noted in earlier chapters, we "see" music as well as hear it, and a musician's appearance helps to guide understandings of his or her sound. Ethnomusicologist Bruno Nettl has even argued that "the correlation between costume and musical category is so strong that a hearing-impaired person could usually identify style and category by noting whether the musicians wear tuxedos, blazers, turtlenecks, robes, dhotis, Elizabethian garb, T-shirts with holes, or leather jackets."[33] Nettl's comments find clear illustration in *Standard Time*, as the "suit look" depicted here has become an integral part of Marsalis's public persona. In contrast to the loose, casual (or Arabic-, Asian-, or African-inspired) garb worn by many "freer"-style players since the 1960s, this trumpeter's groups invariably present a "sharp," ordered appearance that, much like their music, draws on mid-twentieth-century codes of elegance and sophistication.

The cover photo (see figure 7) reveals Marsalis in an expensive home, his trumpet by his side. Behind him an attractive, elegantly clad African-American woman lies on a divan. The image on the back of the booklet shows the same setting, this time with Marsalis playing his instrument while the woman watches him. The album's only other photo, found inside the booklet, depicts the trumpeter engaged in the "Intimacy Calling" suggested in the recording's subtitle: he, alone, serenades the woman by the glass garden doors.

Hearing/Seeing Records as a Cultural Narrative

To recount the sort of jazz identity presented through *Standard Time* we must first hear/see that album as a conscious act of paying homage. This recording serves as a reminder that the "handing down" that Raymond Williams has described of every tradition entails a "respect and duty." For Marsalis and company, names such as Charlie Parker, Louis Armstrong, Clifford Brown, Duke Ellington, and Miles Davis (if only "before rock and roll") not only deserve remembrance but require it if we are to understand the music "correctly."

The album's title, *Standard Time*, is plainly polysemic. The conventional use of that phrase denotes a measure of synchronized chronometric time in America, referring to those winter and fall months enveloping daylight savings time. But both "standard" and "time" may involve multiple interpretations to a jazz reader/listener. "Time" in music can denote divisions of rhythmic emphasis ("'Up Jumped Spring' is a work in three-four time") or describe a musician's ability to project a strong rhythmic pulse ("Ed Blackwell had incredible

Figure 7. Album cover, *Standard Time Vol. 2: Intimacy Calling,* Wynton Marsalis. Courtesy of Columbia Records and Wynton Marsalis.

time"). Time can also mean time for something, that it is the right moment for an event—in this case the presentation and remembrance of the impressive standards set by previous generations of jazz musicians.

I would like to propose yet another notion of time displayed here, that being a "cultural time." Any discussion of *Standard Time* should note that all of the individuals remembered in the album's liner notes are African Americans who worked in the early and middle decades of the twentieth century. This recording presents, above all, a narrative of jazz as a distinctly African-American cultural realm, a celebration of the remarkable achievements of black musicians in this country. *Standard Time* constructs a sense of those past eras and styles when and where jazz seemed to both come from and speak to a broad segment of African-diasporic communities (recall Charles Keil's remark that "style tells you who your home folks are").

This sort of narrative effectively offsets that which Krin Gabbard has called the "sin of erasing black people from jazz," one aspect of the discourse that has surrounded the genre since the 1920s.[34] As white audiences of that decade increasingly gravitated toward jazz and the African-American musicians associated with it, some critics and musicians reacted by espousing an evolutionary model of the genre. Their discourse suggested that jazz was in the process of emerging from its "primitive" roots toward a more "civilized" (to be read "European" or "white"), and therefore acceptable, style. Some white critics promulgated this narrative by wedding jazz to classical musics and performance practices, a whitewashing of the music that helps to explain the coronation of Paul Whiteman as "the King of Jazz."[35]

The following passage, for example, derives from the program notes to Whiteman's famous Aeolian Hall concert of 1924, possessing the very "cultured" title, "An Experiment in Modern Music": "Mr. Whiteman intends to point out, with the assistance of his orchestra and associates, the tremendous strides which have been made in popular music from the day of the discordant Jazz, which sprang into existence about ten years ago from nowhere in particular, to the really melodious jazz of today, which—for no good reason—is still called Jazz."[36] Notice the writer's emphasis on the present and the future of the music, and likewise his refusal to acknowledge any cultural past for jazz at all. The music simply "sprang into existence." *Standard Time* corrects these odious stories, reminding us of jazz's distinguished African-American legacy.

Given the countless instances in which Afro-diasporic peoples have been written out of history, jazz or otherwise, Marsalis's and Crouch's depiction appears understandable. We should keep in mind, however, that their stance is only slightly more historically accurate than the preposterous whites-only jazz narratives. For worse and for better, musicians, audiences, publishers, and record company executives of non-African lineages have played integral roles in the development and dissemination of jazz. In this way, Gabbard is also right when he points out that the distinctive and influential playing of Bix Beiderbecke, Frankie Trumbauer, and others should be considered "as something other than white theft of black capital."[37] Jazz players from all ethnic backgrounds have continually looked to and esteemed musics and musicians beyond those traditionally affiliated with Afro-diasporic communities. We might remember that in 1917 the very first and, though somewhat hokey, highly influential jazz recordings were made by the culturally diverse, but decidedly non–African-American, Original Dixieland Jazz Band.

Meanwhile, Scott DeVeaux has pointed to another issue pertaining to Wynton Marsalis's position in and on jazz:

> Marsalis is careful to present jazz as a cultural heritage and, in a sense, a political reality, entirely separate from the European tradition. But his celebrated feat of winning Grammy awards for both jazz and classical recordings underscores the extent to which jazz has become *another kind* of classical music—one indigenous to black culture and reflecting black values, but following the same pattern of institutionalization in conservatories and repertory groups, and demanding of its musicians an empathetic response to aesthetic sensibilities of the past.[38]

DeVeaux's passage illuminates the other principal theme of *Standard Time:* jazz as "America's classical music." That album, from the elegant dress of Marsalis and his female muse to the controlled performances and Crouch's "heroic" liner notes, suggests jazz as high art. Here we find jazz as "cultured music" (that is to say, "classy") as much as a music culture (in the anthropological sense: the way in which particular groups of people enact identity in their activities). The obvious contempt that Crouch and Marsalis hold for Miles Davis's later work distances the younger trumpeter from what they see as one jazz musician's sellout to crass commercialism. In the world of *Standard Time*, jazz stands above the marketplace. Sophistication, elegance, and, most important, artistic purity distinguish this genre from mere popular music.[39] Recall the fact that the standards on the Marsalis recording originated in Tin Pan Alley—the Jewish-dominated home of American popular music throughout much of this century—yet the liner notes never broach this lineage.[40]

In an interesting twist, *Standard Time* seems to tell a story of jazz not entirely unlike the whitewashed evolutionary narratives of the 1920s. In both cases, one recognizes an attempt to raise the genre from the "lower classes" of its roots (African in the earlier version, popular or commercial in Marsalis's) to a "higher" manner of musicking. On *Standard Time,* the classic jazz instrumentarium, the selection of the tunes and the way these are played, as well as the images and discourse surrounding all of this tell a refined tale of the jazz tradition. The recording narrates the cultural time of a great African-American musical phenomenon that flourished between New Orleans in the 1920s and New York in the late 1950s or early 1960s.

But what are we to make of the present time? If, as Crouch has written, the "entire sweep of jazz" encompasses New Orleans to Coltrane and Coleman, how does Marsalis—over thirty years after Coltrane's death—fit into this sweep? Has the role of the contemporary jazz musician, like that of many of his or her counterparts in the European classical tradition, become that of the interpreter, reviving works and styles from bygone eras? If so, this would represent a very untraditional shift in jazz performance aesthetics as they have developed thus far. For an enduring hallmark of jazz musicians over the course of the twentieth century has been their desire to continually draw on and reshape the sounds, tunes, and genres around them.

FAITH IN WHAT?

Jazz is in a funny place. . . . [Today] when you say something is jazz, it's supposed to fit into some classic idea. But jazz is not just Miles Davis in 1956; it's a whole attitude about feeling

and ideas and what's going on around you. Charlie Parker
used all the information around him, every scrap of it,
from Stravinsky to pop. [Sonny] Rollins did too.

BILL FRISELL,
quoted in Safford Chamberlin, "Bill Frisell: Using All the Information," *Los Angeles View*

Ragtime is a certain type of syncopation and only certain
tunes can be played in that idea, but jazz is a style
that can be applied to any type of tune.

JELLY ROLL MORTON,
quoted in Alan Lomax, *Mister Jelly Roll*

In contrast to *Standard Time,* Bill Frisell's *Have a Little Faith* has no accompanying liner notes. The booklet offers listeners/readers only the production and composition credits along with a series of photographs (discussed below). However, it takes just a cursory glance at the list of compositions listed in table 6 to recognize that these selections reflect a different sense of jazz lineage than the bop-inflected, Tin Pan Alley basis of the Marsalis album.

The composers listed here hail from diverse eras and cultural backgrounds: nineteenth and twentieth centuries, male and female, black and white, North and South. The works span over 125 years of American music, roughly twice that covered on *Standard Time.* Yet, though the compositions on Frisell's album both predate and postdate Crouch's designated "sweep of jazz," historical time is not the only significant difference here, as *Have a Little Faith* opens a decidedly broader cultural field as well. Merely the title of Frisell's opening track carries connotations of a very different America than was evinced on the Marsalis record. Even for those unfamiliar with the name Aaron Copland, his references to *Billy the Kid,* "The Open Prairie," "Street Scene in a Frontier Town," "Prairie Night," and other western images obviously draw on the deeply entrenched (and decidedly white) myth of the "wild, wild West."[41] Copland's work deliberately constructed images of an early America "open and free," destined for "taming" by

TABLE 6   Album Selections, Bill Frisell, *Have a Little Faith*

Composition	Composer and Year
1. *Billy the Kid*	Aaron Copland (1938)
The Open Prairie	
Street Scene in a Frontier Town	
Mexican Dance and Finale	
Prairie Night (Card Game at Night)	
Gun Battle	
Celebration after Billy's Capture	
Billy in Prison	
The Open Prairie Again	
2. The "Saint-Gaudens" in Boston Common	Charles Ives (1911)
"Col. Shaw and His Colored Regiment"	
(Excerpt #1) from *Three Places in*	
New England	
3. Just Like a Woman	Bob Dylan (1966)
4. I Can't Be Satisfied	M. Morganfield (Muddy Waters) (1948)
5. Live to Tell	Madonna/Patrick Leonard (1986)
6. The "Saint-Gaudens" (Excerpt #2)	Charles Ives (1911)
7. No Moe	Sonny Rollins (1953)
8. Washington Post March	John Philip Sousa (1889)
9. When I Fall in Love	Victor Young (1951)
10. Little Jenny Dow	Stephen Foster (1862)
11. Have a Little Faith in Me	John Hiatt (1987)
12. Billy Boy	Traditional

the hardy Euro-American. And while it seems unlikely that a given listener would know that Sousa's "Washington Post March" dates from 1889, few born in this country would fail to identify that work as "an old American song," played as it is at Fourth of July and Memorial Day parades. The inclusion of these early pieces, no less or more than the more recent songs from John Hiatt, Bob Dylan, and Madonna, rub against Marsalis's "classic" understandings of jazz and may startle listeners accustomed to a more circumscribed repertoire.

The Instrumentarium Challenged

Forgoing the traditional jazz rhythm section of acoustic piano, acoustic bass, and drums, Frisell presents a lineup of electric guitar, electric bass, and drum set. While the latter format appears frequently in the American pop and rock genres, it is less common in the jazz field, suggesting perhaps a jazz-rock "fusion." But the presence of clarinet and accordion, along with the "electric" rhythm section, marks this instrumentation as seemingly unique in jazz. As with the album's repertoire, the inclusion of these instruments as the album's front line suggests genre and cultural affiliations quite unlike the "horns = jazz" understandings associated with Marsalis's group.

To be sure, the clarinet once held a prominent position in jazz, and Kernfeld rightly includes it in his instrumentarium. Before the rise of the saxophone with Coleman Hawkins, Lester Young, Johnny Hodges, and—most decisively—Charlie Parker, clarinetists such as Barney Bigard, Benny Goodman, Artie Shaw, and Sidney Bechet stood as the chief woodwind players of the genre, their stature exceeded only by the great trumpet "kings." But that instrument has largely dropped from favor in contemporary jazz; with very few exceptions (Eddie Daniels, Buddy DeFranco, Pete Fountain, Woody Herman, Woody Allen [?]), no clarinetist has maintained a high profile since the Swing era. While a small percentage of jazz adherents may connect the clarinet with the avant-garde work of Joseph Jarman, Anthony Braxton, or the late John Carter, it seems more likely that audiences would associate the look and sound of that instrument with polka bands, klezmer groups, or wind ensembles.

More striking here is the presence of the accordion, which has never enjoyed more than the most tenuous connections to the music. True, accordionists have played jazz; a few, including Art van Damme and Tommy Gumina, even gained some attention in the 1940s, 1950s, and into the 1960s.[42] Still, the ever-changing list of "great figures in jazz" has yet to find an illustrious place for a practitioner of that instrument. Certainly, a critic tracing the jazz-accordion influences on Guy Klucevsek of Frisell's band, as Crouch did for Marsalis's trumpet precursors, would be hard pressed to locate a long line of masters. Instead, understandings of the accordion remain anchored in a range of "ethnic" and "local" sounds, including (again) polkas and klezmer, but also the "delightful" sounds of a French cafe, or the good-time musics of the Southern United States: Tex-Mex, cajun, and zydeco. With the exception of the last of these genres, the accordion's popularity has been limited predominantly to European and Central American musicians and audiences, a fact that is not insignificant to our considerations of cultural identity.

The Performances: Frisell

As I've noted, Frisell chooses as his point of entry for *Have a Little Faith* Aaron Copland's 1938 suite from *Billy the Kid,* originally a ballet based on William H. Bonney, the mythical hero/outlaw who roamed the American Southwest in the later part of the nineteenth century. The composition, an early attempt by Copland to write music in a consciously "American" style, both creates and draws on musical idioms associated with American folk songs, even incorporating such cowboy tunes as "Git Along Little Dogies," "The Old Chisholm Trail," and "Goodbye Old Paint."

The opening of the Frisell version closely follows Copland's score, given the orchestrational challenges inherent in re-creating a large-scale piece with five musicians. But beginning with the "Mexican Dance and Finale" and "Prairie Night" sections, we find a series of extended "free" group improvisations—frantic accordion and clarinet interpolations interweaving with distorted "power chords" from the electric guitar—leading to a nonmetric drum solo in the "Gun Battle."[43] Throughout these sections, the group's interplay draws upon the eclectic vocabulary of the Knitting Factory scene of lower Manhattan more than on either bebop approaches or the Euro-American concert-hall tradition of Copland's suite (or, for that matter, the Hollywood "open prairie" soundtrack style so strongly influenced by Copland).[44] Through these improvisatory passages—interludes that jazz up Copland's score—the group recontextualizes the depression-era composition.

In similar fashion, the opening of Stephen Foster's "Little Jenny Dow" establishes links with the supposed genteel simplicity of its nineteenth-century parlor-song origins through a subdued dialogue between Frisell's "clean" guitar timbre and Klucevsek's accordion. For the improvised sections, however, Frisell's sound turns edgier, more distorted. The rhythmic pulse becomes increasingly pronounced as the performance unfolds: the rubato opening of the tune gives way to a gradual solidifying of the groove by the beginning of the second chorus, ultimately revealing a straight eighth-note pop beat. As in the Copland, the musicians suggest a sense of the roots of the composition, but their rendition facilitates cultural associations that its composer could never have envisioned. Through the stylistic choices made in this version, "Little Jenny Dow" returns as an up-to-date tune, not only as an early American popular song.

A brief look at Frisell's approach to the guitar offers insight into the "contemporizing" conception at work throughout the album. John Scofield, himself a highly skilled and influential jazz guitarist, has called Frisell's "the most unique concept in guitar today." Scofield continues: "Bill [Frisell] is one of the great orchestraters, like [keyboardist] Joe Zawinul; he's a 'painter.'"[45] As Scofield suggests, rather than a bebop-inspired linearity, Frisell's style is based in large measure on sonic colors evoked through his use of electronic technology (effects devices and volume pedals).

One aspect of Frisell's sound that warrants particular discussion is his use of power chords. Until quite recently, jazz guitarists relied solely on a warm, distortion-free timbre. Influential mainstream practitioners including Wes Montgomery, Charlie Christian, and Joe Pass used the amplifier in its most literal way, that is, to increase the loudness of a hollow-bodied instrument. As critic and historian Robert Palmer has shown, however, some musicians after World War II turned to amplification not just to increase volume but also to create a "rawer, more ferocious, and more physical" sound.[46] By manipulating the controls on both instrument and amplifier, a guitarist could achieve a distorted, edgier timbre, one capable of almost unlimited sustain. Few established players in jazz followed this direction (John McLaughlin, Sam Brown, and Larry Coryell were early exceptions). Not until the most recent generation of guitarists—a generation raised on the sounds of Jimi Hendrix and Jimmy Page, as well as on Montgomery, Christian, and Jim Hall—has the "crunch" sound of overdriven amplifiers been heard as a viable option for guitarists playing in jazz. Frisell draws on this sound sparingly (using it only on portions of *Billy the Kid*, "Washington Post March," "Live to Tell," and "Little Jenny

Dow"), but his creative use of distortion signals a shift to a darker and more contemporary musical texture.

Clearly, the guitarist's adoption of these blues and rock techniques into his jazz performances differs sharply from the classic acoustic aesthetic of the Marsalis group, but Frisell also steers clear of a typical "fusion" approach. Most exponents of fusion, a jazz subgenre exemplified on the guitar by McLaughlin, Al DiMeola, and Alan Holdsworth, prize highly animated displays of virtuosity. Indeed, for many fusion musicians and fans, the electric guitar has come to symbolize what Steven Waksman has described as a "technophallus." Waksman coined the term to describe Jimi Hendrix's hypersexual approach, but his description of the guitar as "fusion of man and machine, an electronic appendage that allowed Hendrix to display his instrumental and more symbolically, his sexual prowess," well suits the above-named players as well.[47] And though the worlds of fusion and bebop differ significantly (predominantly in their aesthetics regarding note choice, harmonic structure, rhythmic feel, electricity, and sheer volume but also in stage dress and demeanor), they do share a fundamental attitude regarding the centrality of individual and virtuosic soloing.

By contrast, Frisell and his group emphasize sonic texture. Overt displays of individual "chops" are rare. Drummer Joey Baron, whose experience in jazz includes performances and recordings with the very traditional likes of Carmen McRae, Stan Getz, and Fred Hersch, performs a simple 1960s-style rock 'n' roll beat near the end of their rendition of Madonna's "Live to Tell." This brief stylistic shift—wholly out of place in both bop and fusion styles—serves to draw the music back from the angular, nonmetric improvisation of the previous passages. His gesture re-places that song within the broadly American pop-music tradition of its origins, playfully recalling even the decidedly light sounds of the Partridge Family or the Monkees.

As with their blurring of boundaries among "jazz," "classical," "pop," and "rock" and, more broadly, between "highbrow" and "lowbrow," the musicians here also obscure traditional roles of soloist and accompanist. Somewhat ironically, this group exemplifies its contemporary collective approach most clearly in the one bebop tune on the recording, Sonny Rollins's "No Moe." Compositions such as this commonly serve as "blowing" vehicles at jam sessions where individual soloists may play several choruses over the familiar " 'Rhythm changes." [48] In the *Have a Little Faith* version, however, the group limits itself to four 32-bar choruses, including the melody statements (or "heads"), that open and close the performance. Baron and bassist Kermit Driscoll downplay conventional rhythm-section roles; they rarely outline the groove explicitly, and the group must hold things together as a unit.

Images (Part II): The Open Prairie

The cover photo on *Have a Little Faith* portrays a group of presumably Anglo-American boys and girls competing in a running race in a community park (see figure 8). The original black-and-white photograph has been partially colorized: The sky and trees are green, the ground is purple; only the young people are left unretouched. The full foliage suggests a warm summer day in suburban America. The dress and hairstyles of the children indicate that the photograph was taken sometime in the middle decades of the twentieth century. The leader's name and the album title appear in an uneven scrawl in the upper-right quadrant of the cover. We read in the credits that Monica Frisell, the guitarist's daughter, hand lettered the cover titles. [49]

Three other black-and-white photographs enhance the booklet. One shows a stationary railroad car; a second, by depression-era photographer Walker Evans, offers a tiny view of a mining town with power lines sweeping across the top edge. The remaining photo presents Frisell and his band. All of these images depict a decidedly less opulent setting than Marsalis's jazz "intimacy." In Frisell's group photo, for instance, all five musicians sit for the camera in a makeshift photo studio; they appear relaxed, smiling. The band members have dressed casually: Don Byron (the only African American here) in shorts and Dr. Martens shoes, Joey Baron with shaved head and Birkenstock sandals, Guy Klucevsek looking faintly like an eighth-grade science teacher (except for his high-top sneakers). The leader stands above the band in a denim shirt and patterned vest.

Figure 8. Album cover, *Have a Little Faith,* Bill Frisell. Copyright © 1993 Nonesuch Records. All rights reserved. Used by permission.

Have a Little Faith as Jazz Narrative

We've seen that jazz as Marsalis's album presents it implies sophistication and elegance (not to mention wealth: it takes a lot of money to own a house such as the one he and his companion share on the album cover. For that matter, it takes a fair amount of cash just to buy one of his fine Italian suits). By contrast, all aspects of *Have a Little Faith* contribute to a distinctly vernacular image of jazz. Indeed, the members of Frisell's band don't even look like jazz musicians, at least not the kind of hip, sharply dressed "cats" that Marsalis and Madison Avenue have set as the standard for jazzness.

Yet not only the images convey this impression of unsophistication (antisophistication?); the performances do as well. The guitarist's music certainly doesn't swing in the conventional smooth sense, and with its unusual instrumentation the group doesn't even replicate the timbre traditionally associated with jazz. In the end, the exuberance Frisell's band displays on cuts such as "I Can't Be Satisfied" and "No Moe" or the "falling down the stairs" feeling of the drum entrance in "Little Jenny Dow" seems almost diametrically opposed to the Marsalis group's dignified approach to their material. Even Marsalis's idea of a "Bourbon Street Parade" in New Orleans feels more sedate than Frisell's rollicking "Washington Post March."

If *Standard Time* piously celebrates the rich African-American heritage of the jazz past, *Have a Little Faith* seems less reverent, instead casting an optimistic and at times whimsical view of the present and future. The concept of "faith" mentioned in the album's title suggests an anticipation that "things will work out," that one can look forward with confidence (the words "faith" and "confidence" are both rooted in the Latin *fidere*, to trust). At the very least, the inclusion of "Just Like a Woman," "Live to Tell," and "Have a Little Faith in Me" suggest that jazz musicians might not merely recall great sounds from the first half of this century. They may also reflect sounds from "our own time" as well, which is what jazz musicians had been doing since the music's earliest days. At the same time, "electric" versions of Stephen Foster and John Philip Sousa compositions presented alongside clarinet and accordion renditions of Muddy Waters and Sonny Rollins also display an equivocal, occasionally mischievous view of "the tradition."

Even when drawing on the most recent popular songs and using the latest electronic technology, the album expresses a Frank Capra-esque, "aw shucks" sincerity. As with Capra's depression-era films, jazz in the bucolic, wide open spaces of *Have a Little Faith* does not necessarily memorialize heroic individuals from its past. Instead, it seems to extol a broadly defined, and apparently still breathing American Everyman (recall that Frisell once composed and performed incidental music for the films of comedian Buster Keaton, another "simple" American figure). While the album does not explicitly proclaim an affiliation with popular (populist?) music, neither does it cover up its very deep pop roots.

To understand *Standard Time* and *Have a Little Faith* as contested jazz identities, we should recognize that although Frisell recorded only one generally acknowledged standard (Victor Young's "When I Fall in Love"), he and his band treated their disparate repertoire as standards. "Standards," in this sense, include not only those tunes from the Tin Pan Alley era or even "jazz tunes" that have passed into common use but an entire body of shared American musics: blues tunes, concert works, band pieces. Just as Jelly Roll Morton and the other early New Orleans innovators jazzed all of the musics around them, so too do Frisell and his band. In this sense he narrates jazz not as a collection of names, places, and sounds from the past but as an activity, a verb; these musicians jazz their material.

Yet while Frisell's "faith" points to the possibility of a multivoiced future for American culture, African Americans and other groups who have been excluded—often systematically so—from the histories told in this country may approach *Have a Little Faith* with skepticism. Does this album succeed in mediating the diverse styles, cultures, and eras in American musical history to configure an inclusive narrative of jazz? Or does this, instead, present a naive and ineffectual "We Are the World" type of wishful thinking or, still worse, another whitewashing of the genre such as those circulated in the first half of this century?

CONCLUSIONS: TRADITIONING

Hans-Georg Gadamer has written that "tradition is not simply a permanent precondition; rather we produce it ourselves inasmuch as we understand, participate in the evolution of tradition, and hence further determine it ourselves."[50] We have explored two different models of contemporary jazz identity, but can we hold these musical and cultural texts together as a broadly conceived jazz tradition?

To begin, we should see and hear these musics as enabling new relationships among players and listeners, historical and contemporary, presenting differing visions of past, present, and future. Jazz stands as one of the twentieth century's earliest and most successful activities for bringing disparate racial and cultural groups together, engendering new identities along the way. Perhaps this proud aspect of these musics, more than anything else, explains why Frisell implores us to "have a little faith." Charles Keil has remarked, "Music is our last and best source of participatory consciousness, and it has this capacity not just to remodel but maybe to enact some ideal communities."[51] That jazz musicking has ventured outside the particularities of the cultures of its origins illustrates the tremendous strength of this genre, as people the world over continue to participate in it.

I do not mean to suggest that jazz functions as a *lingua franca,* that everyone everywhere understands these various musics in the same way. I propose, in fact, quite the opposite. As we've seen, jazz both reflects and offers very different worlds, cultural as well as musical. Musicians continually appropriate, modify, or reject aspects of previous styles in an effort to create a work that says something about and to their listening audience. To be sure, how we understand jazz implies a lineage to a cultural past. However, it is not only the past that is at issue. This is the implication of my term "traditioning" in the section heading: How we understand the legacy of the music's forebears depends on the ways in which present-day musicians draw on and recontextualize those earlier styles. As Gadamer suggested, tradition is not an artifact left from the past—a listing of previous players and styles—but a continuously shifting enactment of what and who counts, for whom, and why. In this way, each of these albums—indeed each of the musicians and musics discussed throughout the preceding chapters—present only one way of understanding and presenting jazz, not *the* way. In a sense, multiple jazz traditions are—and always have been—"the tradition."

If jazz holds any hopes of remaining a significant ground of social and cultural renewal in this country or anywhere else, musicians, listeners, teachers, scholars, and critics must remain open to the possibility of still newer jazz identities. Ultimately, jazz traditioning begins anew every time someone picks up an instrument, puts on a record, or walks into a club. It was that way with Jelly Roll Morton and Sidney Bechet; it remains that way nearly a century later. Despite the laments regarding miniscule record sales and the ever-present factional squabbling, if we allow ourselves to trust in our own musical creativity, there is no reason to fear that the twenty-first century won't bring equally vital—though undoubtedly different—jazz sounds, identities, and cultures.

NOTES

INTRODUCTION

1. See, for instance, Anne Shaw Faulkner's "Does Jazz Put the Sin in Syncopation?" *Ladies Home Journal,* August 1921, 16, 34, or Charles Moore, "An Open Letter to Don Ellis," *Jazz,* December 1965. Also see Daniel Goldmark's insightful chapter on the gradual shift in perceptions of race and jazz as they played out in American cartoons, "'Jungle Jive': The Animated Representation of Jazz Music and Swing Culture," in "Happy Harmonies: Music in Hollywood Animated Shorts, 1928–1960" (Ph.D. diss., University of California, Los Angeles, 2001).

2. Paul Gilroy, *The Black Atlantic: Modernity and Double Consciousness* (Cambridge, Mass.: Harvard University Press, 1993), 102.

3. Evan Eisenberg, *The Recording Angel: The Experience of Music from Aristotle to Zappa* (New York: Penguin, 1987), 144.

4. Joseph Kerman, *Contemplating Music: Challenges to Musicology* (Cambridge, Mass.: Harvard University Press, 1985), 20.

5. See Harold Bloom, *The Anxiety of Influence* (New York: Oxford University Press, 1973), and John Murphy, "Jazz Improvisation: The Joy of Influence," *Black Perspective in Music* 18, nos. 1–2 (1990): 7–19. I have more to say on Bloom-inspired music scholarship in the final chapter.

6. Scott DeVeaux, *The Birth of Bebop* (Berkeley: University of California Press, 1997), 3.

7. Women have played jazz since the genre's earliest days, but there can be little question that—as in so many other domains—women have been pushed to

the margins of this music and the historical narratives of it. While the identities presented in this study reflect the male-centricity of various jazz worlds, I do discuss the differing models of masculinity constructed and contested within them. My future work will include an exploration of female jazz singers and the conflicted attitudes toward them by audiences, critics, and instrumentalists.

CHAPTER ONE

1. Gwendolyn Midlo Hall, "The Formation of Afro-Creole Culture," in Arnold R. Hirsch and Joseph Logsdon, eds., *Creole New Orleans: Race and Americanization* (Baton Rouge: Louisiana State University Press, 1992), 59.

2. The term "Creole" has a long and complex history, having been employed by a variety of cultural groups to describe an even broader array of groups. In this case, "Creole," "Creole of color," and *gens du couleur* are synonymous and designate the mixing of African with French or Spanish cultures in New Orleans. For a discussion of the evolution of the term in that city, see Hall, "Formation of Afro-Creole Culture."

3. George "Pops" Foster (as told to Tom Stoddard), *Pops Foster: The Autobiography of a New Orleans Jazzman* (Berkeley: University of California Press, 1971), 64.

4. For discussions of race and jazz, see Norman Mailer, "The White Negro: Superficial Reflections on the Hipster," *Dissent* 4, no. 3 (1957): 276–93; Neil Leonard, *Jazz and the White Americans* (Chicago: University of Chicago Press, 1962); LeRoi Jones (Amiri Baraka), *Blues People* (New York: William Morrow, 1963); Burton W. Peretti, *The Creation of Jazz: Music, Race, and Culture in Urban America* (Urbana: University of Illinois Press, 1992); James Lincoln Collier, *Jazz: The American Theme Song* (New York: Oxford University Press, 1993); Charles Keil and Steven Feld, *Music Grooves* (Chicago: University of Chicago Press, 1994); Gene Lees, *Cats of Any Color: Jazz Black and White* (New York: Oxford University Press, 1994); Ingrid Monson, "The Problem with White Hipness: Race, Gender, and Cultural Conceptions in Jazz Historical Discourse," *Journal of the American Musicological Society* 48 (1995): 396–422, as well as her chapter "Ethnomusicology, Interaction, and Poststructuralism," in *Saying Something: Jazz Improvisation and Interaction* (Chicago: University of Chicago Press, 1996), 192–215; Scott DeVeaux, "What Did We Do to Be So Black and Blue," *Musical Quarterly* 80 (1996): 392–430; and Richard Sudhalter, *Lost Chords: White Musicians and Their Contributions to Jazz, 1915–1945* (New York: Oxford University Press, 1999).

5. Charles Hamm, *Music in the New World* (New York: W. W. Norton, 1983), 507. The André Hodier quotation is from *Jazz: Its Evolution and Essence* (New York: Grove Press, 1956), 7.

6. Hamm, *Music,* 508.

7. Eileen Southern, *The Music of Black Americans* (New York: W. W. Norton, 1983), 376.

8. For a historical sampling of reactions to early jazz, see Robert Walser, ed., *Keeping Time: Readings in Jazz History* (New York: Oxford University Press, 1998).

9. See Collier, *Jazz,* 183–202.

10. Monson, *Saying Something,* 203.

11. See Rudi Blesh, *Shining Trumpets,* 2d ed. (New York: Knopf, 1958); Frederic Ramsey Jr. and Charles E. Smith, eds., *Jazzmen* (New York: Harcourt, Brace, 1939); Jack V. Buerkle and Danny Barker, *Bourbon Street Black: The New Orleans Black Jazzmen* (New York: Oxford University Press, 1973); William J. Schafer, *Brass Bands and New Orleans Jazz* (Baton Rouge: Louisiana State University Press, 1977); or Gunther Schuller, *Early Jazz: Its Roots and Musical Development* (New York: Oxford University Press, 1983). For discussions on problems with some jazz-origin theories, see Henry Kmen's "The Roots of Jazz and the Dance in Place Congo: A Reappraisal," in *Yearbook for Inter-American Musical Research* 8 (1972): 5–16; Donald M. Marquis's *In Search of Buddy Bolden: First Man of Jazz* (Baton Rouge: Louisiana State University Press, 1978); Burton Peretti's *The Creation of Jazz: Music, Race, and Culture in America* (Urbana: University of Illinois Press, 1992); or Lawrence Gushee's notes to the 1977 New World Records *Anthology of American Music* album (Volume 269), *Steppin' on the Gas: Rags to Jazz 1913–1927,* as well as his "The Nineteenth-Century Origins of Jazz," *Black Music Research Journal* 14, No. 1 (Spring 1994): 1–24, and "How the Creole Band Came to Be," *Black Music Research Journal* 8, no. 1 (1988): 83–100.

12. See Bruce Raeburn, "Jewish Jazzmen in New Orleans, 1890–1940: An Overview," *Jazz Archivist* 12 (1997): 1–12. Also see George Lipsitz's important study on the construction and maintenance of the "white" category, *The Possessive Investment in Whiteness: How White People Profit from Identity Politics* (Philadelphia: Temple University Press, 1998).

13. Joseph Roach, "Body of Law: The Sun King and the Code Noir," in Sara E. Melzer and Kathryn Norberg, eds., *From the Royal to the Republican Body: Incorporating the Political in Seventeenth- and Eighteenth-Century France* (Berkeley: University of California Press, 1998), 120. Also see Joseph Roach, *Cities of the Dead: Circum-Atlantic Performance* (New York: Columbia University Press, 1996).

14. St. Domingue (Santo Domingo) is now called Hispaniola and contains the countries of Haiti and the Dominican Republic.

15. Jones, *Blues People,* 72. Congo Square (a.k.a. *Place Congo, Place du Cirque,* and, eventually, Beauregard Square) was a market, meeting, and dancing place for slaves and free blacks during the first three quarters of the nineteenth century. Though that square has since become mythologized as the musical "primordial soup" from which jazz emerged, scholars differ on the degree to

which even the earliest jazz-oriented musicians could have been influenced directly by activities there. See, in particular, Kmen's "Roots of Jazz," 5–16.

16. See the contributions by Hall, Tregel, Logsdon and Bell, and Hirsch in Hirsch and Logsdon, eds., *Creole New Orleans,* or Arthé Agnes Anthony's outstanding "The Negro Creole Community in New Orleans, 1880–1920: An Oral History" (Ph.D. diss., University of California, Irvine, 1978). Physical characteristics did play a role; but hair, its texture and color, seems to have been almost as important as skin tone in these matters. Also see James Haskins, *The Creoles of Color of New Orleans* (New York: Thomas Y. Crowell Company, 1975), 73–74.

17. Johnny St. Cyr, quoted in Alan Lomax, *Mister Jelly Roll* (New York: Pantheon, 1993), 99.

18. Anthony, *Negro Creole Community,* 55, 57.

19. The designations "uptown" and "downtown" do not apply as literally in New Orleans as they do in, say, New York City. Canal Street runs on a diagonal, and "crosstown" would be just as descriptive of that city's geography.

20. Opera exerted an enormous influence on nineteenth-century musical life throughout New Orleans, and that city holds the distinction of producing the first opera company in North America. As Henry Kmen and others have commented, audiences regarded New Orleans' opera productions as the highest quality on this continent, challenging all but the brightest in Europe. For an overview of prejazz musical life in New Orleans, see Kmen's "The Music of New Orleans," in Hodding Carter, ed., *The Past as Prelude: New Orleans 1718–1968* (New Orleans: Tulane University Press, 1968).

21. Dominguez is referring to Storyville, the former red-light section of New Orleans, known to most players as the "District."

22. Paul Dominguez, quoted in Lomax, *Mister Jelly Roll,* 102–6, emphasis in original.

23. Ibid., 99. Ferdinand "Jelly Roll" Morton's original last name has appeared in jazz histories under various guises, including LeMenthe, Lamothe, Lemott, and Lamott. A copy of "a true extract from the Baptismal Register" of St. Joseph's Church in New Orleans is on file at the William Ransom Hogan Jazz Archive at Tulane University. This document clearly records Morton as Ferdinand Joseph Lemott (born October 20, 1890, baptized April 25, 1891). Historians Lewis Porter and Michael Ullman argue—following Lawrence Gushee—that Morton was born Ferdinand Lamothe, suggesting that Morton claimed his name as La Menthe to sound "more impressively French and that Lemott on family records was "probably phonetic" (*Jazz: From Its Origins to the Present* [Englewood Cliffs, N.J.: Prentice Hall, 1993], 36).

24. The remarkable range of Morton's playing is evident on his 1938 Library of Congress recordings. These have been issued on four compact discs by Rounder Records (Rounder CD 1091–94); all are highly recommended.

25. Jelly Roll Morton, quoted in Lomax, *Mister Jelly Roll,* 82. Lomax's misspellings

of the operas and their excerpts have been corrected. Morton's jazz version of "Miserere" can be heard on volume 1 of the aforementioned Rounder series.

26. Women were largely barred from society marching bands (if not always from that informal group of dancers, noisemakers, and revelers that followed behind, known as "the second line") as well as many of these other venues. The few females who did play outside of their own parlors generally performed as pianists and/or singers, often in brothels, and some worked as prostitutes as well as musicians. Despite significant obstacles, women did contribute to the New Orleans scene. Louis Armstrong cites as formidable players pianists Wilhelmina Bart Wynn and Edna Francis (see Louis Armstrong, *Satchmo: My Life in New Orleans* [New York: Da Capo Press, 1986 (1954)], 216); and Jelly Roll Morton claims to have been drawn to the blues through Mamie Desdoumes (see Lomax, *Mister Jelly Roll*, 25). That Crescent City women participated as more than singers and pianists (though perhaps not always in the same circles as the musicians we now regard as jazz players) is demonstrated in a city park "ragtime" concert program from 1911. The program announced that a Mademoiselle S. Berendson—nicknamed "Miss Trombone"—performed both a "comic trombone solo" and a duet with her brother, "Teddy Trombone" (program reprinted in William J. Schafer, *Brass Bands and New Orleans Jazz* [Baton Rouge: Louisiana State University Press, 1977], 19). We should note too that some New Orleans musicians—Sidney Bechet among them—used the terms "ragtime" and "jazz" interchangeably. Jelly Roll Morton usually differentiated between the two.

27. Peretti, *Creation of Jazz*, 29–30. His figures derive from John W. Blassingame, *Black New Orleans, 1860–1880* (Chicago: University of Chicago Press, 1973).

28. John Chilton, *Sidney Bechet: The Wizard of Jazz* (New York: Da Capo, 1996), 16.

29. Johnny St. Cyr, "Jazz as I Remember it. Part One: Early Days," source unknown, 7. In "Johnny St. Cyr" file, Institute for Jazz Studies, Rutgers University, Newark, New Jersey.

30. Antony, *Negro Creole Community*, 71.

31. Chilton, *Sidney Bechet*, 16. Bechet's older brother, Leonard, followed Creole conventions more closely. Though a music lover and performer, Leonard eventually became a respected dentist.

32. From a radio interview conducted by Gabriel Heater, October 31, 1939. Transcript edited November 11, 1970 by Richard B. Allen. Tapes and transcripts now housed at the William Ransom Hogan Jazz Archive of Tulane University, New Orleans.

33. In Lomax, *Mister Jelly Roll*, 31–32.

34. Peretti, *Creation of Jazz*, 29.

35. Scott DeVeaux, *The Birth of Bebop: A Social and Musical History* (Berkeley: University of California Press, 1997), 46.

36. The dubious aura surrounding the professional jazz musician has diminished

somewhat (due, in large part, to the efforts of educators including Billy Taylor and Wynton Marsalis and, perhaps most decisively, by college-level jazz programs). Still, the notion that the musician's life, particularly outside of classical circles, is an unhealthy and difficult one still holds for most middle-class American families. It certainly did in mine when I announced in the late 1970s that I was going to pursue a career as a jazz musician. All were supportive but skeptical, and obviously concerned for my well-being. "All right," my father suggested, "but please go to a university, get a well-rounded education and a degree so that you'll always have something to fall back on in case this music thing doesn't work out." Given the current competitive market for musicologists in academia, it seems somewhat ironic that my performing skills are what I have to fall back on in the event that this "musicology thing" doesn't work out.

37. There is even a street named for Bechet in Paris and a square dedicated to him in Antibes. Four hundred guests attended his 1951 wedding in Cannes, with the American vice consul, the town's mayor, and the well-known French actress Mistinguett acting as witnesses. Similarly, his funeral (May 19, 1959) was accorded semi-State honors, with 3,000 people congregating to pay their respects outside the church of Saint Louis in Garches. Ironically, Bechet's estranged wife, Elisabeth (née Ziegler), barred the playing of jazz at the clarinetist's funeral, claiming that "it wouldn't be dignified to have jazz music" at such a solemn occasion. It hardly needs mentioning that Ms. Bechet was *not* a New Orleans native.

38. For Chilton's discussion of historical inconsistencies, see his *Sidney Bechet,* 290–93. That all facts don't always line up in Bechet's story is a "problem" that all oral histories share. But the realization that not everything related by an interviewee is historically correct does not render their memoirs worthless. What people choose to "remember" (or, indeed, "forget") can tell us a great deal about the values of a given time and place—including our own. We must also consider the role played by editors here: unless we hear Bechet's dictation for ourselves, we have to trust that his words were transcribed faithfully by the book's editors, Desmond Flower, John Ciardi, and Joan Williams. In fact, letters from both Ciardi and Flower housed in the William Ransom Hogan Jazz Archive at Tulane University suggest that Williams (whom the other editors refer to as "a girl just out of college" and "a girl who knew nothing about jazz") interjected a great deal of rather florid prose between Bechet's commentary. Both Ciardi and Flower worked to remove traces of her additions. How much of Bechet's own words remain is unknown. The only tapes extant are those covering his later years (comprising the last chapters of the book); these were recorded when all parties concerned were aware of Bechet's impending passing.

39. Porter and Ullman, *Jazz,* 47. In contrast to Bechet, a recent example of a highly accomplished musician who was sensitive about his inability to read music is heavy-metal guitarist George Lynch. But, as Robert Walser has noted,

Lynch's embarrassment at what he perceives to be his own failing reveals more about the aesthetics and attitudes of the musical culture of which he is a part than of Lynch's ability to play convincingly within that tradition. See Walser's *Running with the Devil: Power, Gender, and Madness in Heavy Metal Music* (Hanover, N.H.: Wesleyan University Press, 1993), 93.

40. Nat Shapiro and Nat Hentoff, eds., *Hear Me Talkin' to Ya* (New York: Rinehart and Company, 1955), 26.

41. Louis Armstrong, the representative par excellence of the Uptown "school" of New Orleans players, did learn to read music—though relatively late in his career—believing that a "good" musician should possess that skill. Was this due to professional necessity or due to perceptions stemming from his increasing interaction with Downtown and European-American players, or a mixture of both?

42. Bechet, *Treat It Gentle,* 45.

43. Ibid., 194.

44. Bechet, quoted in Chilton, *Sidney Bechet,* 284.

45. Bob Wilber, *Music Was Not Enough* (New York: Oxford University Press, 1988), 48. Wilber's comments refer to Theodore Gilmore Bilbo (1877–1947). Bilbo, who served as a state governor and Democratic U.S. Senator from Mississippi (1935–47), called for the deportation of all black Americans to Africa. In 1947 he was barred from a third term in the Senate and charged with voter intimidation and acceptance of bribes.

46. Jelly Roll Morton, quoted in Lomax, *Mister Jelly Roll,* 3.

47. ["Told to RBA at the Mardi Gras Lounge when Lizzie was playing there, . . . in the early 1950s. . . . RBA: saf 8/20/65.]" From a letter in the "Jelly Roll Morton" vertical file, William Ransom Hogan Jazz Archive, Tulane University.

48. Bechet, *Treat It Gentle,* 79 (emphasis in the original). Again, note the use of the term "ragtime" to denote the music we now call "jazz." Bechet also preferred "musicianer" to "musician."

49. Richard Hadlock, "Sidney Bechet: How to Live Music," *San Francisco Examiner,* January 17, 1965, 16.

50. The quotation is from "one wandering singer" cited by Nat Hentoff in *The Jazz Life* (New York: Da Capo, 1975), 140.

51. George Lipsitz has traced the powerful impact of that master bluesman Jimi Hendrix on the music and philosophies of the socially conscious black-Haitian band Boukman Eksperyans (see Lipsitz, *Dangerous Crossroads: Popular Music, Postmodernism, and the Poetics of Place* [New York: Verso, 1994]). That the power of the blues to speak for the ostracized goes beyond racial boundaries can be witnessed in some of the first wave of 1960s' British Invasion musicians—most noticeably Eric Burden. As the sons of working-class poor, Burden and others felt a kinship with Chess Records' more "raw" recording artists, such as Howlin' Wolf and Muddy Waters.

52. In Dwight Andrews, "From Black to Blues," in Richard J. Powell, ed., *The*

Blues Aesthetic: Black Culture and Modernism (Washington, D.C.: Washington Project for the Arts, 1989), 38.

53. Jimmie Rodgers himself represents something of a genre-purist's nightmare. Though Rodgers stands as one of the founding fathers of country music, his style incorporated as many elements of jazz and blues as it did "hillbilly" traits.

54. In his *Stomping the Blues* (New York: Da Capo, 1976), Albert Murray suggests that "blues musician" and "jazz musician" are synonymous. There are many instances in which he'd get no argument from me. However, a great number of fans, critics, record company executives, and musicians would take umbrage at conflating these terms, a phenomenon reflected in and configured by the wide diversity of identities, and a point I address more directly in the next chapter.

55. Bechet, *Treat It Gentle,* 107. This beautiful line echoes Bechet's remark from page 46 of the same book that "the music—it's any damn thing; it's whatever it is you need."

56. Ibid., 209.

57. "Blue Horizon" can be heard on *The Best of Sidney Bechet* (Blue Note CDP 7243 8 2889120), as well as on *The Smithsonian Collection of Classic Jazz.*

58. Richard Hadlock, "Sidney Bechet: How to Live Music," *San Francisco Examiner,* January 17, 1965, 16.

59. "A feature of jazz that seems uniquely African is its penchant for altering sounds to produce roughenings, buzzes, and ringings" (Mark Gridley and Wallace Rave, "Toward Identification of African Traits in Early Jazz," *Black Perspective in Music* 12, no. 1 [Spring 1984]: 51).

60. Frank Tirro's claim that Bechet's "style and sound were highly personal and seemed to have inspired few followers" (in *Jazz: A History,* 2d ed. [New York: W. W. Norton, 1993], 147) appears somewhat dubious when one considers Bechet's considerable influence on Hodges. Hodges's propensity to "scoop" into a note borrows unquestionably from Bechet's approach, and, as Hodges was among the most imitated saxophonists of the pre-bop period, Bechet's style can certainly be said to have inspired a great many others. Even discounting this influence, pioneers Johnny Dodds and Jimmy Noone, among others, as well as "revivalists" including Bob Wilber, have expressed their indebtedness. (See Bechet, *Treat It Gentle,* 94.)

61. DeVeaux, *Birth of Bebop,* 346.

62. Bechet, *Treat It Gentle,* 95.

63. The pseudo gospel and blues gestures found on many of the "hard bop" recordings of the 1950s and 1960s rarely delved as deeply or as unselfconsciously into those "roots" as their songs' titles (i.e., "Moanin'," "The Preacher") suggested.

64. I explore more fully the topic of note choice and phrasing in the chapter entitled "Jazz 'Traning."

65. Bechet, *Treat It Gentle,* 141.

66. Lewis Porter and Michael Ullman, "Sidney Bechet and His Long Song," *Black Perspective in Music* 16, no. 2 (Fall 1998): 148.

67. "Texas Moaner Blues" was originally released on OKeh 8171; it is now available on *Wild Cat Blues: The Essential Sidney Bechet* (Volume 1: 1923–1937) (Music Memoria 879792, 1989), and on Louis Armstrong, *Portrait of the Artist as a Young Man, 1923–1934* (Columbia 57176, 1994). "Old Stack O'Lee Blues" has been rereleased on *The Best of Sidney Bechet* (Blue Note CDP 7243 8 28891 20, 1994).

68. These can be heard on volume 10 of the Media 7 (France) series, *Sidney Bechet: Complete Edition, 1941* (MJCD 127, 1997).

69. Bechet, *Treat It Gentle,* 176.

70. Ralph Ellison, "The Charlie Christian Story," in *Shadow and Act* (New York: Vintage Books, 1972), 234 (article originally published in *Saturday Review,* May 17, 1958).

71. For an outstanding account of the rise of the jazz soloist in the 1930s and 1940s, see, again, Scott DeVeaux's *Birth of Bebop.*

72. Monson, *Saying Something,* 177.

73. Keith Jarrett's recent challenge of Wynton Marsalis to a "blues duel" is only one such example. See Andrew Solomon, "The Jazz Martyr," *New York Times Magazine* (February 9, 1997), 35. I'm not sure a "winner" could ever be decided in that particular battle; though both are exceptional improvisers, neither has recorded any blues that comes close to the powerful work of the players I've mentioned above.

74. For more on bebop as subculture, see Eric Lott's "Double V, Double-Time: Bebop's Politics of Style," in Krin Gabbard, ed., *Jazz among the Discourses* (Durham, N.C.: Duke University Press, 1995), or Scott DeVeaux's definitive study, *Birth of Bebop,* as well as my chapter on Ornette Coleman in this volume.

75. Norman Mailer, "The White Negro: Superficial Reflections on the Hipster," *Dissent* 4, no. 3 (1957): 279.

76. Bechet, *Treat It Gentle,* 4.

77. Ellington, *Music Is My Mistress* (New York: Da Capo, 1976), 47.

78. Bernard Gendron, "'Moldy Figs' and Modernists: Jazz at War (1942–1946)," in Gabbard, ed., *Jazz among the Discourses,* 39.

79. Murray, *Stomping the Blues,* 87.

80. Bechet, *Treat It Gentle,* 204–5.

81. This situation was echoed more recently by pianist Herbie Hancock when he remarked that "look, I didn't start off playing jazz. I hated jazz when I first heard it. It sounded like noise to me. . . . I was a classical player, so I had to learn jazz the way any classical player would. When it came to learning what one feels and hears as soulful nuances in the music, I actually had to learn that technically" (quoted in Rafi Zabor and Vic Gabarini, "Wynton vs. Herbie:

The Purist and the Crossbreeder Duke It Out," *Musician* 77 [1985]: 52–64; reprinted in Walser, ed., *Keeping Time,* 339–51).

82. Jones, *Blues People,* 154.

83. Mary Gehman, *The Free People of Color of New Orleans: An Introduction* (New Orleans: Margaret Media Inc., 1996), 103. I worked for a time with one Creole jazz singer from New Orleans who echoed Gehman's assessments when she told me, "It's not 'official' anymore and it's not something that gets talked about much; it's just something about the way people might talk, or the way they look, or their last name." I asked her if there was still a sense of cultural hierarchy surrounding Creole identity in New Orleans. She responded "yes" immediately (from a telephone interview, June 29, 1998).

84. Sieglinde Lemke, *Primitivist Modernism: Black Culture and the Origins of Transatlantic Modernism* (New York: Oxford University Press, 1998), 41.

CHAPTER TWO

1. Nelson George, *The Death of Rhythm and Blues* (New York: Pantheon Books, 1988); Reebee Garofalo, *Rockin' Out: Popular Music in the USA* (Boston: Allyn and Bacon, 1997); George Lipsitz, *Class and Culture in Cold War America: "A Rainbow at Midnight"* (South Hadley, Mass.: Bergen and Garvey, 1982); and Arnold Shaw, *Honkers and Shouters: The Golden Years of Rhythm and Blues* (New York: Collier Books, 1978).

2. Ted Gioia, *The History of Jazz* (New York: Oxford University Press, 1998); Mark Gridley, *Jazz Styles: History and Analysis,* 7th ed. (Upper Saddle River, N.J.: Prentice Hall, 2000); Lewis Porter and Michael Ullman, *Jazz: From Its Origins to the Present* (Englewood Cliffs, N.J.: Prentice Hall, 1993); Frank Tirro, *Jazz: A History,* 2d ed. (New York: W. W. Norton, 1993); Martin Williams, ed., *The Smithsonian Collection of Classic Jazz,* rev. ed. (Washington, D.C.: Smithsonian Collection of Recordings, 1987).

3. Jonathan Buckley, ed., *Classical Music on CD: The Rough Guide* (New York: The Rough Guides, 1995), 366.

4. For more on the development of cultural hierarchy in and through European art music, see William Weber, "Mass Culture and the Reshaping of European Musical Taste, 1770–1870," *International Review of the Aesthetics and Sociology of Music* 8 (1977): 5–22; Lawrence W. Levine, *Highbrow/Lowbrow: The Emergence of Cultural Hierarchy in America* (Cambridge, Mass.: Harvard University Press, 1988); and Joseph Horowitz, "Sermons in Tones: Sacralization as a Theme in American Classical Music," *American Music* 16 (1998): 311–40.

5. Not everyone concedes that classical music still reigns supreme in terms of prestige. See, for example, Robert Fink, "Elvis Everywhere: Musicology and Popular Music Studies at the Twilight of the Canon," *American Music* 16 (1998): 135–79.

6. United States House of Representatives Bill H7825–27 passed September 23,

1987. For a reprint of the bill, as well as a discussion of the cultural debates and implications surrounding its passage, see Robert Walser, ed., *Keeping Time: Readings in Jazz History* (New York: Oxford University Press, 1999), 332–33.

7. Mark Gridley, "Is Jazz Popular Music?" *The Instrumentalist,* March 1987, 19–22, 26, 85 (my emphasis).

8. Joel Whitburn, *Pop Memories 1890–1954: The History of American Popular Music* (Menomonee Falls, Wisc.: Record Research Inc., 1986), 242–43.

9. For more on the centrality of riffs in Afro-diasporic musics, see Ingrid Monson's "Riffs, Repetition, and Theories of Globalization," *Ethnomusicology* 43 (1999): 31–65.

10. Dud Bascomb, quoted in Stanley Dance, *The World of Swing,* vol. 1 (New York: Charles Scribner's Sons, 1974), 199.

11. Benny Bailey, quoted in Ira Gitler, *Swing to Bop: An Oral History of the Transition in Jazz in the 1940s* (New York: Oxford University Press, 1985), 162.

12. Gridley, *Jazz Styles,* 9–10.

13. See Lawrence Levine, "Jazz and American Culture," *Journal of American Folklore* 102 (1989): 6–22, as well as his previously cited *Highbrow/Lowbrow.*

14. Nick Tosches, "The Hep Cosmogony: Louis Jordan, Forefather of Rock 'n' Roll," *Village Voice,* August 18, 1992, 65, 68.

15. Hughes Panassie and Madeline Gautier, *Guide to Jazz,* trans. Desmond Flower (Boston: Houghton Mifflin Company, 1956), 38.

16. As Ralph Ellison showed in his brilliant short story about a crashed African-American training pilot during World War II, musicians were not the only Northern blacks to dismiss their Southern cousins as yokels. See Ellison's "Flying Home," in Barbara Perkins and George Perkins, eds., *Kaleidoscope: Stories of the American Experience* (New York: Oxford University Press, 1993), 485–99.

17. This phenomenon persists in large measure to this day, whether in the blues, rock, or jazz worlds.

18. Count Basie, *Good Morning Blues: The Autobiography of Count Basie as Told to Albert Murray* (New York: Primus, 1985), 7–8.

19. Francis Davis, *The History of the Blues: The Roots, the Music, the People from Charley Patton to Robert Cray* (New York: Hyperion, 1995); Johnny Otis, *Upside Your Head!: Rhythm and Blues on Central Avenue* (Hanover, N.H.: Wesleyan University Press, 1993). The 1999 boxed set from Rhino Records, *Central Avenue Sounds: Jazz in Los Angeles (1921–1956),* takes a similarly inclusive position. The collection's editors program recordings by Art Tatum, Charles Mingus, and Wardell Gray alongside those by Percy Mayfield, Joe Liggins, and Charles Brown.

20. Grover Sales, *Jazz: America's Classical Music* (Englewood Cliffs, N.J.: Prentice-Hall, 1984), 154.

21. Ibid., 115.

22. Count Basie, quoted in Ernest Tidyman, "Daily Closeup: Count Basie," *New York Post,* October 24, 1958, 26.

23. Composed by Demetruis and Williams. Louis Jordan version issued November 1942 as Decca single #8645. Now available on *Just Say Moe!: Mo' of the Best of Louis Jordan* (Rhino R2 7114, 1992).

24. See Krin Gabbard, *Jammin' at the Margins: Jazz and the American Cinema* (Chicago: University of Chicago Press, 1996), and Daniel Goldmark, "'Jungle Jive': The Animated Representation of Jazz Music and Swing Culture," in "Happy Harmonies: Music in Hollywood Animated Shorts, 1928–1960" (Ph.D. diss., University of California, Los Angeles, 2001). A chapter in George Lipsitz's *Class and Culture in Cold War America* reveals a subversive element underpinning "Ain't Nobody Here but Us Chickens," another of Jordan's hits featuring a seemingly simple character. I find it much more difficult to make such a case for "Mop! Mop!" "Saltpork," and some of the other Jordan tunes. I do recognize, however, that my position as a white male at the start of the twenty-first century may make such "signifyin'" invisible to me. My thanks for raising this issue to Robert O'Meally, Aaron Fox, and the other respondents at Columbia University.

25. "Readers' Poll," *Down Beat,* January 1, 1946, 16.

26. Scott DeVeaux, "Constructing the Jazz Tradition: Jazz Historiography," *Black American Literature Forum* 25 (1991): 544.

27. Gitler, *Swing to Bop,* 6.

28. See *Esquire,* January 1959. For a video account of the making of that legendary photograph, see Jean Bach, *A Great Day in Harlem: A Historic Gathering of Jazz Greats* (ABC Video 41110, 1995).

CHAPTER THREE

1. For discussions of this earlier confrontation, see Bernard Gendron, "'Moldy Figs' and Modernists: Jazz at War (1942–1946)," in Krin Gabbard, ed., *Jazz among the Discourses* (Durham, N.C.: Duke University Press, 1995), or Leonard Feather's memoirs of the period, *The Jazz Years: Earwitness to an Era* (New York: Da Capo, 1987). I've capitalized the word "Swing" in order to differentiate that period of jazz history from "swing," the rhythmic concept.

2. John Litweiler, *Ornette Coleman: A Harmolodic Life* (New York: Morrow, 1992), 82–83.

3. John Lewis, quoted in Martin Williams's liner notes to Ornette Coleman's *The Shape of Jazz to Come* (Atlantic Records 1317, 1959; reissued on Atlantic CD1317–2).

4. Frank Tirro, *Jazz: A History* (New York: W. W. Norton, 1993), 376.

5. Krin Gabbard, *Jammin' at the Margins: Jazz and the American Cinema* (Chicago: University of Chicago Press, 1996), 7.

6. Kaja Silverman, *Male Subjectivity at the Margins* (New York: Routledge, 1992), 53.

7. Eric Lott, "Double V, Double-Time: Bebop's Politics of Style," in Gabbard, ed., *Jazz among the Discourses*, 243–55.

8. Howard Zinn (*The Twentieth Century: A People's History* [New York: Harper Books, 1984], 121) characterized the situation in the 1940s:

> There seemed to be widespread indifference, even hostility, on the part of the Negro community to the war despite the attempts of Negro newspapers and Negro leaders to mobilize black sentiment. . . . A student at a Negro college told his teacher: "The Army Jim-crows us. The Navy lets us serve as messmen. The Red Cross refuses our blood. Employers and labor unions shut us out. Lynchings continue. We are disenfranchised, Jim-crowed, spat upon. What more could Hitler do than that?"

9. Lott, "Double V," 247.

10. In jazz terminology, to "cut" someone is to outplay another musician in an unofficial, onstage competition. The term derives, of course, from knife fighting, an arena in which one could "cut or be cut" quite literally.

11. Jelly Roll Morton, quoted in Alan Lomax, *Mister Jelly Roll* (New York: Pantheon, 1993), 7.

12. Nat Hentoff, liner notes for Dexter Gordon, *Our Man in Paris* (Blue Note CDP 7 46394 2, 1986 [originally 1963]).

13. Marvin Freeman, "Here's the Lowdown on 'Two Kinds of Women,'"*Down Beat*, February 1, 1941, 9. Reprinted in Robert Walser, ed., *Keeping Time: Readings in Jazz History* (New York: Oxford University Press, 1999), 119–20.

14. Ben Sidran, *Black Talk* (New York: Da Capo, 1981), 121.

15. Dizzy Gillespie and Charles Mingus stand as two important exceptions to the "junky cool" demeanor described above. We should recognize, however, that while both of these musicians were perceived as gregarious, they rarely engaged in behavior that could be seen as "Tomming," a charge frequently leveled against pre-bop jazz "entertainers," particularly Louis Armstrong (though Gillespie's antics did cause some concern at times). See Miles Davis's critique of Gillespie, in Miles Davis with Quincy Troupe, *Miles: The Autobiography of Miles Davis* (New York: Touchstone, 1989), 83, 163.

16. Arguments could be made for the "cool" school of the early 1950s as a precursor to Coleman's challenge. However, with the exception of Miles Davis (briefly) and John Lewis (permanently), that moment created little impact on the playing style of most bop-type players except, perhaps, to goad them toward a "harder" bop sound. Further, racial considerations enter here, as "cool" and "white" have long remained linked in jazz narratives, despite the participation of Davis, Lewis, and others. The question of race as it pertains to jazz gendering is discussed more fully near the end of this chapter.

17. Coleman recorded *Something Else! The Music of Ornette Coleman* (C3551, 1958) and *Tomorrow Is the Question* (M3569, 1959) for Contemporary.

18. Coleman plays "Klactoveedsedsteen" on *Live at the Hillcrest Club* (Inner City IC 1007; now out of print).

19. Coleman also paid homage to his musical forebear with song titles "Word from Bird" and "Bird Food."

20. LeRoi Jones (now Amiri Baraka), *Black Music* (New York: Morrow, 1968), 73.

21. This tune has been covered by, among others, Geri Allen, the Kronos Quartet, John Zorn, John Lewis, Branford Marsalis, and Lester Bowie. The inclusion of "Lonely Woman" in the *Smithsonian Collection of Classic Jazz*—by far the most widely distributed collection of its kind—contributed further to that tune's popularity.

22. To be sure, Coleman was not the first to offer such titles. Duke Ellington's "Sophisticated Lady" seems to present a similarly sympathetic stance (his *A Drum Is a Woman* and "The Clothed Woman" may present a different vision, however).

23. For perceptive discussions of the difficulty of notating this composition/performance, see Lynette Westendorf, "Analyzing Free Jazz" (Ph.D. diss., University of Washington, 1994), chap. 3, or, especially, Charles O. Hartman, *Jazz Text: Voice and Improvisation in Poetry, Jazz, and Song* (Princeton: Princeton University Press, 1991), chap. 3.

24. Martin Williams, *The Jazz Tradition,* 2d ed. (New York: Oxford University Press, 1993), 240.

25. Coleman's "vocal" style certainly influenced many of the "New Thing" musicians who emerged in his wake. His approach is particularly echoed in the works of Dewey Redman and Pharoah Sanders.

26. For insightful discussions of the connection between masculinity and the jazz trumpet, see Gabbard, *Jammin',* or his "Signifyin(g) the Phallus: *Mo' Better Blues* and Representations of the Jazz Trumpet," in *Representing Jazz* (Durham, N.C.: Duke University Press, 1995), 104–30. Gabbard is one of the first scholars to address at length the topic of gender representations in jazz. His important research canvasses a broad range of stylistic periods and an equally broad range of jazz media (recordings, of course, but also film, television commercials, and print). Ingrid Monson may be right to argue that Gabbard's "Freudian accented framework is too narrow to account for the enormous diversity of gender constructions in jazz" (see her review of Gabbard's *Representing Jazz* and *Jazz among the Discourses* in *American Music* 15 [1997]: 111). However, as Monson herself also points out, an understanding of the interrelationships of race, gender, and class remains vital to an understanding of jazz as a cultural activity, and Gabbard stands as one of the few to consider this interplay in any depth. Also relevant to the topic is Robert Walser's "'Out of Notes': Signification, Interpretation, and the Problem of Miles Davis," in Gabbard, ed., *Jazz among the Discourses,* 165–88, and Sherrie Tucker, "Nobody's Sweethearts: Gender, Race, and the Darlings of Rhythm," *American Music* 16 (1998): 255–88.

27. The term "s(t)imulate" was coined by Andrew Dell'Antonio in his article "The Sensual Sonata: Constructions of Desire in Early Baroque Instrumental Music," *Repercussions* 1 (1992): 52–83. His term conveys a sense of the simultaneous representation and enactment of meaning that take place in effective musical performances.

28. Quoted in Williams, *Jazz Tradition,* 242. On the one hand, I am aware that citing Martin Williams in a project such as this may surprise some readers: Williams remained, after all, quite formalistic in his commentaries on jazz and might have been skeptical about exploring gender representations in the genre. On the other hand, Martin Williams was one of the first writers to recognize Coleman's contributions; indeed, Williams stood as an early and active crusader on the saxophonist's behalf. Clearly, the writer sensed that Coleman's approach to jazz represented something new and refreshing, and he expressed that belief in the manner most prevalent at that time.

29. When I asked Billy Higgins about his approach to Coleman's music as opposed to that of other leaders for whom he had worked, he replied, "Well, you know, Ornette's music is different, it's about playing in a zone rather than a pocket" (private conversation, May 13, 1997).

30. We should note that *Playboy* stood as one of the leading proponents of jazz in the American press at this time. An interesting project for further study would be an exploration of the interrelationship of *Playboy*'s jazz coverage and the evolution of "sexy" images in jazz. For more on this American publishing institution and its role in reshaping notions of manhood, see Barbara Ehrenreich's *The Hearts of Men: American Dreams and the Flight from Commitment* (New York: Anchor Press, 1983).

31. Litweiler, *Ornette Coleman,* 48.

32. Ornette Coleman, quoted in ibid.

33. Perhaps a more appropriate deity here would be Loki, the androgynous, shape-shifting trickster of Norse mythology, or, better, Esu-Elegbara (Legba), among whose many qualities Henry Louis Gates Jr. lists "individuality, open-endedness, and sexuality." See Gates's *The Signifying Monkey: A Theory of African-American Literary Criticism* (New York: Oxford University Press, 1988), 6.

34. Ornette Coleman, quoted in Litweiler, *Ornette Coleman,* 48 (my emphasis).

35. Ornette Coleman, quoted in A. B. Spellman, *Four Lives in the Bebop Business* (New York: Pantheon, 1966), 139.

36. For an account of Coleman's flirtation with castration, see Litweiler, *Ornette Coleman,* 48, or the film *Ornette: Made in America,* directed by Shirley Clarke. As aberrant as this desire sounds, Coleman is not the first artist to wish for an end to his sexual desires. See, for example, the depiction of poet William Cowper's self-mutilation in Helen Deutsch's "Symptomatic Correspondences: The Author's Case in Eighteenth-Century Britain," *Cultural Critique* 42 (1999): 40–103.

37. For other Coleman statements on jazz and sexuality, see Valerie Wilmer, *As Serious as Your Life: The Story of the New Jazz* (London: Allison and Busby, 1980), or, especially, Litweiler, *Ornette Coleman.*

38. In Wilmer, *As Serious as Your Life,* 198.

39. Steven T. Katz's "The Conservative Character of Mystical Experience," in Steven T. Katz, ed., *Mysticism and Religious Traditions* (New York: Oxford University Press, 1983), provides a powerful demonstration of the cultural basis of all human experiences, even the most "transcendent." For more on jazz and mysticism/spirituality, see my discussions of John Coltrane and Keith Jarrett in the following chapters.

40. From Eduard Hanslick's *On the Musically Beautiful,* trans. Geoffrey Payzant (Indianapolis: Hackett, 1986), 64 (originally published 1854):

    > The most significant factor in the mental process which accompanies the comprehending of a musical work and makes it enjoyable will most frequently be overlooked. It is the mental satisfaction which the listener finds in continuously following and anticipating the composer's designs. . . . Only such music as brings about musing . . . of the imagination, will provide fully artistic satisfaction.

    In recent years, a great deal of musicological scholarship has pointed to the problems of viewing music as such an "autonomous" entity. Among the most persuasive of these studies are Susan McClary's *Feminine Endings* (Minneapolis: University of Minnesota Press, 1991), Lawrence Kramer's *Music as Cultural Practice: 1800–1900* (Berkeley: University of California Press, 1990), Christopher Small's *Music of the Common Tongue: Survival and Celebration in Afro-American Music* (New York: Riverrun Press, 1987), and Jacques Attali's *Noise: The Political Economy of Music* (Minneapolis: University of Minnesota Press, 1985). In particular, McClary's work remains essential reading for anyone concerned with music's role in constructing gender identities, while Small's book is relevant to jazz studies in its exploration of African and African-American musics and the cultural and social values that are expressed in these.

41. Cootie Williams, quoted in Wilmer, *As Serious as Your Life,* 199.

42. Of course, as Susan McClary and others have demonstrated, sexuality and music have been connected since long before the emergence of jazz. See, for instance, McClary's *Feminine Endings.*

43. Charles Mingus, quoted in Brian Priestley's *Mingus: A Critical Biography* (New York: Da Capo, 1983), 48. There are countless other examples of jazz musicians' cross-genre listening. Among these are Art Lange's interview with Keith Jarrett in *Down Beat,* June 1984, 17, Ira Gitler's interview with Al Cohn in *Swing to Bop: An Oral History of the Transition in Jazz in the 1940s* (New York: Oxford University Press, 1985), 198, and Ben Sidran's discussions in *Talking Jazz: An Oral History,* exp. ed. (New York: Da Capo, 1995) with McCoy Tyner (page 231) and Willie Ruff (page 97).

44. A possible route of further exploration is the ways in which Coleman's "Free Jazz"/"New Thing" followers configured their jazz masculinity. Archie

Shepp—though clearly influenced by Coleman's approaches—seems to have returned to many of the gender codes I have described of the bop-era musicians (I thank one of *American Music's* anonymous referees for this observation). At the same time, another Coleman protégé, the late clarinetist John Carter, embraced wholeheartedly the new jazz identities opened by his mentor.

For an outstanding study of the effects of institutionalized racism during this period, see George Lipsitz, *The Possessive Investment in Whiteness: How People Profit from Identity Politics* (Philadelphia: Temple University Press, 1998).

45. Neither, on the other hand, does it sound dated. That most jazz radio station programmers and jazz educators still consider this record to be "pretty far out" attests to the fact that the music maintains at least some of its original capacity to upset.

CHAPTER FOUR

1. The fact that Evans passed away in 1980 but Jarrett still performs presents the historian with a dilemma of tense selection. Rather than remaining case specific for each player in each instance, I shuttle back and forth between past and present tenses as the occasion seems to warrant.

2. Robert Walser, "Deep Jazz: Notes on Interiority, Race, and Criticism," in Joel Pfister and Nancy Schnog, eds., *Inventing the Psychological: Toward a Cultural History of Emotional Life in America* (New Haven: Yale University Press, 1997), 272.

3. As Nelson Goodman has shown, music notation can never specify all parameters of humanly performed musical works, nor can humans ever perform "perfectly" all aspects of notation. The goal, then, of the "perfect realization of the score," much less the goal of realizing the composer's intentions in writing that score, seems always doomed to failure to some degree. Therefore, rather than viewing the score as a fixed blueprint for sonic reconstruction, teachers may more productively serve their students by showing the many culturally and historically based options of musical gesture, affect, and the like dormant in every score. See Nelson Goodman, *Languages of Art: An Approach to a Theory of Symbols* (New York: Bobbs-Merrill Company, Inc., 1968), 179–92. For a related discussion exploring the problems involved in re-creating "authorial intention," see Hans-Georg Gadamer, *Truth and Method,* 2d rev. ed. (New York: Continuum, 1994).

4. For a discussion of the deceptively "open-ended" nature of apparently self-evident words and the culturally grounded semantic competence necessary to make it at all possible to communicate with them, see Stanley Fish, *Is There a Text in This Class?: The Authority of Interpretive Communities* (Cambridge, Mass.: Harvard University Press, 1980).

5. See Robert Walser, "The Body in the Music: Epistemology and Musical Semi-

otics," *College Music Symposium* 31 (1991):118–26, or his *Running with the Devil: Power, Gender, and Madness in Heavy Metal Music* (Hanover, N.H.: Wesleyan University Press, 1993).

6. See Michael Ventura's insightful meditations on Elvis's gyrations and other healings of the Western mind-body split in his chapter "Hear That Long Snake Moan," in *Shadow Dancing in the USA* (Los Angeles: Jeremy P. Tarcher, 1985).

7. There are exceptions to this, of course. One of Richard Wagner's ideas for his concert hall at Bayreuth was to enhance the power and mystery of his music by hiding the orchestra from the view of the audience. Earlier, Antonio Vivaldi's all-female ensembles in Venice played behind a screen—it was thought unseemly for women to play in public—and this is said to have evoked a disembodied, "heavenly" experience for many listeners. Of course, the deafness and/or blindness of some audience members and musicians (Beethoven, Ray Charles) also preclude them from directly experiencing the coupling of the seen and the heard.

8. I return in a later chapter to the significant role played by Wynton Marsalis's wardrobe in modeling current understandings of jazz as an upscale and sophisticated artform.

9. Richard Leppert, *The Sight of Sound: Music, Representation, and the History of the Body* (Berkeley: University of California Press, 1993), xxii. The role of the human body (or perceived lack thereof) in music remains one of the central battle lines dividing proponents of the "new musicology" from their "traditional" colleagues. The former camp discusses music as an activity involving physical experiences and social and cultural enactments ("musicking," as Christopher Small would say), while the latter camp regards such discussions as subjective and unverifiable, opting, instead, to explain only that which can be readily authenticated. In the end, I hope that the distinctions between the "new musicology" and the "old musicology," among ethno-, historical-, and systematic musicologies, and between music history and music theory will gradually become only matters of disciplinary emphasis rather than jealously guarded claims to methodological correctness. The best scholarship has always artfully combined elements of each of these emphases anyway.

10. The death of bassist Scott LaFaro in a 1961 auto accident robbed the jazz world of a young man with huge potential. Only twenty-five at the time of his passing, LaFaro had already set new standards for technical facility on the instrument as well as paved the way for a more flexible rhythmic conception. His death came as a tremendous shock to Evans, who, it could be argued, never fully recovered from the loss.

11. Frank Tirro, *Jazz: A History,* 2d ed. (New York: W. W. Norton, 1993), 415.

12. Mark Gridley, *Jazz Styles: History and Analysis,* 7th ed. (Upper Saddle River, N.J.: Prentice Hall, 2000), 313.

13. Orrin Keepnews, liner notes to Bill Evans Trio, *Sunday at the Village Vanguard* (Riverside OJCCD-140-2, 1987, originally RLP-9376, recorded June 25, 1961).

14. Leonard Feather, questionnaire for *Encyclopedia Yearbook of Jazz* in "Bill Evans" file at the Institute for Jazz Studies, Rutgers University, Newark, New Jersey.

15. Bill Evans, quoted in John Mehegan, "Bill Evans," *Jazz,* January 1965, 5.

16. Miles Davis with Quincy Troupe, *Miles Davis: The Autobiography* (New York: Touchstone, 1989), 226.

17. Lewis Porter and Michael Ullman (with Edward Hazell), *Jazz: From Its Origins to the Present* (Englewood Cliffs, N.J.: Prentice Hall, 1993), 340. These authors are somewhat less accurate in their assessments of Evans's famous 1961 recording of "Solar," the composition of which they credit to Miles Davis. The authors write on page 340 that "the title, 'Solar,' referring to the sun, is a Davis joke, since it's based on 'How High the Moon.'" In fact, we might describe "Solar" more correctly as an "altered" twelve-bar blues in C minor rather than as a variation of the 32-bar "How High the Moon" form, typically played in G major. Also, there is some question as to whether Miles Davis actually wrote "Solar" at all; the late guitarist Chuck Wayne claimed credit for it. Given Davis's well-known penchant for taking composer's credit for songs on which he may have had only minor (if any) input—Evans's "Blue in Green" is only one such example—Wayne's claim should be considered seriously. As any Ellingtonian will tell you, however, Miles Davis was neither the first nor even the most famous jazz musician to "borrow" other composers' works and call them his/her own.

18. "Alice in Wonderland" (take 2) from Bill Evans Trio, *Sunday at the Village Vanguard* (Riverside OJCCD-140-2, 1987). Recorded June 25, 1961. Originally released on Riverside RLP-9376.

19. James Lincoln Collier, *The Making of Jazz: A Comprehensive History* (Boston: Houghton Mifflin, 1978), 396.

20. Ibid.

21. Scott DeVeaux, *The Birth of Bebop: A Social and Musical History* (Berkeley: University of California Press, 1997), 264.

22. A notable exception to Evans's typical approach to rhythm is his early trio recording, *Everybody Digs Bill Evans,* on which he used the very bop-rooted rhythm section of "Philly" Joe Jones and Sam Jones and seemed to respond by playing more "straight ahead." This recording illustrates that, as with Billy Higgins's and Charlie Hadens's work behind Ornette Coleman, Evans's sidemen contributed to and enhanced significantly the rhythmic conception of the leader. For insightful commentary on the roles, responsibilities, and views of rhythm-section players, see Ingrid Monson's *Saying Something: Jazz Improvisation and Interaction* (Chicago: University of Chicago Press, 1996).

23. Joe Goldberg, liner notes to Bill Evans Trio, *Waltz for Debby* (Riverside

OJCCD-210-2). Recorded live at the Village Vanguard, New York, June 25, 1961.

24. Scott LaFaro, quoted in Martin Williams, "Introducing Scott LaFaro," in *Jazz Panorama* (New York: Collier, 1964), 279.

25. Bill Evans Trio, *Everybody Digs Bill Evans* (Riverside Records RLP-1129, released 1959, rereleased Riverside OJCCD-068-2, 1987).

26. Davis, *Miles,* 231.

27. H. W. Janson (*History of Art,* 2d ed. [Englewood Cliffs, N.J.: Prentice-Hall, 1977], 615) reproduces a twelfth-century Byzantine sculpture of Adam similar to Rodin's brooding work. The piece demonstrates that the conceptual roots of this contemplative pose go back at the very least to early Christian iconography.

28. "A glance into Evans' library provides an indication of what his mind is up to. The diversity of titles shows how many avenues he has explored to reach his 'something'—Freud, Whitehead, Voltaire, Margaret Meade, Santayana, and Mohammed are here, and, of course, Zen" (Don Nelson, "Bill Evans," *Down Beat,* December 8, 1960, 16).

29. Ian Carr, *Miles Davis: A Biography* (New York: Quill, 1984), 97.

30. Davis, *Miles,* 231.

31. Walser, "Deep Jazz," 271, 272.

32. Bill Evans, quoted in Len Lyons, *The Great Jazz Pianists: Speaking of Their Lives and Music* (New York: Quill, 1983), 223.

33. When Ben Sidran (*Talking Jazz: An Oral History,* exp. ed. [New York: Da Capo, 1995], 285) described Keith Jarrett as a "mantra groove player," he did not single out this aspect of the pianist's playing, but the term seems especially appropriate to these passages.

34. Keith Jarrett, quoted in ibid., 285–86.

35. Jarrett did play the occasional standard as an encore to his concerts—he can be seen and heard playing "Somewhere over the Rainbow" on the *The Last Solo* video (Tokyo, 1984), as well as on the more recent recording from *La Scala* (ECM 1640, 1997)—but these encores remain the exception.

36. I wonder if it is not the musicians' move away from Tin Pan Alley–type song-forms in the late 1950s and early 1960s that proved most responsible for the "anti-jazz" controversy surrounding that period's "New Thing." By tearing down established forms—effectively removing the predictable eight- or twelve-bar "nodal points"—some listeners found themselves cast adrift in a wash of sound. It seems to me that this factor, as much as or more than the oft-cited elements of looser rhythm, louder volume, longer solos, or denser harmonic structures, may have alienated some audiences who found nothing else to hold onto.

37. See Andrew Dell'Antonio, "The Sensual Sonata: Constructions of Desire in Early Baroque Instrumental Music," *Repercussions* 1 (1992): 52–83. Dell'Antonio writes: "Constructing an ebb and flow of musical tension and release, and

setting up and toying with expectations, are components in the creation of musical desire" (53), and "The fluid state of sacred and erotic ecstasy in the early seventeenth century allowed for the incorporation of musical ecstasy into the continuum" (56). See also Susan McClary, "Unruly Passions and Courtly Dances: Technologies of the Body in Seventeenth-Century Music," in Sara Melzer and Kate Norberg, eds., *From the Royal to the Republican Body: Incorporating the Political in Seventeenth- and Eighteenth-Century France* (Berkeley: University of California Press, 1998), 85–112, as well as her groundbreaking *Feminine Endings: Music, Gender, and Sexuality* (Minneapolis: University of Minnesota Press, 1991).

38. Jim Aiken, "Keith Jarrett: Redefining the Solo Piano in Jazz and Beyond," *Contemporary Keyboard,* September 1979, 39.

39. Jack DeJohnette, quoted in Ian Carr, *Keith Jarrett: The Man and His Music* (New York; Da Capo, 1992), 190.

40. John Litweiler, quoted in ibid. For an insightful discussion of the nineteenth-century aesthetics underlying contemporary critiques of Jarrett's performance style, see Jairo Moreno, "Body 'n' Soul?: Voice and Movement in Keith Jarrett's Pianism," *Musical Quarterly* 83 (1999):75–92. By the way, Moreno and I came upon the "Body and Soul" subtitle independently of each other.

41. Keith Jarrett, quoted in Art Lange, "The Keith Jarrett Interview," *Down Beat,* June 1984, 17.

42. Quoted in Susan McClary, "Unruly Passions," 97.

43. C. P. E. Bach, *Essay on the True Art of Playing Keyboard Instruments,* trans. and ed. William J. Mitchell (New York: W. W. Norton, 1949), 152. Bach originally published Part One of this work in 1753.

44. Richard Leppert, "The Virtuoso as Fetish: Desirous Looking and the Production of Meaning in Music," paper presented at UCLA Department of Musicology Distinguished Lecture Series (February 17, 1998), 20–21.

45. Peter Ruedi, "The Magician and the Jugglers" (liner notes) in *Keith Jarrett Concerts* (ECM-3-1227, 1982).

46. Frank Conroy, "Mr. Epiphany," *New Times,* April 1, 1977, 53; Edward Strickland, "Keith Jarrett and the Abyss," *Fanfare* March/April 1983, 92.

47. Keith Jarrett, quoted in Josef Woodard, "Keith Jarrett: In Search of the Perfect E Minor Chord," *Down Beat,* February 1989, 19.

48. Keith Jarrett, quoted in Sidran, *Talking Jazz,* 286.

49. Ibid. (my emphasis).

50. The only exception here to naming his concerts after the city in which he performed them would be *The Sun Bear Concerts,* a set comprising five complete solo concerts recorded in Japan in 1976; ECM originally released these as ten LPs and recently rereleased them on six CDs (ECM 78118-21100-2). Ostensibly, Jarrett recognized a kinship between himself and the animal that gave its name to the album title—a species of small Japanese bear possessed of a gentle face but a ferocious temperament.

51. Keith Jarrett, quoted in Lange, "Keith Jarrett Interview," 19.
52. Strickland, "Keith Jarrett," 91.
53. James Lincoln Collier, "Jazz in the Jarrett Mode," *New York Times Magazine*, January 7, 1979, 39.
54. Sidran, *Talking Jazz,* 283.
55. See Albert Murray, *Stompin' the Blues* (New York: Da Capo, 1976), 87–90, 98.
56. Lyons, *Great Jazz Pianists,* 295.

CHAPTER FIVE

1. The Notre Dame festival dates to 1959 and has become a major showcase for college jazz bands. For more on this Midwestern jazz institution, see Joseph Kuhn Carey's *Big Noise from Notre Dame: A History of the Collegiate Jazz Festival* (Notre Dame, Ind.: Notre Dame University Press, 1986).
2. A colleague informed me that as recently as the early 1990s, she and her fellow clarinet majors at a major Midwestern university were forbidden to play jazz: classical instructors feared that such musicking would "destroy" their embouchures. Ironically, this attitude persists at a school with a long-running jazz program, which demonstrates that although jazz has established a foothold in the academy, a cultural hierarchy remains in place.
3. Bruno Nettl, *Heartland Excursions: Ethnomusicological Reflections on Schools of Music* (Urbana: University of Illinois Press, 1995), 107. I recommend Nettl's engaging and insightful book for anyone considering a life in America's music schools as student, teacher, or administrator. Meanwhile, Nettl's observation that the big band's presence in colleges remains disproportionate to the larger group's viability in the outside world clearly relates to our topic of jazz pedagogy and musical values. While I touch on this topic throughout the chapter, a more in-depth exploration of this jazz aggregation will have to be taken up elsewhere.
4. Jeff Jarvis, "The Improvised Jazz Solo: An Endangered Species," *Jazz Educators Journal* 22, no. 4 (spring 1990): 70–74; Scott Reeves, "Don't Neglect Improvisation," *Jazz Educators Journal* 23, no. 3 (winter 1991): 65–67. As with any broad overview, there are exceptions to the characterizations outlined throughout this chapter. Though jazz remained largely ignored in institutions of higher learning well into the 1960s, various programs and courses had surfaced, some as far back as the early decades of this century. Marshall Stearns, for instance, taught a jazz history course at New York University in 1950 (his rather incredible list of guest lecturers and performers included Louis Armstrong, Duke Ellington, Benny Goodman, Count Basie, Dizzy Gillespie, and author Ralph Ellison!). Robert Walser reprints Stearns's syllabus in Robert Walser, ed., *Keeping Time: Readings in Jazz History* (New York: Oxford University Press, 1999), 195–99. Meanwhile, the Berklee School of Music (now the Berklee College of Music) in Boston and the Westlake College of Music in Los An-

geles (no longer in operation) both opened in 1945 offering private instruction in jazz. Two years later, North Texas State Teachers College (later North Texas State University and now the University of North Texas) developed an outstanding program starting with a major in Dance Band. A lesser-known but highly influential individual in jazz pedagogy was Len Bowden, who as a student/teacher led a band at the Tuskegee Institute as early as 1919. Bowden later taught at Georgia State College (now Savannah State College) and Alabama State Normal College, and held the directorship of the black musicians at Great Lakes Naval Air Station outside of Chicago during World War II. For more on Bowden, the players and teachers he inspired, and other early educators, see Dr. Dan Murphy, "Jazz Studies in American Schools and Colleges: A Brief History," *Jazz Educators Journal* 26, no. 3 (March 1994): 34–38. Also see William T. McDaniel Jr., "The Status of Jazz Education in the 1990s: A Historical Commentary," *International Jazz Archives Journal* 1 (1993): 114–39.

5. Murphy, "Jazz Studies," 34.
6. From *Music Data Summaries 1997–98* (Reston, Va.: Higher Education Arts Data Services, 1998). My thanks to Gail Crum, information services manager of the Music Educators National Conference, for providing these documents.
7. Unfortunately, some students have found to their dismay that not everyone who can "do" can teach.
8. Some jazz educators raised these concerns as early as the 1960s. See Dave (now David) Baker, "Jazz: The Academy's Neglected Stepchild," *Down Beat,* September 23, 1965, 29–32.
9. See, for example, Mark Gridley's *Jazz Styles: History and Analysis,* 7th ed. (Upper Saddle River, N.J.: Prentice Hall, 2000), 5–10.
10. See Charles Hamm, *Music in the New World* (New York: W. W. Norton, 1983), 398–99.
11. Anne Shaw Faulkner, "Does Jazz Put the Sin in Syncopation?" *Ladies Home Journal,* August 1921, 16; the article was reprinted in Walser, ed., *Keeping Time,* 34.
12. Peter Dykema and Karl Gehrkens, *The Teaching and Administration of High School Music* (Boston: C. C. Birchard, 1941), 455.
13. Sieglinde Lemke, *Primitivist Modernism: Black Culture and the Origins of Transatlantic Modernism* (New York: Oxford University Press, 1998), 92.
14. Ibid., 92–93. The quotation appeared originally in "Jazz Bitterly Opposed in Germany," *New York Times,* March 11, 1928, "Amusements" section, 8.
15. See Lawrence W. Levine, "Jazz and American Culture," *Journal of American Folklore* 102, no. 403 (January–March 1989): 6–22.
16. See Robert Walser, "Deep Jazz: Notes on Interiority, Race, and Criticism," in Joel Pfister and Nancy Schnog, eds., *Inventing the Psychological: Toward a Cultural History of Emotional Life in America* (New Haven: Yale University Press, 1997), 271–96.
17. Which is why the producer's reference to "timeless classics by Duke Elling-

ton" in the liner notes to my own album, *Sound and Time* (Posi-tone 1423-15, 1998), remain the source of a great deal of embarrassment to me.

18. For more on the hazards of attempted expressive nuance within an orchestral setting, see Carl A. Vigeland, *In Concert: Onstage and Offstage with the Boston Symphony Orchestra* (Amherst: University of Massachusetts Press, 1991).

19. College Music Society, *1997–98 Directory of Music Faculties in Colleges and Universities, U.S. and Canada* (Missoula: College Music Society, 1997).

20. Max Roach, "What 'Jazz' Means to Me," *Black Scholar* 3 (Summer 1972): 3–6; reprinted in Walser, ed., *Keeping Time*, 308.

21. See David Baker, *Jazz Pedagogy: A Comprehensive Method of Jazz Education for Teacher and Student* (Chicago: Music Workshop Publications, 1981).

22. Aebersold offers new titles constantly. The summer/fall 1998 edition of his catalog featured eighty-four volumes of the "Play-a-Long" series and hundreds of other instructional guides, videos, and recordings.

23. Governor James A. Martin proclaimed September 14 through September 27, 1986, as "John Coltrane Days in North Carolina." In 1983, the General Assembly of North Carolina passed "a joint resolution honoring the life and memory of John Coltrane." Copies of both official documents are in the "John Coltrane" file at the Institute of Jazz Studies at Rutgers University in Newark. Coltrane was born in Hamlet, North Carolina (September 23, 1926), and raised in High Point, North Carolina, until 1943, when he moved with his family to Philadelphia.

24. Biographies include J. C. Thomas, *Chasin' the Trane: The Music and Mystique of John Coltrane* (Garden City, N.Y.: Doubleday and Co., 1975); C. O. Simpkins, *Coltrane: A Biography* (New York: Herndon House Publishers, 1975); Bill Cole, *John Coltrane* (New York: Schirmer Books, 1976); Eric Nisenson, *Ascension: John Coltrane and His Quest* (New York: Da Capo, 1995); Lewis Porter, *John Coltrane: His Life and Music* (Ann Arbor: University of Michigan Press, 1998); and Frank Kofsky, *John Coltrane and the Jazz Revolution of the 1960s* (New York: Pathfinder, 1998).

25. Author's telephone discussion with Ravi Coltrane, July 30, 1998.

26. For more on Coltrane representations in some of these films, see Michael Bruce McDonald's "Traning the Nineties, Or the Present Relevance of John Coltrane's Theophany and Negation," in *African American Review* 29 (1995): 275–82.

27. We should note that John Coltrane's surviving family strongly opposes St. John's Church. Alice Coltrane has stated, "In his own way, John was religious, but he never proclaimed himself to be a minister. Why can't they just retain the memory of him, cherish that in their hearts and not desecrate his name?" (quoted in David Beer's "The Coltrane Church," *Image*, March 6, 1988, 18, 20). For more on that church and understandings of Coltrane in it, see the video documentary *The Church of Saint Coltrane*, produced by Jeff Swimmer and Gayle Gilman for Tango Films, 1996.

28. Michel Foucault, "What Is an Author?" trans. Josue V. Harari in *The Foucault Reader,* ed. Paul Rabinow (New York: Pantheon, 1984), 106, 107.

29. David Liebman, introduction to Aebersold, *John Coltrane,* i (my emphasis).

30. For detailed discussions of the compositional evolution of "Giant Steps" through its recording, see Porter, *John Coltrane,* 145–58. For a guide to practicing this chord progression, see Andy Laverne, "Twelve Steps to Giant Steps," *Keyboard,* November 1996, 56–75.

31. Just ask pianist Tommy Flanagan. Flanagan, an outstanding bop-style improviser and accompanist, served as the "guinea pig" on Coltrane's first release of this piece and was clearly unprepared for what was at the time a highly unusual harmonic obstacle course. This and other takes are available on the seven-disc *The Heavyweight Champion: The Complete Atlantic Recordings* (Rhino/Atlantic R2 71984, 1995).

32. During an interview with Lewis Porter, Jimmy Heath demonstrated a number of patterns and exercises that Coltrane and he had practiced together in their formative years. After noting that "Trane liked four-note patterns; we did them all around the keys," Heath illustrated his point by playing a series of the 1–2–3–5 patterns (in Porter, *John Coltrane,* 66).

33. The more explorational jazz of the 1960s was dubbed, variously, "free," "Avant Garde," or "New Thing."

34. Tommy Flanagan, quoted in Porter, *John Coltrane,* 155.

35. Thomas, *Chasin' the Trane,* 101–3. Coltrane's practicing ethic has even reached into contemporary fiction. A comparison is made between Coltrane and the title character of *The Bear Comes Home* after the latter enters a period of intensive "woodshedding." See Rafi Zabor, *The Bear Comes Home* (New York: W. W. Norton, 1997), 348.

36. McCoy Tyner, quoted in David Wild, "McCoy Tyner: The Jubilant Experience of the Classic Quartet," *Down Beat,* July 12, 1979, 18ff.

37. John Coltrane, quoted in Nat Hentoff, liner notes to John Coltrane, *Giant Steps* (original album released as Atlantic SD-1311, January 1960; reissued on Rhino/Atlantic R2 75203, 1998).

38. In fact, Mintzer and Liebman earn much of their incomes through teaching workshops, writing manuals, and composing school-oriented big-band charts. Meanwhile, Michael Brecker appears on the cover of the summer/fall edition of Aebersold's 1998 catalog.

39. Porter, *John Coltrane,* 216. For more on Coltrane's approach to scales, modes, and patterns, see chapters 16 and 17 of that book, as well as Porter's earlier piece, "John Coltrane's *A Love Supreme:* Jazz Improvisation as Composition," *Journal of the American Musicological Society* 38 (1985): 593–621. C. L. Hanon's *The Virtuoso Pianist,* arranged in sixty exercises, has served as a workbook for generations of aspiring pianists.

40. John Coltrane, quoted in Benoit Quersin, "Entretiens: La Passe Dangereuse," *Jazz Magazine,* January 1963, 40. Interview transcribed by Lewis Porter and

Carl Woideck, printed in Porter, *John Coltrane,* 203; the bracketed editorial is Porter's.

41. *The Avant Garde* was not originally released until April 1966 on Atlantic (1451). It is now available in Rhino/Atlantic's boxed set, *The Heavyweight Champion* (R2 71984, 1995).

42. In *Down Beat*'s annual Reader's Poll, Coltrane was named Jazzman of the Year and Tenor Saxophonist of the Year. His *A Love Supreme* was selected Record of the Year, and he was voted to the magazine's Hall of Fame.

43. Tynan, columnist for *Down Beat* in the early 1960s, wrote, "Go ahead, call me reactionary. I happen to object to the musical nonsense currently peddled in the name of jazz by John Coltrane and his acolyte, Eric Dolphy. At Hollywood's Renaissance Club recently, I listened to a horrifying demonstration of what appears to be a growing anti-jazz trend exemplified by these foremost proponents of what is termed avant garde music" (John Tynan, "Take Five," *Down Beat,* November 23, 1961, 40). Tynan's review sparked a heated debate between pro- and anti-Coltrane factions, leading to Don DeMichel's double interview, "John Coltrane and Eric Dolphy Answer the Jazz Critics," *Down Beat,* April 12, 1962, 20–23.

44. Jazz critic Ira Gitler coined the term "sheets of sound" to describe Coltrane's seemingly nonstop series of scalar substitutions and superimpositions. The term first appeared in Gitler's liner notes to Coltrane's *Soultrane* (Prestige LP 7142), recorded in February 1958.

45. "Review of *John Coltrane Quartet Plays,*" *Jazz Journal,* February 1969, 24.

46. Thomas, *Chasin' the Trane,* 172–73.

47. Author's telephone interview with Andrew White, September 9, 1998.

48. Four different versions of "India" can be heard on the four-volume *Coltrane: The Complete 1961 Village Vanguard Recordings* (Impulse IMPD4-232).

49. Ekkehard Jost, *Free Jazz* (New York: Da Capo, 1994), 89.

50. Archie Shepp, quoted in A. B. Spellman, liner notes to original release of *Ascension* (Impulse Records 95). Also cited by David Wild in his notes to *The Major Works of John Coltrane* (GRP Records GRD-2-113), 6–7.

51. Frank Kofsky, *Black Nationalism and the Revolution in Music* (New York: Pathfinder, 1970).

52. Coltrane was reticent to express anger or outrage in the media, even despite inflammatory or leading questions such as those Kofsky asked Coltrane in his famous interview. The piece originally appeared as "John Coltrane: An Interview," *Jazz and Pop,* September 1967, 23–31; it was republished in *Black Nationalism and the Revolution in Music.* Kofsky revised that book shortly before his death; it was published posthumously as *John Coltrane and the Jazz Revolution of the 1960s* (New York: Pathfinder, 1998).

53. Pete Welding, "Spotlight Review: John Coltrane: Coltrane at the Village Vanguard Again!" *Down Beat,* February 1967, 26.

54. In fact, much of Coltrane's work from the early 1960s was heard as angry by many critics and listeners, a response that seemed to diminish with the introduction of more "peaceful" and "spiritual" titles later on.

55. David Borgo, "Music, Metaphor, and Mysticism: Avant-Garde Jazz Saxophone and the Ecstatic State," paper delivered at Society for Ethnomusicology Southern California Chapter Meeting, Northridge, California, February 1997.

56. In Ben Sidran, *Talking Jazz: An Oral History,* exp. ed. (New York: Da Capo, 1995), 302.

57. We should note that jazz education's Eurocentricism may be coming into question among some musicians and institutions. For instance, during the 1980s, saxophonist Steve Coleman taught students at the Banff Summer Jazz Workshops his oftentimes extremely intricate compositions by ear. Likewise, the Vail Jazz Foundation workshops for promising high school players rely solely on aural skills. Bill Cunliffe, one of the program's teachers, said of this pedagogical approach: "Learning by ear and performing in front of an audience really increases their confidence level. I've seen some miraculous development." See Bill Kohlhasse, "All That Jazz: In Vail, Young Musicians Learn by Doing," *Los Angeles Times,* August 28, 1998, F14. Most promising, the Music Educators National Conference recently published *Teaching Jazz: A Course of Study.* Their four-page section on "Skills and Concepts" recommends that teachers develop students' rhythmic and aural skills as well as their knowledge of scales and harmony. See Music Educators National Conference, *Teaching Jazz: A Course of Study* (Reston, Va.: Music Educators National Conference, 1996), 26–29.

CHAPTER SIX

1. Scott DeVeaux, "Constructing the Jazz Tradition: Jazz Historiography," *Black American Literature Forum* 25 (1991): 551.

2. John Gennari, "Jazz Criticism: Its Development and Ideologies," *Black American Literature Forum* 25 (1991): 451. Writers have spilled much ink over Marsalis's high-profile position in jazz. While many of the issues raised elsewhere will be broached here, this essay focuses on a specific recording and will by and large not enter the ongoing fray. For a sampling of the debates surrounding Marsalis and his fellow "neo-traditionalists," see Scott DeVeaux, "What Did We Do to Be So Black and Blue?" *Musical Quarterly* 80 (1996): 392–430; Keith Jarrett, "The Virtual Jazz Age: A Survival Manual," *Musician,* March 1996, 34–36, 102; Gene Lees, *Cats of Any Color: Jazz, Black and White* (New York: Oxford University Press, 1995); Tom Moon, "Chief of the Jazz Police?" *Roanoke Times,* Wednesday, June 16, 1999, "Extra" (entertainment) Section, 1, 5; Lewis Porter, *Jazz—A Century of Change: Readings and New Essays* (New York: Schirmer, 1997); Thomas Sancton, "The New Jazz Age: Horns of

Plenty," *Time,* October 22, 1990, 64–71; and Richard Woodward, "A Rage Supreme: The Feud That's Shaking Up Lincoln Center," *Village Voice,* August 9, 1994, 27–34.

3. Advertising insert for *Bill Frisell/Kermit Driscoll/Joey Baron Live* (Gramavision Records GCD 79504).

4. See Gene Santoro, *Dancing in Your Head: Jazz, Blues, Rock, and Beyond* (New York: Oxford University Press, 1994), 299, or Richard Gehr, "Sold American: Bill Frisell," *Village Voice,* December 13, 1994, 60. The Knitting Factory is a downtown New York nightclub and a forum for a wide range of improvising musicians not typically thought of among the jazz "mainstream." Along with Frisell, frequent Knitting Factory performers include Tim Berne, the Jazz Passengers, and John Zorn.

5. Charles Keil and Steven Feld, *Music Grooves* (Chicago: University of Chicago Press, 1994), 291.

6. Herbie Hancock, *Headhunters* (Columbia/Legacy CK 65123, 1997 [1973]).

7. Or at least of tunes that borrow the Tin Pan Alley model, which generally consists of a series of ii-V-I harmonic progressions usually structured in some type of 32-bar form.

8. *The Real Book* has clearly extended the "lives" of a number of tunes that would not likely have survived otherwise. Notable examples include Steve Swallow's "Falling Grace" and Ralph Towner's "Icarus."

9. Robert Walser, "Out of Notes: Signification, Interpretation, and the Problem of Miles Davis," *Musical Quarterly* 77 (1993): 351. See also Henry Louis Gates Jr., *The Signifying Monkey: A Theory of African-American Literary Criticism* (New York: Oxford University Press, 1988). Gates's theory has proven to be extraordinarily useful for jazz scholars. In addition to Walser's work, see Samuel A. Floyd Jr., *The Power of Black Music: Interpreting Its History from Africa to the United States* (New York: Oxford University Press, 1995), and "Ring Shout! Literary Studies, Historical Studies, and Black Music Inquiry," *Black Music Research Journal* 11 (1991): 265–87, as well as John P. Murphy, "Jazz Improvisation: The Joy of Influence," *Black Perspective in Music* 18, nos. 1–2 (1990): 7–19. Indeed, Murphy uses Gates to critique another theorist, Harold Bloom. Murphy turns around Bloom's theory regarding *The Anxiety of Influence* (New York: Oxford University Press, 1973), arguing that jazz musicians feel less threatened by their forebears than poets do, according to Bloom's depiction of them, and engage instead in a celebration of their musical ancestors. He cites the obvious affection that tenor saxophonist Joe Henderson displays for the music of Charlie Parker.

    While Murphy's essay helps to dispel some of the more darkly romantic and/or hyper-Freudian notions surrounding jazz musicians (and all "artists"), we should bear in mind that the influences that some musicians exerted on others have not always been "joyful" ones. Murphy chooses as his model Joe

Henderson, now an established figure in the music (Bloom would call him a "strong" musician). But what of the many young and not so young performers during the 1940s and 1950s who could not find their own sound, drawn in by the artistic and charismatic gravity of Charlie Parker, oftentimes to devastating psychological and physical consequences (i.e., heroin addiction)? It may have proven more illuminating for Murphy to investigate the ways in which the not-yet-established Joe Henderson dealt with the influence of tenor sax giant John Coltrane. Coltrane would have presented a more difficult figure to handle because, by the mid-1960s, when Henderson was coming up, Charlie Parker had already become somewhat passé. Most eyes and ears at that time focused on Coltrane, Ornette Coleman, and Miles Davis.

For a discussion of Gates's theories as they may apply to music outside of the jazz domain, see Steve Waksman, "Black Sound, Black Body: Jimi Hendrix, the Electric Guitar and the Meanings of Blackness," in *Instruments of Desire: The Electric Guitar and the Shaping of Musical Experience* (Cambridge, Mass.: Harvard University Press, 2000). Also see Richard Taruskin's unfavorable take on some recent Bloom-inspired musicological studies in his "Review: Kevin Korsyn, 'Towards a New Poetics of Musical Influence'," and Joseph N. Straus, *Remaking the Past: Musical Modernism and the Influence of the Tonal Tradition,* in *Journal of the American Musicological Society* 46 (1993): 114–38.

10. "Effective history" *(Wirkunsgeschichte)* derives from philosopher Hans-Georg Gadamer. The term describes the inescapable reality that one never approaches a situation objectively. Meanings accrue and evolve around events and artifacts, and thus all understanding is always already culturally, historically, and socially grounded. See Hans-Georg Gadamer, *Truth and Method,* 2d rev. ed., trans. and rev. by Joel Weinsheimer and Donald G. Marshall (New York: Continuum, 1994).

11. A very partial list of musicians releasing either tributes or standards-oriented material since the early 1980s includes Terence Blanchard, Anthony Braxton, Joe Henderson, Fred Hersch, Keith Jarrett, Diana Krall, Joe Lovano, Brad Mehldau, Paul Motian, and Marcus Roberts. Meanwhile, the role of Keith Jarrett—who has released more standards albums than any of these others—in this phenomenon appears somewhat ironic, given his much-publicized quarrel with Wynton Marsalis, who, as we will see, also holds very strong views on the interconnectedness of standards and tradition. See Jarrett's comments in Andrew Solomon, "The Jazz Martyr," *New York Times Magazine,* February 9, 1997, 35, or Keith Jarrett, "Virtual Jazz Age."

12. Kevin Eubanks, quoted in Tom Moon, "Jazz Special: Jazz Becomes Big-Biz," *Musician,* November 1994, 44.

13. Crouch, former columnist for the *Village Voice,* has not only served as Wynton Marsalis's personal essayist (including Marsalis's Jazz at Lincoln Center

program notes). He has also written liner notes for the entire Marsalis family (saxophonist Branford, trombonist Delfeayo, and their father/pianist, Ellis), as well as for the recordings of many of their sidemen.

14. Stanley Crouch, liner notes to Wynton Marsalis, *Standard Time Vol. 2: Intimacy Calling* (Columbia CD Ck47346, 1991), 6.

15. Wynton Marsalis, quoted in ibid., 6–7.

16. Marsalis, quoted in ibid., 6.

17. Ibid., 2.

18. Marsalis, quoted in ibid., 6.

19. Ibid., 6.

20. See Dizzy Gillespie's comments on Armstrong in his *To Be or Not to Bop* (Garden City, N.Y.: Doubleday, 1979), 295–96, as well as Miles Davis's criticisms of Armstrong (and Gillespie!) in Miles Davis with Quincy Troupe, *Miles: The Autobiography* (New York: Touchstone, 1989), 83, 313.

21. Following the failure of the Jacobite uprising in the 1740s, the English government proclaimed it unlawful for Scots to bear arms or to wear the tartan. In 1746, Scotsman James Reid was brought before the court, charged with possession of a deadly weapon. He pleaded innocent, claiming he was carrying only his bagpipes. The judge ruled that the sound of that instrument inspired rebellion in the Scottish people and, as such, was an implement of war. Reid died by hanging on November 6, 1747. See Seumas MacNeill and Frank Richardson, *Piobaireachd and Its Interpretation: Classical Music of the Highland Bagpipe* (Edinburgh: John Donald Pub. Ltd., 1987), and *The Highland Bagpipe: Its History, Literature, and Music* (London: Alexander Gardener Publishers, 1901).

22. For insightful accounts of the central role of instruments in jazz-based Hollywood films, see Krin Gabbard's *Jammin' at the Margins: Jazz and the American Cinema* (Chicago: University of Chicago Press, 1996).

23. Barry Kernfeld, *What to Listen For in Jazz* (New Haven: Yale University Press, 1996), 166–67.

24. The synthesizer became such a fixture in the jazz groups of the 1970s (Mahavishnu Orchestra, Return to Forever, Weather Report, Head Hunters) that pianist Keith Jarrett's all-acoustic stance was seen as a rebellious statement. See my discussion of the piano in the previous chapter.

25. For more on instrumentation and genre purity, see Steve Waksman's discussion of Bob Dylan's "electric" appearance at the 1965 Newport Folk Festival in "Going Electric: An Introduction," in *Instruments of Desire.*

26. Crouch, liner notes to Marsalis, *Standard Time,* 6.

27. The terms "stroll" and "lay out" refer to songs or sections of songs in which individual musicians do not play.

28. In "stop-time," the band—particularly the rhythm section—breaks up their steady rhythmic flow with a series of "kicks" or "hits" that serve to highlight a soloist.

29. The "New Thing" was another name for the 1960s avant-garde jazz scene based in New York.

30. Crouch, liner notes to Marsalis, *Standard Time,* 3.

31. Albert Murray, *Stomping the Blues* (New York: Vintage Books, 1982), 87, 90.

32. See chapter 5, "Jazz 'Traning."

33. Bruno Nettl, *Heartland Excursions: Ethnomusicological Reflections on Schools of Music* (Urbana: University of Illinois Press, 1995), 33.

34. Gabbard, *Jammin' at the Margins,* 14.

35. See Gabbard's excellent discussion of Whiteman's all-white jazz narrative in *Jammin' at the Margins.* Of this discourse, Gabbard writes that "a more elaborate, more thorough denial of the African American role in jazz is difficult to imagine" (10).

36. Hugh C. Ernst, "An Experiment in Modern Music," program notes. Concert presented on February 12, 1924, in Aeolian Hall, New York City. Program reprinted in Walser, ed., *Keeping Time: Readings in Jazz History* (New York: Oxford University Press, 1999), 39–40.

37. Gabbard, *Jammin' at the Margins,* 15.

38. DeVeaux, "Constructing the Jazz Tradition," 552.

39. Miles Davis had his own view of his later music: "Jazz today is closer to classical music than it is to folklore music, and I'd rather stay closer to folklore music." See Keith Jarrett (interviewed by Kimihiko Yamashita), "In Search of Folk Roots," *Antaeus* 71/72 (autumn 1993): 114.

40. Gene Lees has pointed to a not-so-subtle anti-Semitism underlying certain comments by both Wynton Marsalis and Stanley Crouch, which may account for the reticence of those two to credit the Jewish origins of so many Tin Pan Alley standards. See Gene Lees, *Cats of Any Color: Jazz Black and White* (New York: Oxford University Press, 1994), 195.

41. Though perhaps Will Smith's portrayal of Jim West in the 1999 film version of *Wild Wild West* will inspire new understandings of that time and place.

42. Tommy Gumina (along with clarinetist Buddy DeFranco) even participated in one of Leonard Feather's famous "Blindfold Tests" for *Down Beat* magazine. Gumina's comments on John Coltrane's "Up 'gainst the Wall" reveal that accordionist to have been well acquainted (if not wholly in accord) with the latest jazz developments. See Leonard Feather's two-part "Blindfold Test: Tommy Gumina and Buddy DeFranco," *Down Beat,* October 24, 1963, 34 (part one), and November 7, 1963, 37 (part two).

43. "Power chords result from distortion of the chord voicings most often used in [heavy] metal [music] and hard rock, an open fifth or fourth on the lower strings" (Robert Walser, *Running with the Devil* [Hanover, N.H.: Wesleyan University Press, 1993], 43). I will have more to say regarding this musical device below.

44. Listen, for example, to John Barry's scoring of the "Buffalo Hunt" scene in the 1990 film *Dances with Wolves.*

45. James Scofield, quoted in James Rotondi, "Bill Frisell and John Scofield: A Meeting of Spontaneous Minds," *Guitar Player,* July 1992, 55.

46. Robert Palmer, *Deep Blues* (New York: Penguin Books, 1982), 16.

47. See Waksman, *Instruments of Desire,* 207.

48. In jazz, a "chorus" is one cycle of the harmonic form. "Rhythm changes" refers to the form and harmonic sequence borrowed from George Gershwin's "I Got Rhythm."

49. Bill Frisell, booklet to *Have a Little Faith* (Electra-Nonesuch Records 79301-2, 1993), 5.

50. Gadamer, *Truth and Method,* 293.

51. In Keil and Feld, *Music Grooves,* 20.

INDEX

Numbers in italics indicate figures and tables.

Coleman, Ornette *(continued)*
ogy," 68; Coltrane and, 130–31, 135, 136; "cool" school and, 189n16; as cultural outsider, 73–80; in Francis Davis history, 51; "Donna Lee," 77; Ellington and, 71, 190n22; *The Empty Foxhole,* 142; Evans comparisons to, 92, 96; "Eventually," 68; "free jazz" and, 63, 81, 136, 139, 142, 192–93n44; Higgins and, 69–70, 73, 191n29; on jazz as "art of the improviser," 154; "Lonely Woman," 69–73; Marsalis and, 158, 164; New York arrival of (1959), 7, 65, 68, 76–77; and sexuality, 62, 72–82, 191n36, 192–93n44; *The Shape of Jazz to Come,* 63, 68–74, 76, 82; timbral manipulations of, 120; Martin Williams and, 71, 73, 191n28; youth of, 74–75

Coleman, Steve, 115, 203n57

college music departments, 112–27, 198–203; and chord-scale system, 122–27, 131–32, 134; and Coltrane, 4, 112, 131–45; and Eurocentrism, 119–20, 121–22, 203n57; and harmony, 116, 122, 126, 131–34; and improvisation, 114, 116–17, 120–23, 131–34, 144–45; and "New Thing," 142–44; and notation, 120–27; Notre Dame Intercollegiate Jazz Festival, 112, 114, 198n1

College Music Society, 121

Colley, Scott, ix

Collier, James Lincoln, 13–14, 93

colonies: British, 16; French, 15–17

Coltrane, Alice, 127, 140, 200n27

Coltrane, John, 96, 112, 126–45, 200–3; "Amen," 141; *Ascension,* 135, 138, 139; "Ascent," 141; *The Avant Garde,* 136; *Ballads,* 158; Bechet compared with, 32; "Big Nick," 141; college music departments and, 4, 112, 131–45; *Coltrane Live at the Village Vanguard Again!* 141; "Compassion," 141; "Countdown," 133; early life of, 200n23; "Giant Steps," 129–33, *131,* 134, 135, 136, 138; and harmony, 122, 129–34, *131,* 135, 138–39, 201n31; *The Heavyweight Champion,* 135–36; Henderson and, 205n9; honors, 127–29,

136–37, 200n23, 202n42; "Impressions," 129, 133–34, *133,* 139; "India," 139; *Kulu Se Mama,* 135; later works of, 135–45; "Lazy Bird," 141; "Like Sonny," 141; *Live at Birdland,* 4; *A Love Supreme,* 127, 128, 135, 138, 141, 202n42; *The Major Works of John Coltrane,* 135; Marsalis and, 158, 164; *Meditations,* 135, 141; modalities and, 133, 139; "My Favorite Things," 150; *Om,* 135, 138, 141; "pattern" playing and, 134, 135, 201n32; practicing ethic of, 131–32, 143, 201n35; "Psalm," 127; "Satellite," 133; sound as structure and, 138–40; spirituality and, 79, 127–29, 137, 141–42, 200n27; *Sun Ship,* 135; "26–2," 133; "Up 'gainst the Wall," 207n42. *See also* John Coltrane Quartet

Coltrane, Ravi, ix, 200n25

Columbia Records, 146

competition: aesthetics of, 66–67; "cutting contest," 35, 67, 72, 189n10

complexity, aesthetics of, 47–49, 51, 54

Congo Square (New Orleans), 16, 179–80n15

Congressional Act (1987), 45

Connick, Harry, Jr., 88, 97

Conroy, Frank, 107

Contemporary label, 68

"cool" style, 97, 189n16

Copland, Aaron, 165–66; *Billy the Kid,* 165, 166, 168, 169–70; "The Gun Battle," 168; "Mexican Dance and Finale," 168; "The Open Prairie," 165; "Prairie Night," 165, 168; "Street Scene in a Frontier Town," 165

Corea, Chick, 88, 93, 111, 117

Coryell, Larry, 169

Count Basie. *See* Basie, Count

Creoles: in New Orleans, 10–41, 178n2, 181n31, 186n83

Crosby, Bing, 46

Crouch, Stanley, 153–67, 205–6n13, 207n40

Crump, Bill, *58–59*

cultural hierarchies: among African Americans, 10–11, 16–20, 22, 25–26, 40–41,

George, Nelson, 42–43
Gershwin, George: "Embraceable You," 154; "I Got Rhythm," 149, 208n48
Getz, Stan, 51, 142, 148–49, 170
Gibbs, Gerry, ix
Gillespie, Dizzy, 53, 63, 189n15; in *Down Beat's* readers' poll (1946), 57; influence on Marsalis of, 155; in Kane photograph, *58–59*, 60; on pop music charts (1945), 54; "Salt Peanuts," 54; on Torin radio show, 60
Gilroy, Paul, 3
Gioia, Ted, 43
Gitler, Ira, 57–58, 60, 202n44
Glenn, Tyree, *58–59*
Goldberg, Joe, 94–95, 135
Goldmark, Daniel, 55
Golson, Benny, *58–59*
Goodman, Benny, 55, 57, 167
Goodman, Nelson, 193n3
Gordon, Dexter, 67, 73
Grammy Awards: and Marsalis, 147, 163
"gravity" of the saxophonist, 7
Greer, Sonny, *58–59*
Gridley, Mark, 53; on Evans, 89; "Is Jazz Popular Music?" 45–46; *Jazz Styles,* 48; and Jordan, 43
Griffin, Johnny, *58–59*, 96, 126
Grossman, Steve, 134
Gryce, Gigi, *58–59*
guitar, 169–70
Gumina, Tommy, 167, 207n42

Haden, Charlie, 69–70, 73, 115, 136
Hadlock, Richard, 27, 30, 38
Haines, Roy, 132
Hall, Gwendolyn Midlo, 10
Hall, Jim, 169
Hamm, Charles, 117; *Music in the New World,* 11–13, 20
Hammond organ, 111
Hampton, Lionel, 43
Hancock, Herbie, 93, 94, 111; classical beginnings of, 185n81; Evans influence on, 88; "Watermelon Man," 149
Hanslick, Eduard, 192n40
Harlem, 50, *58–59,* 60

harmony, 126; "chorus" and, 208n48; college music departments and, 116, 122, 126, 131–34; Coltrane and, 122, 129–34, *131,* 135, 138–39, 201n31; Evans and, 91–92; Jarrett and, 103
Harper, Philip, ix
Harris, Wynonie, 51
Hart, Lorenz, Rodgers (Richard) and, 150, 157
Hartman, Johnny, 158
Hawes, Hampton, 29
Hawkins, Coleman, 55, *58–59,* 121, 139, 167
Heard, J. C., *58–59*
Heath, Jimmy, 201n32
Henderson, Joe, 204–5n9
Hendrix, Jimi, 169, 170, 183n51
Hentoff, Nat, 25
Herman, Woody, 57, 114, 167
heroin, 67–68, 99, 205n9
Hersch, Fred, 170
Hiatt, John, 166
hierarchies. *See* cultural hierarchies
Higginbotham, Jay C., *58–59*
Higgins, Billy, 69–70, 73, 115, 191n29
Hines, Earl, 87–88
Hinton, Milt, *58–59*
"historical trauma" of identity, 65, 81–82
historiography, jazz: and European music, 80–81; Jordan missing in, 42–61. *See also* Gridley, Mark; jazz scholarship; Porter, Lewis; Tirro, Frank; Ullman, Michael; Williams, Martin
Hodes, Art, 29
Hodges, Johnny, 29, 30–31, 53, 57, 184n60
Hodier, André, 12
Holdsworth, Alan, 170
Holiday, Billie, 54–55
Hollywood: Coltrane and, 127, 202n43; standards from, 152
Howlin' Wolf, 28, 183n51
Hubbard, Freddie, 155
humanities scholars, 1–2
Hurt, Mississippi John, 29

identity, 3, 81; blues, 27–28; Coleman's personal, 74–75; cultural/musical, 10–41, 175; "historical trauma" of, 65, 81–82;

identity *(continued)*
  and musical participation, 23. *See also*
  gender codes; genre labeling; jazz identity; racial identity
"If I Were a Bell," 149–50
"I'll Remember April," 154, 159
images, 3. *See also* liner notes; photography;
  recordings
improvisation: Bechet and, 19, 25, 33; Coleman on jazz as "art of the improviser,"
  154; college music departments and, 114,
  116–17, 120–23, 131–34, 144–45; Coltrane and, 129–34; Copland and, 168;
  "ear" players and, 25; Jarrett and, 103,
  106–11, 185n73; Marsalis and, 159,
  185n73; "note choice" approach, 123;
  Uptown New Orleans players and, 19;
  "vertical" approach and, 126, 129, 130
Impulse Records, 135, 158
income of jazz professional, 21–24, 54, 114,
  115, 201n38. *See also* economics
"inner being": musician's, 83–84, 110, 111,
  159. *See also* deep jazz; interiority; mysticism; spirituality
instrumentarium, jazz: accordion, 167–68;
  acoustic, 110–11, 206n24; amplification,
  169–70; clarinet, 26, 167; drums, 32–33,
  53–54; electronic, 111, 156–57, 169–70,
  206n24; Frisell album, 166–68, 169–70;
  guitar, 169–70; Marsalis album, 156–57,
  164; trumpet, 71, 156, 167, 190n26. *See
  also* piano; saxophone
interiority, 99–101. *See also* deep jazz; "inner being"
International Association of Jazz Educators, 114
intonation: of Coleman group, 70–71; college music departments and, 119–20
introducing fellow musicians, 97
Irvis, Charlie: "Texas Moaner Blues" with
  Bechet and Armstrong, 34
Ives, Charles, 83, 146

Jackson, Chubby, *58–59*
James, Bob, 111
Jarman, Joseph, 167
Jarrett, Keith, 83, 84, 101–11, 193n1; acous-

tic instruments and, 110–11, 206n24;
  Evans and, 93, 103, 110–11; jazz identity
  and, 110–11; *Köln Concert,* 110; "mantra
  grooves" of, 103, 196n33; Marsalis chal-
  lenged to "blues duel" by, 185n73; physical movements of, 104–6; spontaneous
  performance and, 102, 106–11; standards
  and, 103, 196n35, 205n11; *The Sun Bear
  Concerts,* 197n50; titles for recordings
  by, 108; vocalizations of, 104–5, 106
Jazz Educators Journal, 114
jazz identity, 3, 6–7, 11, 37, 41; bebop and,
  9, 54, 57; Coleman and, 76–77, 81–82;
  deep jazz and, 90–91, 96–101, 110–11;
  Frisell album and, 146–47, 174; gender
  codes and, 62–82, 177–78n7, 190n26;
  Marsalis album and, 146–47, 160–61,
  174; "sensitive intellectual," 99–101;
  "soul," 29, 83–111; Swing-era, 37, 54;
  traditioning and, 174–76. *See also* black
  jazz; genre labeling; white jazz
jazz scholarship, 1, 12–14, 159; and performance ability, 5, 182n36. *See also* college
  music departments; DeVeaux, Scott;
  Gabbard, Krin; historiography, jazz
Jefferson, Hilton, *58–59*
Jerry McGuire (film), 127
Jews: and Tin Pan Alley, 164, 207n40
jobs. *See* professionalism
"John Coltrane Days in North Carolina,"
  200n23
John Coltrane Quartet, 132; *The John Col-
  trane Quartet Plays,* 135, 136–37. *See also*
  Coltrane, John
Johnson, Manzie, 29, 32–33
Johnson, Osie, *58–59*
Johnson, Robert, 28–29, 50, 51; "Dust My
  Broom," 51
Jones, Elvin, 132, 140
Jones, Hank, *58–59*
Jones, Jimmy, *58–59*
Jones, Jo, *58–59*, 143
Jones, LeRoi (Amiri Baraka), 16–17, 38–
  39, 69, 76
Jones, "Philly" Joe, 195n22
Jones, Sam, 195n22
Jones, Thad, 114

Marsalis, Wynton (*continued*)
   Jarrett challenges to "blues duel,"
   185n73; "Lover," 157; and standards, 154–
   55, 205n11; *Standard Time Vol. 2: Inti-
   macy Calling*, 146, 148, 153–64, *153, 161,
   165–67*, 171, 172–74; and Tin Pan Alley,
   153, 164, 207n40; wardrobe of, 160;
   "When It's Sleepytime Down South,"
   155, 157, 158
Martin, Gilbert, 15
Martin, James A., 200n23
masculinity: "cutting contest" and, 67, 72;
   Evans and, 96; jazz world and, 62–82,
   96, 192–93n44; trumpet and, 71, 190n26
MCA/Impulse, 135
McCann, Les, 51
McClary, Susan, 103, 192n40, 192n42
McLaughlin, John, 169, 170
McLean, Jackie, 76
McPartland, Marian, *58–59*
McRae, Carmen, 170
Mehldau, Brad, 88
Metheny, Pat, 148–49
Miles, Lizzie, 26
Miley, Bubber, 71
Mills Brothers, 47
Mingus, Charles, 31, *58–59,* 70, 92; book-
   smart identity of, 98; "cool" style and,
   189n16; Parker story of, 80
Mintzer, Bob, 134, 201n38
modernism, 57
Modern Jazz Quartet, 63, 95
Mole, Miff, *58–59*
Monder, Ben, ix
Monk, Thelonious, 49, *58–59,* 60, 63, 89;
   "Blue Monk," 154; "Crepuscule with
   Nellie," 154; *Dobie Gillis* and, 112; Evans
   and, 92, 94, 96; Higgins with, 73; Mar-
   salis album and, 154; piano tone of, 94;
   "Round Midnight," 154; "Straight, No
   Chaser," 154
Monkees, 170
Monson, Ingrid, 14, 35, 190n26
Montgomery, Wes, 100, 152, 169
Morgan, Frank, 76
Morgan, Lee: "The Rump Roller," 69
Morton, Jelly Roll, 12, 38, 87–88; family's

attitude toward activities of, 22–23; gen-
   der codes and, 67; "Miserere," 181n25;
   original name of, 180n23; and racial hierarchies, 19–20, 25–26; and ragtime,
   23, 165, 181n26; source material of, 148,
   174; traditioning and, 175–76
Motian, Paul, 89, 93
Mr. Holland's Opus (film), 127
MTV, 86
Mulligan, Gerry, *58–59*
Murphy, John P., 6–7, 204–5n9
Murray, Albert: *Stomping the Blues,* 38,
   109–11, 159, 184n54
Musical Courier, 117
Musical Observer, 117
Music Educators National Conference
   (1998), 115
musicologists, 1, 192n40, 198n3; ethnomusicologists, 1, 159–60; new vs. traditional, 194n9. *See also* jazz scholarship;
   teachers
"My Favorite Things," 150
"My Funny Valentine," 150
mysticism: Coleman and, 79; Coltrane
   and, 79, 137, 141–42; Jarrett and, 107–
   11. *See also* spirituality

Nanton, Joe "Tricky Sam," 71, 120
Navarro, Fats, 155
NBC: Tonight Show band, 151
Nettl, Bruno, 114, 120, 159–60, 198n3
Neumann, Scott, ix
"New Age" musicians, 103
New Orleans, 10–41; Canal Street, 18; college music departments and, 143, 144;
   Coltrane and, 130; Creoles in, 10–41,
   178n2, 181n31, 186n83; Downtown, 18–
   41, 180n19, 183n41; Eurocentrism of
   music from, 17, 18–20, 23–27, 35, 148;
   Marsalis album and, 155, 158, 164; masculinity of musicians in, 67; slaves/slave
   descendants in, 10, 15–20, 25, 179–
   80n15; source material for musicians
   in, 148, 174; Tulane University's William Ransom Hogan Jazz Archive, 26,
   180n23, 182n38; two "black" cultures in,
   10–41, 179–80n15; two "black" musics

in, 18–37; Uptown, 18–31, 35–39,
180n19, 183n41; women in, 181n26
"New Thing," 82, 130, 201n33, 207n29;
anti-jazz controversy and, 196n36; college music departments and, 142–44;
and masculinity, 192–93n44; Shepp
and, 139, 192–93n44. *See also* "free jazz"
New York, ix–x, 60; Atlantic Records, 68,
135–36, 141; Coleman's arrival in (1959),
7, 65, 68, 76–77; Five Spot jazz club,
63, 68; Harlem, 50, *58–59*, 60; jazz
world of (1940s and 1950s), 65–68;
Knitting Factory (lower Manhattan),
147, 168, 204n4; Lincoln Center, 119,
147; Marsalis album and, 164. *See also*
"New Thing"
New York Times: "Jazz Bitterly Opposed in
Germany," 118–19
Nicholas, Albert "Nick": "Old Stack O'Lee
Blues" with Bechet, 34
Nichols, Herbie, 89
Night and Day (film), 154
Nobel, Ray: "Cherokee," 149
Noone, Jimmy, 184n60
North Carolina: Coltrane honors, 200n23
North Texas State University, 114, 199n4
notation: college music departments and,
120–27; Coltrane and, 138; and perfor-
mance, 84–85, 193n3; transcription
problems, 31–32, 138. *See also* reading
music
"note choice" improvisational approach, 123
Notre Dame Intercollegiate Jazz Festival,
112, 114, 198n1

Oklahoma (Rodgers and Hammerstein),
152, 153
Oliver, Joe/King, 11, 12, 73, 158
Original Dixieland Jazz Band (O.D.J.B.),
12, 163
Ory, Kid, 11, 38
ostinatos: Jarrett and, 102–3
Otis, Johnny, 51

Page, Jimmy, 169
Panassie, Hughes, 49
Paris, jazz musicians in, 24, 182n37

Parker, Charlie, 9, 11, 29, 49, 57, 63; book-
smart identity of, 98; Coleman and, 68–
69, 75, 76; and European tradition, 80;
Evans's rhythm compared to Parker's,
94; Frisell and, 165; "gravity" of, 7; Henderson and, 204–5n9; "Klactoveedsedsteen," 68; Marsalis and, 160; note selections of, 126; "Now's the Time," 52–53;
Roach and, 121; Sales on, 52–53, 54; saxophone, 7, 53, 167; solitary practicing
tale, 143; on Torin radio show, 60
Partridge Family, 170
Pass, Joe, 169
pastoralists, British, 95
Pastorious, Jaco, 29
"pattern" playing, 134, 135, 201n32
Patton, Charley, 51
PBS: *Jazz* documentary (Burns), 147
Pepper, Art, 76
Peretti, Burton, 21–22, 23
Perez, Emanuel, 19
performance, 4; deep jazz and, 83–111;
Frisell album and, 168–71, 173; jazz
scholar's ability at, 5, 182n36; physical,
55, 83–111, 155, 189n15, 194n6, 194n9;
"ragged" style, 21; stage announcements,
97, 99. *See also* sexuality; virtuosity
Peterson, Oscar, 92, 99
Pettiford, Oscar, *58–59*
Phillips, Little Esther, 51
photography: album, 159–60, 171, *172;* of
Art Kane, *58–59*, 60
piano, 87–89; acoustic, 110–11; bebop, 88,
97; with Miles Davis, 94; electric, 111;
Evans, 87–101, 110–11; grand, 111; Jarrett, 101–11; masculinity of, 67; vs. reed
playing, 26; "rootless voicings," 91, 93;
solo, 101–11; women players, 181n26
Picou, Alphonse, 23
"Play-a-Long" series, Aebersold's, 122, 129–
30, 133, 200n22
Playboy, 74, 191n30
polyphony: college music departments and,
143; piano, 88
popular music: charts, 46, 54, 55; Frisell
album and, 173–74; vs. "highbrow," 48;
jazz distinguished from, 45–46, 48–49,

171, 173; harmony, 126; "No Moe," 171, 173; "Plain Jane," 69; rhythmic conception of, 92; solitary practicing of, 143; "The Surrey with the Fringe on Top," 152, 153

romanticism, 95, 107

"rootless voicings," Evans's, 91, 93

Rushing, Jimmy, *58–59*

Russell, George, 94, 95

Russell, Pee Wee, *58–59*

St. Cyr, Johnny, 17, 22

Saint John Coltrane African Orthodox Church (San Francisco), 127–28, 137, 200n27

Sales, Grover, *Jazz: America's Classical Music,* 51–54

Sanders, Pharoah, 135, 139

saxophone: Coleman, 71; Coltrane, 138, 139, 141–42; "gravity," 7; jazz genre signaled by, 156; Jordan, 53; Parker, 7, 53, 167; piano vs., 26; rise of, 167

"Scale Syllabus," Aebersold's, 122–23, *124–25,* 134. See also chord-scale system

scholarship: humanities, 1–2; "music appreciation," 159. See also jazz scholarship; musicologists; teachers

Schroeder, John, ix

Scofield, John, 169

Seattle Times, 147

sexuality, 118, 191n30, 192n40, 192n42, 196–97n37; Coleman and, 62, 72–82, 191n36, 192–93n44; guitar and, 170; horns and, 156; Jarrett and, 104–6, 109; jazz world and, 62–82, 96, 192–93n44. See also masculinity

Shapiro, Nat, 25

Shaw, Arnold, 42–43

Shaw, Artie, 57, 167

Shaw, Woody, 155

Shepp, Archie, 11, 135, 139, 140, 192–93n44

Shihab, Sahib, *58–59*

Shorter, Wayne, 148–49

Sidran, Ben, 68, 88, 109, 112, 196n33

signification theory, 150

Silver, Horace, 60, 70, 92, 94, 96

Silverman, Kaja: *Male Subjectivity at the Margins,* 65, 66, 81–82

Simeon, Omer, 12

Sinatra, Frank, 54–55

singers: female, 178n7; pianist, 88; vs. "real" musicians, 54–61

Singleton, Zutty, *58–59*

slaves/slave descendants: in New Orleans, 10, 15–20, 25, 179–80n15

Smith, Bessie, 28–29, 50

Smith, Stuff, *58–59*

Smith, Will, 207n41

social status: of jazz musicians, 21–24. See also cultural hierarchies; identity

soloist: Coltrane as, 132; Frisell album and, 170–71; jazz educators and, 143; piano, 101–11; rise of, 4, 35

sonic feedback, 85–86

"soul": in Bechet recordings, 29; body and, 83–111. See also deep jazz; spirituality

sound: Coltrane's, 138–42; Evans's, 91–96; as search, 140–42; as structure, 138–40

Sound and Time (Ake), 199–200n17

source material, 55, 148–51. See also genre labeling; standards

Sousa, John Philip, 146, 173; "Washington Post March," 166, 169–70, 173

Southern, Eileen, 12–13; *The Music of Black Americans,* 12, 20

"So What": Evans chords on, 91

"spinning" standards, 152–55

spirituality: Coleman and, 79; Coltrane and, 79, 127–29, 137, 141–42, 200n27; Jarrett and, 107–11. See also church; mysticism

Stags at Bay, 154

standards, 149–52, 205n11; Frisell and, 174; Jarrett and, 103, 196n35, 205n11; Marsalis and, 154–55, 205n11; "spinning," 152–55

Stearns, Marshall, 198n4

stereotypes: gender, 79; racial, 55, 118, 155, 189n15. See also black jazz; primitivism; white jazz

Steward, Rex, *58–59*

Stitt, Sonny, 126

Strauss, Johann, Jr., 44–45

Strickland, Edward, 107, 109

style, 31; Marsalis and, 162; performing, 21, 83–111, 148. *See also* African-American forms and styles; formalism and jazz

Sullivan, Arthur, 44–45

Sullivan, Maxine, *58–59*

Sun Ra, 49

"The Surrey with the Fringe on Top," 152, 153

Swing era: in ads, 119; bebop and, 53, 54, 63; college music departments and, 117–18; harmony, 126; jazz identity, 37, 54; Jordan and, 53, 55; Marsalis album and, 157. *See also* rhythmic conception

symphonies, genre labeling and, 44–45

synthesizers, 156–57, 206 n24. *See also* electronic instruments

Taj Mahal (Henry Saint Clair Fredericks), 29

Tatum, Art, 57, 88, 99; "Tiger Rag," 51

Taylor, Billy, 182 n36

Taylor, Cecil, 51, 92

teachers: in college music departments, 114, 115, 121, 142–43

"technophallus," 170

"territory bands," 47

Terry, Clark, 155

Tesh, John, 60–61

Thiele, Bob, 135

Thomas, J. C., 132, 137

Thomas, Joe, *58–59*

Threadgill, Henry, 49

timbral manipulation: college music departments and, 119–20, 121

time, 160–61; cultural, 161–62; drummers and, 53; Evans group and, 94; Jarrett and, 103. *See also* rhythmic conception

Timmons, Bobby, 94

Tin Pan Alley, 196 n36; Coleman and, 72, 73; Coltrane and, 139; Evans and, 93–94, 95; Harlem-based, 50; Jarrett and, 103; Jews and, 164, 207 n40; Marsalis album and, 153, 164, 207 n40; standards and, 151

Tio, Lorenzo, 19

Tirro, Frank: on Bechet, 184 n60; and blues, 50, 51; and Coleman, 63–64, 80;

on Evans, 89, 91; *Jazz: A History,* 51, *52;* and Jordan, 43

"Tomming," 155, 189 n15. *See also* stereotypes

Tonight Show band (NBC), 151

Torin, "Symphony Sid," 57–60

Tosches, Nick, 48–49

Townshend, Pete, 85–86

traditioning, 174, 175; jazz, 146–76

transcription problems from recordings, 31–32, 138

Tristano, Lennie, 51, 70, 97

Trumbauer, Frankie, 163

trumpet, 71, 156, 167, 190 n26

Turner, Big Joe, 29

Tympany Five, 46–47, 56. *See also* Jordan, Louis

Tynan, John, 136, 202 n43

Tyner, McCoy, 91, 92, 132, 140, 150

Ullman, Michael: and Bechet, 25, 34; and Evans, 93, 195 n17; and Jordan, 43; and Morton's name, 180 n23

van Damme, Art, 167

Vaughan, Sarah, 55, 88

Veal, Reginald, 157, 158

"vertical" approach, 126, 129, 130

vibratos: exaggerated, 30–31; thinner, 31

Village Vanguard, 89–90, 96

Village Voice, 48–49, 205 n13

Vinson, "Cleanhead," 50

virtuosity: classical, 105–6; Coltrane, 132, 135; Evans, 88–89; fusion, 170; Leppert on, 101, 105; Marsalis album and, 157, 159; and masculinity, 66–68, 82

visual performance. *See* body, performing

vocalists. *See* singers

vocalizations, Jarrett's, 104–5, 106

Wagner, Richard, 107, 194 n7; *Tristan und Isolde,* 103

Wake Up and Dream, 154

Waksman, Steven, 170

Walker, T-Bone, 50, 51

Waller, Fats, 43, 87–88, 97, 99

Text:	12/14.5 Adobe Garamond
Display:	Perpetua and Adobe Garamond
Compositor:	G & S Typesetters, Inc.
Printer and binder:	Edwards Brothers, Inc.